D1593174

This Prayer Book is Presented

to _____

by _____

date _____

Our Family Prayer Book

Edited by
Rev. Bernard F. McWilliams
C.SS.R

NIHIL OBSTAT
    Alfred Rush, C.SS.R., S.T.D.
    Lawrence Everett, C.SS.R., S.T.D.

IMPRIMI POTEST
    Ronald Conners, C.SS.R.
    Provincial

NIHIL OBSTAT
    Donald Tracey, S.T.D.
    Censor Librorum

IMPRIMATUR
    ✠ John J. Carberry
    Administrator of Lafayette-in-Indiana

#0510 ISBN 1-58087-051-1
#0511 ISBN 1-58087-052-X

©1965 C.D. Stampley Enterprises, Inc.
Charlotte, North Carolina

Prayer for the Great Jubilee

The following prayer was written by His Holiness Pope John Paul II to mark the Great Jubilee inaugurating the third millenium – a New Springtime for the Church.

Blessed are you, Father,
who, in your infinite love,
gave us your only-begotten Son.
By the power of the Holy Spirit he became incarnate
in the spotless womb of the Virgin Mary
and was born in Bethlehem
two thousand years ago.
He became our companion on life's path
and gave new meaning to our history,
the journey we make together
in toil and suffering,
in faithfulness and love,
towards the new heaven and the new earth
where You, once death has been vanquished,
will be all in all.

Praise and glory to You, Most Holy Trinity,
you alone are God most high!

By your grace, O Father, may the Jubilee Year
be a time of deep conversion
and of joyful return to you.
May it be a time of reconciliation between people,
and of peace restored among nations,
a time when swords are beaten into ploughshares
and the clash of arms gives way to songs of peace.
Father, grant that we may live this Jubilee Year
docile to the voice of the Spirit,
faithful to the way of Christ,
diligent in listening to your Word
and in approaching the wellsprings of grace.

Praise and glory to You, Most Holy Trinity,
you alone are God most high!

Father, by the power of the Spirit,
strengthen the Church's commitment
to the new evangelization
and guide our steps along the pathways of the world,
to proclaim Christ by our lives,
and to direct our earthly pilgrimage
towards the City of heavenly light.
May Christ's followers show forth their love
for the poor and the oppressed;
may they be one with those in need
and abound in works of mercy;
may they be compassionate towards all,
that they themselves may obtain indulgence
and forgiveness from you.

Praise and glory to You, Most Holy Trinity,
you alone are God most high!

Father, grant that your Son's disciples,
purified in memory
and acknowledging their failings,
may be one, that the world may believe.
May dialogue between the followers of the
great religions prosper,
and may all people discover the joy of being
your children.
May the intercession of Mary,
Mother of your faithful people,
in union with the prayers of the Apostles,
the Christian martyrs,
and the righteous of all nations in every age,
make the Holy Year a time of renewed hope
and of joy in the Spirit
for each of us and for the whole Church.

Praise and glory to You, Most Holy Trinity,
you alone are God most high!

To you, Almighty Father,
Creator of the universe
and of mankind,
through Christ, the Living One,
Lord of time and history,
in the Spirit who makes all things holy,
be praise and honour and glory
now and forever.
Amen!

—Pope John Paul II

Our Family Record

We

_____   _____
HUSBAND   WIFE

received the Sacrament of Holy Matrimony

on _____
           DATE

at _____
           CHURCH

Our marriage was officially witnessed by

_____
           PRIEST

in the presence of

_____   _____
BEST MAN   MAID OF HONOR

Others taking part in the ceremony included

_____

_____

_____

God blessed them saying, "Be fertile and multiply."
GENESIS 1:28

HUSBAND'S FAMILY TREE

❖ HUSBAND   ❖

❖ DATE OF BIRTH   ❖

❖ PLACE OF BIRTH   ❖

❖ DATE OF BAPTISM   ❖

❖ PLACE OF BAPTISM   ❖

❖ DATE OF CONFIRMATION   ❖

PLACE OF CONFIRMATION

Father	Mother
Date of birth	Date of birth
Place of birth	Place of birth

Paternal Grandmother	Maternal Grandmother
Date of birth	Date of birth
Place of birth	Place of birth

Paternal Grandfather	Maternal Grandfather
Date of birth	Date of birth
Place of birth	Place of birth

WIFE'S FAMILY TREE

❖ WIFE _____ ❖

❖ DATE OF BIRTH _____ ❖

❖ PLACE OF BIRTH _____ ❖

❖ DATE OF BAPTISM _____ ❖

❖ PLACE OF BAPTISM _____ ❖

❖ DATE OF CONFIRMATION _____ ❖

PLACE OF CONFIRMATION _____

Father	Mother
Date of birth	Date of birth
Place of birth	Place of birth
Paternal Grandmother	Maternal Grandmother
Date of birth	Date of birth
Place of birth	Place of birth
Paternal Grandfather	Maternal Grandfather
Date of birth	Date of birth
Place of birth	Place of birth

❖ OUR CHILDREN ❖

Name   *Date and place of birth*

Was baptized at   *on*

The Godparents were

Date and place where the Sacrament of Penance was first received

Date and place of First Holy Communion

Was confirmed by   *on*   *at*

The Confirmation Sponsor was

Married

On   *at*

Received Holy Orders or made Religious Profession

On   *at*

Received the Sacrament of the Anointing of the Sick

On   *at*

Died on

Is buried at

❖ OUR CHILDREN ❖

Name   Date and place of birth

Was baptized at   on

The Godparents were

Date and place where the Sacrament of Penance was first received

Date and place of First Holy Communion

Was confirmed by   on   at

The Confirmation Sponsor was

Married

On   at

Received Holy Orders or made Religious Profession

On   at

Received the Sacrament of the Anointing of the Sick

On   at

Died on

Is buried at

❖ OUR CHILDREN ❖

Name

Date and place of birth

Was baptized at   *on*

The Godparents were

Date and place where the Sacrament of Penance was first received

Date and place of First Holy Communion

Was confirmed by   *on*   *at*

The Confirmation Sponsor was

Married

On   *at*

Received Holy Orders or made Religious Profession

On   *at*

Received the Sacrament of the Anointing of the Sick

On   *at*

Died on

Is buried at

❖ OUR CHILDREN ❖

Name *Date and place of birth*

Was baptized at *on*

The Godparents were

Date and place where the Sacrament of Penance was first received

Date and place of First Holy Communion

Was confirmed by *on* *at*

The Confirmation Sponsor was

Married

On *at*

Received Holy Orders or made Religious Profession

On *at*

Received the Sacrament of the Anointing of the Sick

On *at*

Died on

Is buried at

❖ OUR CHILDREN ❖

Name | Date and place of birth

Was baptized at | on

The Godparents were

Date and place where the Sacrament of Penance was first received

Date and place of First Holy Communion

Was confirmed by | on | at

The Confirmation Sponsor was

Married

On | at

Received Holy Orders or made Religious Profession

On | at

Received the Sacrament of the Anointing of the Sick

On | at

Died on

Is buried at

❖ OUR CHILDREN ❖

Name   *Date and place of birth*

Was baptized at   *on*

The Godparents were

Date and place where the Sacrament of Penance was first received

Date and place of First Holy Communion

Was confirmed by   *on*   *at*

The Confirmation Sponsor was

Married

On   *at*

Received Holy Orders or made Religious Profession

On   *at*

Received the Sacrament of the Anointing of the Sick

On   *at*

Died on

Is buried at

❖ OUR GRANDCHILDREN ❖

Name   *Date and place of birth*

Parents

Name   *Date and place of birth*

Parents

Name   *Date and place of birth*

Parents

Name   *Date and place of birth*

Parents

Name   *Date and place of birth*

Parents

Name   *Date and place of birth*

Parents

Name   *Date and place of birth*

Parents

Name   *Date and place of birth*

Parents

❖ OUR GRANDCHILDREN ❖

Name   *Date and place of birth*

Parents

Name   *Date and place of birth*

Parents

Name   *Date and place of birth*

Parents

Name   *Date and place of birth*

Parents

Name   *Date and place of birth*

Parents

Name   *Date and place of birth*

Parents

Name   *Date and place of birth*

Parents

Name   *Date and place of birth*

Parents

❖ **OTHER SIGNIFICANT EVENTS** ❖

_____

_____

_____

_____

_____

_____

_____

_____

_____

_____

_____

_____

_____

_____

_____

_____

_____

_____

_____

_____

_____

_____

_____

Contents

Introduction

AN ATTEMPT has been made in this book to produce a manual that may be used as an all-purpose prayer book for the family. Not included, therefore, are prayers that would be liturgical or designed for congregational use. However, some sections, such as the visits to the Blessed Sacrament and The Way of the Cross, are for personal rather than family devotion. This book has for this reason been kept to a size convenient for carrying to church by any member of the family. The wording of many of the prayers, in keeping with the purpose of the book, is simple, informal, direct. Indeed, as noted frequently in the text, the prayers are often only suggestions as to the form in which the head of household might lead his family in conversing with God. It is better, if only for the education of his children, that a father speak what is in his heart rather than mouth the words of others, however elegant or expressive. Bearing in mind that, in many American homes, one parent will not be Catholic, we have made an effort to keep the prayers as nonsectarian as possible without in any way compromising Catholic teaching or practice. We feel that almost any non-Catholic parent will have little conflict with his conscience while leading his Catholic family in the family prayers to be found in this book.

The color plates, while conforming to acceptable artistic standards, have been chosen more for their devotional than esthetic value.

Finally, this book may be a great help to those who wish to introduce the custom, long out of general use but most helpful for wholesome Christian family life, of reading the Bible aloud. Selections from the Bible text with brief explanations have been made for each day of the year that will not ordinarily be too incomprehensible to the average youngster in the family.

It is to be hoped that this book will help parents to make family prayer in the home a natural, unstilted, unembarrassing conversation with their Father in Heaven and also with other members of His celestial family.

Prayer

WHILE THE PURPOSE of this book is to provide the family with suitable devotions for the home, it should be noted that family prayer should have the same essential characteristics as congregational prayer. In both instances, prayer should be above all a matter of adoration. In the home we adore, that is, we acknowledge our dependence as a family upon God our Father. Public prayer in church can be viewed as simply a broader expression of that dependence, a community act wherein we acknowledge publicly that all of us, butcher and baker, white and colored, are members of the family whose Father is God. It is always easier in public worship to sense our solidarity with others under God if we come from a home where our consciousness of solidarity is heightened from early childhood by the prayer of the family together.

Prayer is an attitude of the mind, a yearning of the heart. Prayer is thus, not the making of many words, but the mind accepting the fact of God's fatherhood, the heart yearning for the coming of his Kingdom wherein the divided and separated family of God will become one. Nevertheless, we have a psychological need to put our attitudes and yearnings into words and gestures. It was for this reason that Christ taught us in the Our Father suitable words to use, thereby suggesting the form and content that our prayer ought to have. Theoretically, we need not be explicit in expressing our needs to God; nor do we need to thank him for each individual benefit; nor need we ask pardon for our offenses in all their minute details; but we are creatures of detail and it would be helpful to spell out in detail our needs, to regret, fault by fault, our failures to do our Father's will, to be grateful for, that is, to acknowledge, the source of each blessing that comes to us.

This book is offered in the hope that it will help families, that is, small units of the great family of God, to do all this together.

Marriage and the Family*

Marriage and Family in the Modern World

47. The well-being of the individual person and of human and Christian society is intimately linked with the healthy condition of that community produced by marriage and family. Hence Christians and all men who hold this community in high esteem sincerely rejoice in the various ways by which men today find help in fostering this community of love[152] and perfecting its life, and by which spouses and parents are assisted in their lofty calling. Those who rejoice in such aids look for additional benefits from them and labor to bring them about.

Yet the excellence of this institution is not everywhere reflected with equal brilliance. For polygamy, the plague of divorce, so-called free love, and other disfigurements have an obscuring effect. In addition, married love is too often profaned by excessive self-love, the worship of pleasure, and illicit practices against human generation. Moreover, serious disturbances are caused in families by modern economic conditions, by in-

---

152. A notable feature of the Council's teaching on Christian marriage is the repeated emphasis on the centrality of conjugal love. It is important, of course, to recall that Pius XI made much the same emphasis in a less-known passage of his encyclical "Casti Connubii." The present treatment is nonetheless remarkable.

*From *The Documents of Vatican II*, Part II, Chapter I, Sections 47-48, published by Guild Press, America Press, Association Press, Herder and Herder. Copyrighted 1966, The America Press.

fluences at once social and psychological, and by the demands of civil society. Finally, in certain parts of the world problems resulting from population growth are generating concern.

All these situations have produced anxious consciences. Yet, the power and strength of the institution of marriage and family can also be seen in the fact that time and again, despite the difficulties produced, the profound changes in modern society reveal the true character of this institution in one way or another.

Therefore, by presenting certain[153] key points of Church doctrine in a clearer light, this Council wishes to offer guidance and support to those Christians and other men who are trying to keep sacred and to foster the natural dignity of the married state and its superlative value.

The Sanctity of Marriage and the Family

48. The intimate partnership of married life and love has been established by the Creator and qualified by His laws. It is rooted in the conjugal covenant of irrevocable personal consent. Hence, by that human act whereby spouses mutually bestow and accept each other, a relationship arises which by divine will and in the eyes of society too is a lasting one. For the good of the spouses and their offspring as well as of society, the existence of this sacred bond no longer depends on human decisions alone.

For God Himself is the author of matrimony, endowed as it is with various benefits and purposes.[154] All of these have a very decisive bearing on the continuation of the human race, on the personal development and eternal destiny of the individual members of a family, and on the dignity, stability, peace, and prosperity of the family itself and of human society as a whole.

---

153. It is important to an understanding of the entire section on Christian marriage and family life to realize that the Council intends to discuss "certain" key points only and not to give an exhaustive treatment of all matters in this area. Thus, it clearly intended to leave untouched those aspects of birth control and related themes that are under debate in the special commission set up by Paul VI to study them.

154. *Cf. St. Augustine, "De bono coniugii": PL 40, 375-376 and 394; St. Thomas, "Summa Theol.," Suppl. Quaest. 49, Art. 3 ad 1; Decretum pro Armenis: Denz.-Schoen. 1327; Pius XI, encyclical letter "Casti Connubii": AAS 22 (1930), pp. 547-548; Denz.-Schoen. 3703-3714.*

By their very nature, the institution of matrimony itself and conjugal love are ordained for the procreation and education of children,[155] and find in them their ultimate crown.

Thus a man and a woman, who by the marriage covenant of conjugal love "are no longer two, but one flesh" (Mt. 19:6), render mutual help and service to each other through an intimate union of their persons and of their actions. Through this union they experience the meaning of their oneness and attain to it with growing perfection day by day. As a mutual gift of two persons, this intimate union, as well as the good of the children, imposes total fidelity on the spouses and argues for an unbreakable oneness between them.[156]

Christ the Lord abundantly blessed this many-faceted love, welling up as it does from the fountain of divine love and structured as it is on the model of His union with the Church. For as God of old made Himself present[157] to His people through a covenant of love and fidelity, so now the Savior of men and the Spouse[158] of the Church comes into the lives of married Christians through the sacrament of matrimony. He abides with them thereafter so that, just as He loved the Church and handed Himself over on her behalf,[159] the spouses may love each other with perpetual fidelity through mutual self-bestowal.

Authentic married love is caught up into divine love and is governed and enriched by Christ's redeeming power and the saving activity of the Church. Thus this love can lead the spouses to God with powerful effect and can aid and strengthen them in the sublime office of being a father or a mother.[160]

For this reason, Christian spouses have a special sacrament

---

155. Here, as elsewhere when the question arises, the Council sedulously avoids the terminology of primary and secondary ends of marriage. It insists on the natural ordering of marriage and conjugal love to procreation but without recourse to such formulations. The same teaching is repeated in Art. 50, and the Council's care to avoid distinguishing "primary" and "secondary" is again evident.

156. *Cf. Pius XI, encyclical letter "Casti Connubii": AAS 22 (1930), pp. 546-547; Denz.-Schoen. 3706.*

157. *Cf. Os. 2; Jer. 3:6-13; Ezek. 16 and 23; Is. 54.*

158. *Cf. Mt. 9:15; Mk. 2:19-20; Lk. 5:34-35; Jn. 3:29; cf. also 2 Cor. 11:2; Eph. 5:27; Apoc. 19:7-8; 21:2 and 9.*

159. *Cf. Eph. 5:25.*

160. *Cf. Second Vatican Council, dogmatic constitution "Lumen Gentium": AAS 57 (1965), pp. 15-16; 40-41; 47.*

by which they are fortified and receive a kind of consecration in the duties and dignity of their state.[161] By virtue of this sacrament, as spouses fulfill their conjugal and family obligations, they are penetrated with the spirit of Christ. This spirit suffuses their whole lives with faith, hope, and charity. Thus they increasingly advance their own perfection, as well as their mutual sanctification, and hence contribute jointly to the glory of God.

As a result, with their parents leading the way by example and family prayer, children and indeed everyone gathered around the family hearth will find a readier path to human maturity, salvation, and holiness. Graced with the dignity and office of fatherhood and motherhood, parents will energetically acquit themselves of a duty which devolves primarily on them,[162] namely education, and especially religious education.

As living members of the family, children contribute in their own way to making their parents holy. For they will respond to the kindness of their parents with sentiments of gratitude, with love and trust. They will stand by them as children should when hardships overtake their parents and old age brings its loneliness. Widowhood, accepted bravely as a continuation of the marriage vocation, will be esteemed by all.[163] Families will share their spiritual riches generously with other families too. Thus the Christian family, which springs from marriage as a reflection of the loving covenant uniting Christ with the Church,[164] and as a participation in that covenant, will manifest to all men the Savior's living presence in the world, and the genuine nature of the Church. This the family will do by the mutual love of the spouses, by their generous fruitfulness, their solidarity and faithfulness, and by the loving way in which all members of the family work together.

---

161. *Pius XI, encyclical letter "Casti Connubii": AAS 22 (1930), p. 583.*
162. The Council speaks also of the primary right and duty of parents with respect to the education of their children in its Declaration on Christian Education.
163. *Cf. 1 Tim. 5:3.*
164. *Cf. Eph. 5:32.*

Calendar of
The Church Year

For the convenience of the user, missals, breviaries (the official prayer book of priests) and almost all prayer books are furnished with a calendar of the church year. The calendar, rich and glowing with color and found in the following pages, is surely one of the most beautiful such calendars ever produced. Readers of this book will most certainly find themselves turning time and time again to these fascinating pages of calendar art.

Originally commissioned in the late 1400's, its feasts will not perfectly coincide with those that are celebrated at the local parish. Still, this calendar shows in loving detail the Church's keen interest in marking the passage of time, and how, through special feasts and fasts, through penitential seasons and through jubilees, she draws us to contemplate ever more deeply the different facets of our faith.

Flemish artist Hans Memling (1458–?), known the world over for the warmth and richness of his canvases, created paintings which are found in the breviary of Cardinal Grimani. Those paintings have been beautifully photographed for **Our Family Prayer Book** by the masterful camera of noted photographer C. Harrison Conroy.

For each of the twelve months of the year the artist painted scenes depicting life as it was lived month by month in 15th century France. Perhaps he has glamorized and over-romanticized that life, but it was a good life that he saw and captured with his brush. These are not overtly religious pictures and may seem not to belong in a prayer book. They have been included precisely to make the point that life was meant to be good, to be enjoyed and that the Lord God has placed a bountiful world at our disposal.

The ornate pages of the calendar itself are the work of several contributors, possibly Gerard de Gand and Liéven d'Anvers, among others. (We are indebted to Miss Julia B. Cannon for our information.) These pages, frankly religious, depict incidents in the lives of the Lord, of Mary and of many of the saints, together with vignettes mirroring the daily life of the common people. Of special interest is the highly ornate title page. With fantastically intricate detail, the artist has made a superb decorative page by illustrating creation scenes from the first chapter of Genesis in one column and with the letters from the French word for calendar (*calendrier*) in the other. Around the border are other scenes from the early chapters of Genesis. So incredibly minute are the details that one needs a magnifying glass to discover that the artists have depicted here the creation of woman, the fall of man, the expulsion of Adam and Eve from the garden of Eden, Adam earning his daily bread by the sweat of his brow, Cain and Abel offering their sacrifices to God, Cain killing Abel, Cain fleeing the wrath of God. Finally, the ghostly figure riding across the sky at the top of each month-picture very probably represents Father Time, speeding on his way.

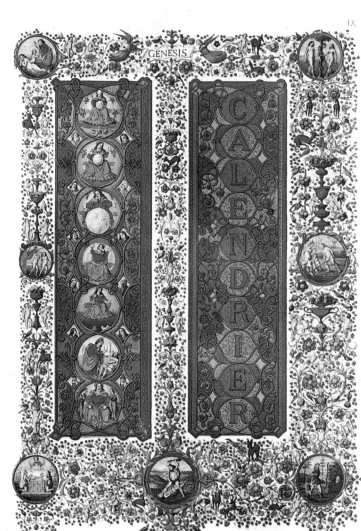

GENESIS

CALENDRIER

Janvïer.

l	Circoncision	xvi	S. Marcel
	S. Fulgence	xvii	S. Antoine Abb
ii	S. Basile	xviii	S. Paul er et es co
iii	Ste Geneviève	xix	S. Sulpice
iiij	S. Tite	xx	S. Sébastien
v	S. Siméon Stil	xxi	Ste Agnès
vi	Epiphanie	xxii	S. Vincent
	S. Pierre Abbé	xxiii	S. Ildefonse
vii	S. Lucien	xxiiij	S. Timothée
viii	S. Séverin	xxv	S. Maximin
ix	S. Honoré	xxvi	Ste Paule
x	S. Marcien	xxvii	S. Julien
xi	S. Théodose	xxviii	S. Cyrille
xii	S. Arcade	xxix	S. Franc. de Sal
xiii	Ste Véronique	xxx	Ste Bathilde
xiiij	S. Félix	xxxi	Ste Marcelle
xv	S. Paul Ermite		

Février

I	S. Ignace	xvi	Ste Julienne
II	Purification	xvii	S. Théodule
	S. Laurent de C.	xviii	S. Siméon E.
III	S. Blaise	xix	S. Barbat
IV	S. Aventin	xx	S. Eleuthère
V	Ste Agathe	xxi	S. Sévérien
VI	S. Amand	xxii	Ste Isabelle
VII	S. Romuald	xxiii	S. Gérénus
VIII	S. Jean de Math.	xxiv	S. Mathias A.
IX	Ste Appolline	xxv	S. Victorin
X	Ste Scolastique	xxvi	S. Porphire
XI	S. Saturnin	xxvii	Ste Honorine
XII	Ste Eulalie	xxviii	S. Romain
XIII	S. Martinien	xxix	S. Séver
XIV	S. Valentin		
XV	S. Faustin		

Mars

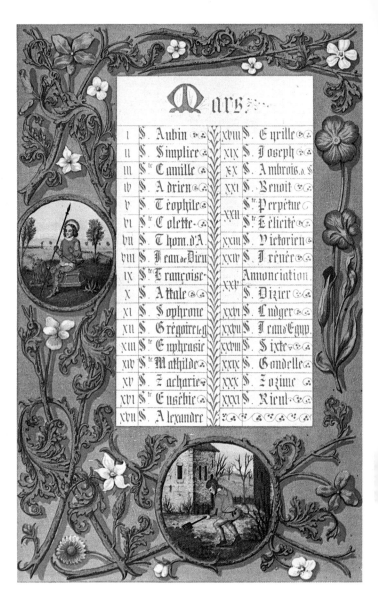

I	S. Aubin	XVIII	S. Cyrille
II	S. Simplice	XIX	S. Joseph
III	Ste Camille	XX	S. Ambrois.
IV	S. Adrien	XXI	S. Benoit
V	S. Téophile		Ste Perpétue
VI	Ste Colette	XXII	Ste Félicité
VII	S. Thom. d'A.	XXIII	S. Victorien
VIII	S. Jean de Dieu	XXIV	S. Irénée
IX	Ste Françoise		Annonciation
X	S. Attale	XXV	S. Dizier
XI	S. Sophrone	XXVI	S. Ludger
XII	S. Grégoire le g.	XXVII	S. Jean d'Egyp.
XIII	Ste Euphrasie	XXVIII	S. Sixte
XIV	Ste Mathilde	XXIX	S. Gondelle
XV	S. Zacharie	XXX	S. Zozime
XVI	Ste Eusébie	XXXI	S. Rieul
XVII	S. Alexandre		

Avril

i	S. Hugues	xvi	S. Fructueux
ii	S. François de P.	xvii	S. Anicet
iii	S. Ambroise D.	xviii	S. Apollonius
iv	S. Isidore	xix	S. Léon Pape
v	S. Vincent Fer.	xx	S. Marcellin
vi	S. Célestin	xxi	S. Anastase
vii	S. Clotaire	xxii	Ste Opportune
viii	S. Denis	xxiii	S. Georges
ix	Ste Marie d'Egn.	xxiv	S. Léger
x	S. Pallade	xxv	S. Marc Evang.
xi	S. Léon le Grand	xxvi	S. Clet
xii	S. Jules	xxvii	S. Antime
xiii	Ste Hermenigilde	xxviii	S. Vital
xiv	S. Lambert	xxix	S. Robert
xv	S. Paterne	xxx	Ste Cather. de S.

Mai

	S. Philippe	xvi	S. Jean-Népo
	S. Jacques Ap.	xvii	S. Pascal
ii	S. Germain	xviii	S. Venant
iii	S. Juvénal	xix	Ste Prudentien
iv	Ste Monique	xx	S. Bernardin
v	S. Hilaire	xxi	S. Hospice
vi	S. Jean Damas	xxii	S. Aigulfe
vii	S. Stanislas	xxiii	Ste Julie
viii	S. Victor	xxiv	S. Donatien
ix	S. Grég. de Na.	xxv	S. Urbain
x	S. Désiré	xxvi	S. Phil. de Ner.
xi	S. Mamert	xxvii	S. Eutrope
xii	Ste Flavie	xxviii	S. Germain
xiii	S. Servais	xxix	S. Conon
xiv	S. Boniface	xxx	S. Ferdinand
xv	S. Euphraise	xxxi	Ste Pétronille

Juin

I	S. Pamphile		XVII	S. Avit
II	S. Pothin		XVIII	Sᵗᵉ Marine
III	Sᵗᵉ Clotilde		XIX	S. Gervais
IV	S. Gautier			S. Protais
V	Sᵗᵉ Dorothée		XX	S. Sylvère
VI	S. Claude		XXI	S. Louis de G.
VII	S. Paul		XXII	S. Paulin
VIII	S. Médard		XXIII	Sᵗᵉ Ethelrède
IX	Sᵗᵉ Pélagie		XXIV	S. Jean-Bapt.
X	Sᵗᵉ Marguerite		XXV	S. Prosper
XI	S. Barnabé		XXVI	S. Lambert
XII	S. Omphre		XXVII	S. Ladislas
XIII	S. Antoine de P.		XXVIII	Sᵗ Irénée
XIV	S. Basile le g.		XXIX	S. Pierre-Apôt.
XV	Sᵗᵉ Crescence		XXX	S. Paul-Apôt.
XVI	S. Franc.Reg.			

Juillet

i	S. Thibault	xvii	S. Alexis
ii	Ste Éléonore	xviii	S. Frédéric
iii	S. Thierry	xix	S. Vincent de P
iv	Ste Berthe	xx	S. Juste
v	Ste Zoé	xxi	S. Victor
vi	S. Pallade	xxii	Ste Marie-Mad
vii	S. Pantène	xxiii	S. Apollinaire
viii	S. Procope	xxiv	S. Loup
ix	S. Éphrem	xxv	S. Jacques l.m
x	Ste Amalberge	xxvi	Ste Anne
xi	Ste Félicité	xxvii	S. Pantaléon
xii	S. Jean Gualbert	xxviii	S. Nazaire
xiii	S. Eugène	xxix	S. Lazare
xiv	S. Bonaventure	xxx	Ste Juliette
xv	S. Henry	xxxi	S. Ignace de L
xvi	S. Fulrad		

Aout

i	S. Pierre aux liens	xvi	S. Hyacinthe
ii	S. Etienne	xvii	S. Libérat
iii	S. Nicodème	xviii	Ste Hélène
iv	S. Dominique	xix	S. Louis Evêq
v	Ste Afre	xx	S. Bernard
vi	S. Juste	xxi	Ste Jeanne d.C.
vii	S. Donat	xxii	S. Symphorin
viii	S. Cyriaque	xxiii	Ste Sidonie
ix	S. Numidique	xxiv	S. Barthélemy
x	S. Laurent	xxv	S. Louis Roi
xi	Ste Suzanne	xxvi	S. Zéphirin
xii	Ste Claire	xxvii	S. Césaire
xiii	S. Hippolyte	xxviii	S. Augustin
xiv	S. Eusèbe	xxix	S. Sabin
xv	Assomption Ste Marie	xxx	S. Fiacre
		xxxi	Ste Gutherge

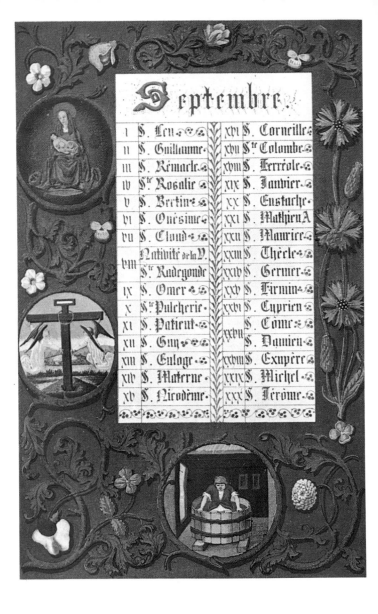

Septembre

i	S. Leu	xvi	S. Corneille
ii	S. Guillaume	xvii	Ste Colombe
iii	S. Rémacle	xviii	S. Ferréole
iv	Ste Rosalie	xix	S. Janvier
v	S. Bertin	xx	S. Eustache
vi	S. Onésime	xxi	S. Mathieu A
vii	S. Cloud	xxii	S. Maurice
viii	Nativité de la V. Ste Radegonde	xxiii	S. Thècle
		xxiv	S. Germer
ix	S. Omer	xxv	S. Firmin
x	Ste Pulcherie	xxvi	S. Cyprien
xi	S. Patient	xxvii	S. Côme
xii	S. Guy		S. Damien
xiii	S. Euloge	xxviii	S. Exupère
xiv	S. Materne	xxix	S. Michel
xv	S. Nicodème	xxx	S. Jérôme

Octobre

i	S. Rémy	xvii	S. Austrude
ii	S. Thomas	xviii	S. Luc Évang.
iii	S. Denis l'Aré.	xix	S. Aquilin
iv	S. Franc. d'As.	xx	Ste Zénobie
v	S. Placide	xxi	Ste Ursule
vi	S. Bruno	xxii	S. Népotien
vii	S. Serge	xxiii	S. Théodoret
viii	Ste Brigitte	xxiv	S. Magloire
ix	S. Denis de P.	xxv	S. Crépin
x	S. François de B.	xxvi	S. Évariste
xi	S. Nicaise	xxvii	S. Frumence
xii	S. Séraphin	xxviii	S. Simon Apô.
xiii	S. Édouard	xxix	S. Narcisse
xiv	S. Calixte	xxx	S. Lucain
xv	Ste Thérèse	xxxi	S. Quentin
xvi	S. Gall		

Novembre

I	Toussaint	xv	S. Didier
	S. Bénigne	xvi	S. Edmond
II	Trépassés	xvii	S. Grégoire
	S. Marchien	xviii	Ste Hilde
III	S. Hubert	xix	Ste Elisabeth
IV	S. Charles B.	xx	Ste Maxence
V	Ste Bertille	xxi	S. Colomban
VI	S. Léonard	xxii	Ste Cécile
VII	S. Florent	xxiii	S. Clément
VIII	S. Godefroid	xxiv	S. Jean de la C.
IX	S. Mathurin	xxv	Ste Catherine
X	Ste Florence	xxvi	S. Conrad
XI	S. Martin	xxvii	S. Virgile
XII	S. Réne	xxviii	S. Etienne
XIII	S. Brice	xxix	S. Saturnin
XIV	S. Albéric	xxx	S. André Apô.

Décembre.

i	S. Éloi	xvii	Ste Olympiade
ii	Ste Bibiane	xviii	S. Gratien
iii	S. François X.	xix	S. Némésion
iv	Ste Barbe	xx	S. Philogone
v	S. Sabas	xxi	S. Thomas
vi	S. Nicolas	xxii	S. Sigon
vii	S. Fare	xxiii	Ste Victoire
viii	Immacule Conc.	xxiv	Ste Émilienne
	S. Romain		Noël
ix	Ste Léoradie	xxv	Ste Eugénie
x	Ste Eulalie	xxvi	S. Étienne
xi	S. Damase	xxvii	S. Jean Évang
xii	S. Valéry		Sts Innocents
xiii	Ste Luce	xxviii	S. Antoine
xiv	Ste Valère	xxix	S. Thom. de C
xv	S. Mesmin	xxx	S. Sabin
xvi	Ste Adélaïde	xxxi	S. Sylvestre

Basic Prayers

Herein are to be found a number of prayers that every Catholic should know. They are used in the home and in public gatherings of all sorts. They represent our universal language of prayer, our common prayer vocabulary.

THE SIGN OF THE CROSS

The sign of the cross is an outward gesture of our inner belief in the mystery of the Blessed Trinity and our redemption through the Cross of Christ.

In the name of the Father and of the Son and of the Holy Spirit. Amen.

THE OUR FATHER

Our Father who art in heaven, hallowed be Thy Name; Thy Kingdom come; Thy will be done on earth as it is in heaven. Give us this day our daily bread; and forgive us our trespasses as we forgive those who trespass against us; and lead us not into temptation, but deliver us from evil. Amen.

THE HAIL MARY

Hail Mary, full of grace, the Lord is with thee, blessed art thou among women and blessed is the fruit of thy womb, Jesus. Holy Mary, Mother of God, pray for us sinners now and at the hour of our death. Amen.

THE GLORY BE TO THE FATHER

Glory be to the Father and to the Son and to the Holy Spirit, as it was in the beginning, is now, and ever shall be, world without end. Amen.

THE APOSTLES CREED

This creed differs from the creed to be found in the Mass. Dating from the third century, it is a simpler and more compact summation of Christian beliefs.

I believe in God, the Father Almighty, creator of heaven and earth and in Jesus Christ, his only son, our Lord, who was conceived by the Holy Ghost, born of the Virgin Mary, suffered under Pontius Pilate, was crucified, died, and was buried. He descended into hell. The third day He arose again from the dead. He ascended into Heaven and sitteth at the right hand of God, the Father Almighty. From thence He shall come to judge the living and the dead. I believe in the Holy Ghost, the Holy Catholic Church, the communion of saints, the forgiveness of sin, the resurrection of the body and life everlasting. Amen.

THE ANGELUS

If the family lives within the sound of the Angelus Bell of the parish church, it is a pious and profitable custom to recite the Angelus together while the bell is being rung. The prayer recalls the coming of the Son of God to this world and honors Mary for her role in his coming.

V. The angel of the Lord declared unto Mary.
R. And she conceived of the Holy Spirit.
  Hail Mary, etc.
V. Behold the handmaid of the Lord.
R. Be it done unto me according to thy word.
  Hail Mary, etc.
V. And the Word was made flesh.
R. And dwelt among us.
  Hail Mary, etc.
V. Pray for us, O holy Mother of God,
R. That we may be made worthy of the promises of Christ.

Let Us Pray

Pour forth, we beseech Thee, O Lord, Thy grace into our hearts, that we to whom the Incarnation of Christ, Thy Son, was made known by the message of an angel, may by His passion and cross be brought to the glory of His resurrection, through the same Christ our Lord. Amen.

REGINA COELI

This prayer is said in place of the Angelus during the Easter season.

V. O Queen of Heaven, rejoice, Alleluia.
R. For he whom you were made worthy to bear, Alleluia.

V. Has risen again as he said, Alleluia.
R. Pray for us to God, Alleluia.
V. Rejoice and be glad, O Virgin Mary, Alleluia.
R. For the Lord has arisen indeed, Alleluia.

Let us pray

O God, who by the resurrection of your Son, our Lord Jesus Christ, saw fit to give joy to the world, grant, we beg you, that through his Mother, the Virgin Mary, we may obtain the joys of everlasting life. Through the same Christ, Our Lord. Amen.

THE HAIL HOLY QUEEN

Hail, Holy Queen, Mother of Mercy, our life, our sweetness and our hope, to thee do we cry, poor banished children of Eve. To thee do we send up our sighs, mourning and weeping in this vale of tears. Turn then, most gracious advocate, thine eyes of mercy toward us and, after this our exile, show unto us the blessed fruit of thy womb, Jesus. O clement, O loving, O sweet Virgin Mary.

MEMORARE

Remember, O gracious Virgin Mary, that never was it known that anyone who fled to your protection, implored your help or sought your intercession was left unaided. Inspired by this confidence, I fly to you, O Virgin of Virgins, our Mother; to you I come, before you I stand, sinful and sorrowful; O Mother of the Word incarnate, despise not my petitions but in your mercy, hear and answer me. Amen.

Family Prayers

THERE IS no obligation to say prayers upon arising in the morning or before going to bed at night, and no sin is committed when we fail to pray at either time. However, we cannot do without prayer; we need constantly to remind ourselves that we are children of our Father in Heaven and are thus completely dependent upon him. Because this matter is so important to us, the Church recommends that we pray at fixed times so as not to forget our need to pray. It is well, therefore, that parents train themselves and, in turn, their children to the practice of morning and night prayers. It is suggested that this Family Prayer book be left open by the head of the household the night before in some sort of "prayer nook" in the house where everyone going to bed at night or coming in for breakfast in the morning can pause and kneel for a moment to pray. The prayers on the following pages are suggestions as to the form the morning or evening prayer might take. If the family schedule permits, perhaps these, or similar prayers, could be recited by the family all together.

Morning Prayers

In the name of the Father and of the Son and of the Holy Spirit. Amen.

I acknowledge you, God, to be my true Father. I acknowledge you in the person of your Son to be my brother, friend and redeemer. In the person of your Holy Spirit I acknowledge you to be my sanctifier.

THE APOSTLES CREED

I believe in God the Father Almighty, creator of heaven and earth, and in Jesus Christ, his only son, Our Lord, who was conceived by the Holy Ghost, born of the Virgin Mary, suffered under Pontius Pilate, was crucified, died, and was buried. He descended into Hell. The third day He arose again from the dead. He ascended into Heaven and sitteth at the right hand of God the Father Almighty. From thence He shall come to judge the living and the dead. I believe in the Holy Ghost, the Holy Catholic Church, the communion of saints, the forgiveness of sins, the resurrection of the body and life everlasting. Amen.

6

My Father, I trust you because I know you not only want me to come home to you someday, but that you will continually offer me the strength to get there.

My God, I wish to love you above all things by giving my whole self to you in the gift of my will to you. I will try to do your will all this day.

My Father, I thank you for having watched over me during the night and for having given me the priceless gift of another new day.

And I am sorry, my Father, that I have not always done what you wanted me to do. Today I will try harder. Help me to do so. Hail Mary, etc.

SPIRITUAL COMMUNION

> Those in the family who will not be able to go to daily Mass might make a spiritual communion, that is, to put into words their unfulfillable desire to receive Holy Communion that day. Granting the impossibility of their getting to Mass, we see no reason why a generous measure of grace would not be given them.

My Jesus, I believe that you are present in the most Holy Sacrament. I love you above all things and I desire to receive you into my soul. Since I cannot now receive you sacramentally, come at least spiritually into my heart. I unite myself wholly to you; never permit me to be separated from you.

Evening Prayers

As previously mentioned, a fixed time for prayer is recommended. Since we go to bed nearly every night of our lives, we would do well indeed to make the time of our retiring one of the fixed points of our prayer life. It is better that we improvise the night prayer, speaking from the heart. Below will be found merely a suggestion as to the form prayer might take.

Thank you, my Father, for the day that is ending. Because I am tired, help me to sleep well. Looking back over the day, I can plainly see that I did not do too well. There were things I should not have done, things I could have done for you that were left undone. I am sorry about this. Help me, Father, to do better tomorrow, to be less harsh to people, more gentle, more patient. Help me to give of myself for the sake of others and to be more cheerful about it. Mary, my Mother, keep an eye on all of us in this household.

PRAYER FOR HUSBAND AND WIFE

To be said together before retiring or alone if the other is absent.

Father, we beg you to continue to bless us and to help us to be thankful for what we already have. We are one through the sacrament of matrimony. Grant that we may truly be of onc hcart and mind, that we may respect the person in each other, that we may love each other in you, remembering that it was you who gave us our love because we were to be parents of your children. Help us to give of ourselves more completely to each other and to be less selfish. Let us trust one another. Let us in our difficulties trust in you and in the guarantee you gave us in your sacrament of matrimony. (Help us to be good parents.) If it be your will, give us the health and strength we need for our jobs. In the happiness we know in our love for each other, let us not forget that it is but a foretaste of Heaven. Through the merits of Jesus Christ, Our Lord and Savior. Amen.

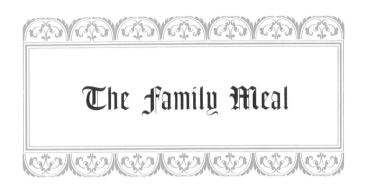

The Family Meal

THE FAMILY MEAL is a necessary and most effective instrument in the training of children. One of the great flaws in American family life is that the members of the family so seldom get to eat together. Consequently, unaccustomed to doing things together, the children grow up with no profound sense of belonging to a family. Not seeing their father presiding at the table, they fail to understand that the father must be the head of the family. Furthermore, the dinner table is the indispensable school for teaching children good manners, deference and consideration for others and, above all, the relation between their own supper and the Lord's Supper. It is most desirable, therefore, to have the family eat together once a day at least. The main family meal should begin with a prayer, recited always by the father.

There is never any obligation to pray before or after meals. However, the omission of prayer at this time should be the exception rather than the rule. Although the father would do well to improvise his own prayers, he may find helpful the following blessings before meals and grace after meals for each day of the week.

SUNDAY

Father in Heaven, you watch over the tiniest sparrow. Please watch over us and bless our food.

After the Meal

We thank you, Father, for the food which you have provided for us. May we never lose sight of the fact that every good thing comes from your hands.

MONDAY

Our Brother, Christ, be with us in spirit here at the table that we may love one another. Bless what we have here that we may use it to our advantage.

After the Meal

Christ, our Brother, we thank you for the two kinds of bread you provide us with—the bread we have eaten at this table and the bread of eternal life we eat at your table.

TUESDAY

Holy Spirit of God's Love, fire our hearts with the fire of your love so that our coming together for food will bring our hearts together.

After the Meal

Holy Spirit, may we leave the table with a deeper realization that we are brothers and sisters not only to each other but to all whom we meet. Inspire us to do all that we can about the needs of others.

WEDNESDAY

Heavenly Father, although we know we have worked hard to be able to buy this food, we recognize that you have sustained us every moment of our working hours.

After the Meal

Now that we have dined so well, Father, we ask that the injustice of men will not continue to deprive the hungry of the world of the abundance that you have placed in the world.

THURSDAY

Christ, our Brother, help us to live worthily enough to be able one day to sit down with you at your Heavenly table.

After the Meal

Christ, our Savior, may we ever be mindful of the great sorrow and pain it caused you in order to give us the bread of eternal life.

FRIDAY

Holy Spirit of Wisdom, teach us to know that the good things of life that we enjoy are to be used thankfully but not to be desired for themselves

After the Meal

Come, Holy Spirit, to all of us gathered here at this table as you came down on those gathered at the table in the Upper Room and fill us with the strength and courage to be like Christ.

SATURDAY

Bless us, Lord, and these your gifts, which we are about to receive from the bounty of your hands. Through Christ Our Lord. Amen.

After the Meal

We give you thanks, Heavenly Father, for all your benefits who live and reign with the Son and the Holy Spirit, world without end. Amen.

Blessing of Children

The father of the family should know
that he is empowered to bless his children. It is therefore recommended that,
if possible, he bless his children before
going to work. As he gathers the children about him, he should avoid for-
malism, undue solemnity or a routine
approach. It is preferable that the words
of the blessing be informal, varied, and
improvised by him. Here is a suggested
form that the blessing might take.

Children, may your good Father in
Heaven watch over you today while
your Daddy is gone; may He help
you to work hard at school and to be
kind to the other children. In the
name of the Father and of the Son
and of the Holy Spirit. Amen.

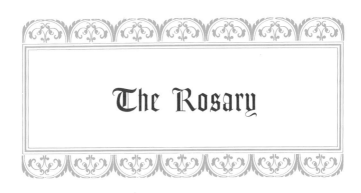

The Rosary

FOR CENTURIES it has been the custom of devout Catholics to recite daily five decades of the highly indulgenced Rosary of our Mother Mary. It is thought that the Rosary was introduced to a laity, unable to read the psalms, as a simple substitution for the Divine Office of the clergy. Now that laymen in most areas are literate, more stress has been made on the reading of scripture, especially as a family project. It would not be out of place, however, for the family to recite together at least once a week, perhaps on Saturday, (Mary's day) after the evening meal, five decades of the Rosary. Where there are several small children, one decade would be enough.

Whoever presides at the table should announce the intention for which the Rosary will be said and begin by making the sign of the Cross. He then recites the first half of the Apostles' Creed and the rest of those present recite the second half, beginning with the words, "I believe in the Holy Spirit." Then the leader announces: "for an increase of our faith, hope and love." After this, he says the first half of the Our Father, and the others answer with the second half. This is followed by three Hail Marys and the Glory Be to

the Father, recited in the same way as the Our Father. Then
the leader announces the mystery to be meditated upon during the first decade. He may, if he wishes, read a short meditation about the mystery, examples of which may be found
in the following pages. Then one Our Father, ten
Hail Marys and the Glory Be to the Father are recited as
indicated above, after which the group proceeds to the second mystery which is recited in the same fashion as the first;
and so are the remaining three mysteries. An effort should
be made by all to avoid a mechanical, rapid, and undevout
recitation of the many Hail Marys. The group may stand or
kneel or sit at the table throughout the recitation. Even a
devout recitation should not take more than twelve to fifteen
minutes. As with all family prayer, the family rosary will
undoubtedly give the members a deeper consciousness of
the fact that God is the real Father of them all and, in this
case, that Mary is their Mother.

On the following pages will be found suggested meditations to be read by the leader. The colorful illustrations ac-
companying the text may be shown to young children present as an aid to their efforts to meditate upon the great
events highlighted by the mysteries. It is further recommended that the head of the family employ other devices
to hold the interest of the children. For example, one child
could be appointed to turn the page of the book after each
mystery, another could lead the group in the Hail Marys.
But stern reprimands for inattention are out of place. Family prayer should always be a pleasant experience for children. If there hangs over them the constant threat of pa-
rental anger, they will come to dread not only prayer with
the family but prayer in general.

The Mysteries of the Rosary

If one has the laudable custom of saying five decades of the Rosary every day, one should meditate on the joyful mysteries on Monday and Thursday, on the Sorrowful Mysteries on Tuesday and Friday, and on the Glorious Mysteries on Wednesday and Saturday. On Sundays from Advent to Lent, the Joyful Mysteries are to be chosen; from Lent to Easter, the Sorrowful Mysteries; and from Easter to Advent, the Glorious Mysteries. For family recitation on Saturdays, use the Joyful Mysteries from Advent to Lent, the Sorrowful Mysteries during Lent and the Glorious Mysteries from Easter to Advent.

The
Joyful Mysteries

The First Mystery

THE ANNUNCIATION

The angel Gabriel comes and tells Mary that she is going to have a baby who will be the Son of God. She remains humble at the news of this great honor to come to her because she realizes clearly, as we all should, that we are nothing without God.

The
Joyful Mysteries

The Second Mystery

THE VISITATION

Mary, although she will soon have her own baby to take care of, travels up into the hill country to help her cousin Elizabeth. She wishes to tell us that we must do what we can for our neighbor despite the hardships that might be involved.

The
Joyful Mysteries

The Third Mystery

THE BIRTH OF
JESUS

God sends Mary her baby at a time when she and Joseph have been forced to spend the night in a stable. Her baby is the Son of Almighty God, but He doesn't mind the stable. Big, expensive houses are not important to Him. He had less than any of us.

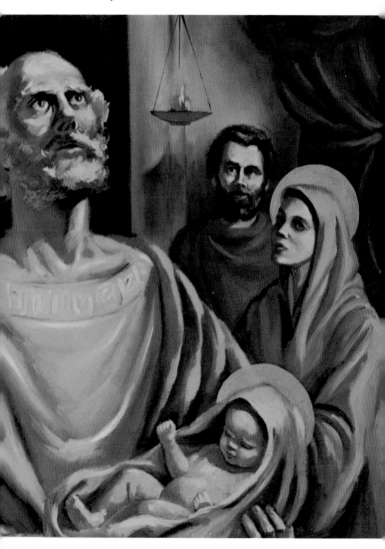

The Joyful Mysteries

The Fourth Mystery

THE PRESENTATION

When we go to Mass on Sunday, we tell our Father in Heaven that we are willing to accept anything He has in store for us. That is just what the baby Jesus did when His mother took Him to the temple.

The Joyful Mysteries

The Fifth Mystery

Her boy Jesus was lost but Mary kept looking and looking until she found Him. If we lose Jesus, we should not give up until we have found Him. We will find Him easily if we really go looking for Him.

The Sorrowful Mysteries

The First Mystery

THE AGONY
IN THE GARDEN

Jesus was terrified at the thought of what He would have to suffer the next day. He asked his Father to spare Him this suffering, but then He said "Father, not my will be done, but Yours." We should often say this.

The Sorrowful Mysteries

The Second Mystery

THE SCOURGING

The terrible beating they gave Jesus is a senseless thing except to those who, like Christ, understand that the harm we do to ourselves by sin had to be repaired in some mysterious way by His great pain.

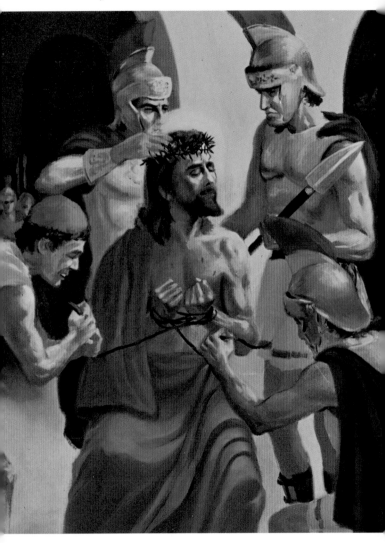

The Sorrowful Mysteries

The Third Mystery

THE CROWNING
WITH THORNS

The soldiers thought that they were making fun of Christ but they were really helping to make Him King by inflicting this cruel pain upon Him. He is our King precisely because of what He suffered for us.

The Sorrowful Mysteries

The Fourth Mystery

THE ROAD OF
THE CROSS

We must learn to see that Christ still carries His Cross along the roads of the world in the person of the suffering and needy. We must step forward and help them as Simon of Cyrene helped Christ, our Brother.

The Sorrowful Mysteries

The Fifth Mystery

CHRIST DIES

Since love is the gift of self, no one can love more than he who gives his whole self in death for his friends. How can we doubt that God loves us when we know that He made the gift of Himself by dying for us?

The Glorious Mysteries

The First Mystery

Christ came back from the tomb not as a ghost, but as a man who could eat and drink and be seen clearly by all His friends. If we are one with Him, we also shall rise again from the dead, to live forever with Him.

The Glorious Mysteries

The Second Mystery

THE ASCENSION

Jesus left us and went up in to Heaven —His friends saw him go—so that we would have to live by faith. He told Thomas that those who believe without seeing are better off than those who insist on seeing with their eyes.

The Glorious Mysteries

The Third Mystery

THE COMING OF THE HOLY SPIRIT

Getting us in shape for the happiness of Heaven is the work of the Father and the Son and the Holy Spirit. That is why Christ told his Apostles that He would see to it that the Holy Spirit would also come to make us good.

The
Glorious Mysteries

The Fourth Mystery

THE ASSUMPTION
OF MARY

Because of original sin our bodies are returned to dust when we die. However, because God kept Mary free from original sin, her body did not decay. Instead, God sent His angels to transport her, body and soul, to the splendor of Heaven.

The Glorious Mysteries

The Fifth Mystery

THE CORONATION

Mary, the dear Mother of us all, is the greatest woman that ever lived. God crowned our Mother Queen of Heaven and of the world. But we must remember that, despite her greatness, she cares deeply and tenderly for each one of us.

Novenas

A NOVENA is a nine day prayer similar in spirit to the prayer of Mary and the Apostles before Pentecost. Many people affirm that after nine days of prayer to a favorite saint, their special request is answered in a startling way. There is ample room here for speculating as to why this would seem to be so. One could dismiss the matter as being purely a question of coincidence—a much needed raise in salary, for example, just happens to come on the ninth day of prayer. Or one could say the dramatic answers to Novena prayers are God's way of rewarding our perseverance in prayer. Whatever the explanation, it is hardly to be doubted that the Novena is a valid form of prayer, well suited to the psychological needs of many of the faithful.

The prayer itself does not have to follow a set formula; one may improvise his own prayer; however, the following pages contain a number of Novenas that have gained favor with the faithful. The prayer may be said for nine consecutive days or on one day of the week for nine consecutive weeks. If the intention being prayed for involves the whole family, all should be invited to make the Novena together.

THE DESCENT OF THE HOLY SPIRIT *by an Antwerp Mannerist*
National Gallery of Dublin, Ireland

NOVENA TO

Christ Jesus

MY BROTHER JESUS, according to the clear words of your Holy Scriptures, you are in truth our advocate before your Father. Because you are one of us, you look out for us all the time.

You said at the grave of Lazarus that the Father always hears you. Filled with faith and confidence in your compassionate heart, I come to plead my cause. I am in the present need (here mention your intentions) where only the power of the Father can help me. For the salvation of my soul, I sorely need this grace. May it come to me from the riches of your Father.

Christ Jesus, from your throne in Heaven, go to your Father and to my Father, to your God and to my God and reconcile me with Him. I repent sincerely of ever having turned away from Him. Obtain for me the help in my present trial that I need so much.

In the Our Father, you have composed a prayer with which I will now approach the Father. Because you pray so well, I ask you to please say along with me, Our Father who art in Heaven, hallowed be Thy name, etc.

NATIONAL SHRINE OF THE IMMACULATE CONCEPTION
Washington, D.C.

NOVENA TO

The Holy Spirit

HOLY SPIRIT OF GOD, love of God, silent, secret,
strengthening, breathing where you will,
expressing our longings.
You are wisdom, you are love, you are strength
and constancy.
I am none of these—I need them all.
Sincerely I want them,
I do believe sincerely I want them.
You are the Father of the poor,
you do not fail. Will you fail me?
Grant that I may never fail you. I cannot trust myself.
Grant that I may never do wrong—
that I may be wise according to my place in life,
that I may love truly, not falsely,
that I may be faithful to God, to men,
that I may have strength sufficient for the tasks
you gave me and may I use it.

THE HOLY TRINITY
by El Greco
Museo del Prado, Madrid, Spain

NOVENA TO

Our Mother of Perpetual Help

BEHOLD AT YOUR FEET, Mother of Perpetual Help, a pitiful sinner who has recourse to you and confides in you; Mother of Mercy, have pity on me. I hear you called by all the refuge and the hope of sinners; be then my refuge and my hope. Assist me for the love of Jesus Christ, stretch forth your hand to a miserable, fallen creature who recommends himself to you and who devotes himself to your service forever.

I bless and thank Almighty God who in His mercy has given me this confidence in you which I hold to be a pledge of my eternal salvation. It is true, dearest Mother, that in the past I have miserably fallen into sin because I had no recourse to you. I know that, with your help, I shall conquer. I know, too, that you will assist me if I recommend myself to you.

But I fear, dear Mother, that in time of danger I may neglect to call on you and thus lose my soul. This grace, then, I ask of you and this I beg with all the fervor of my soul that, in all the attacks of hell, I may ever have recourse to you. O Mary, help me. O Mother of Perpetual Help, never suffer me to lose my God.

NOVENA TO

Our
Lady of Lourdes

HOLY MARY, Immaculate Mother of God, we have come to implore your help and to honor you during this Novena under your beautiful title of Our Lady of Lourdes. Mary, we need your help and protecting care.

In the spiritual and material struggle of life, in the thick of temptation, and the trying hours of worry and affliction, we need you to console and strengthen us. During these days of special grace, therefore, we want to re-awaken our love and affection for you so that you will care for us in a special way. Abide with us, dearest Mother, during these days and draw us close to you. Intercede for us with Christ, your divine Son, and obtain for us the favors we ask in this Novena. (Here mention your intentions.)

St. Bernadette, humble child of Jesus and Mary, join with us in asking Jesus and Mary to bless us and to answer our prayers during these grace-filled days.

NOVENA TO

St. Joseph

ST. JOSEPH, the just man, the perfect man of Nazareth,
the husband of Mary, the foster father of Jesus,
the patron of labor, the patron of a happy death,
the patron of the whole Church,
sinless, selfless, unflinchingly generous,
I am a poor beggar.
I am in need—my record is against me.
I am very disappointing.
I have no excuse, I deserve nothing.
Even for the future how much can I promise?
I cannot be sure of myself, but I wish it were otherwise.
I wish to be faithful to Jesus and you can help,
for Jesus hears you.
Ask Him to forgive, ask Him to forget,
ask Him to make me sinless like you,
to make me selfless like you,
to make me generous.
Take me as your companion and Mary's and His.

ST. JOSEPH AND THE CHRIST CHILD *by Francisco Meneses Osorio*
The Baltimore Museum of Art

NOVENA TO

St. Jude

ST. JUDE, blood cousin of our Brother Jesus,
apostle, martyr, obtain for us
from the giver of every good and perfect gift
all the graces whereof we stand in need,
especially (here mention your intentions)
Help us to take seriously, and to live by,
the divinely inspired words in your epistle,
praying by the grace of the Holy Spirit
to keep ourselves in the love of God
by every means available to us,
and to help them that go astray.
May we be patient in finding out God's holy will
and courageous in carrying it out.
Through Christ our Lord. Amen.

St. Anthony of Padua

WONDERFUL ST. ANTHONY, you had the happiness of receiving in your arms our Blessed Lord disguised as a small child. From His goodness, obtain for me this favor which I desire with all my heart. (Here mention your intention.)

You were so gracious to poor sinners. Do not look upon the unworthiness of him who calls on you but upon the glory of God which through you will be exalted once again through the salvation of my soul and through the granting of my earnest request.

As a sign of my gratitude, I beg you to accept my promise to live from now on more perfectly in accord with the teachings of the Gospel and to be devoted to the service of the poor whom you loved and still love so much.

Look favorably upon my resolution and obtain for me the grace to be faithful to it even until death. Amen.

ST. ANTHONY OF PADUA
by Bartolomé Murillo

St. Anne

DEAR ST. ANNE, filled with compassion for those who, weighed down with many troubles, call upon you, we humbly ask you to do what you can about our present difficulty. (Here mention your intention.)

Please recommend this to your daughter, the Blessed Virgin Mary, and lay it before the throne of your grandson, Jesus, so that He may take care of it. Please keep asking until the matter is settled according to God's will.

Above all, obtain for us the grace of one day being united with the whole wonderful family of God. Amen.

SAINT ANNE
by Leonardo da Vinci

St. Francis Xavier

OUR MOST LOVABLE and loving St. Francis Xavier, in union with you I reverently adore the Divine Majesty. While joyfully giving thanks to God for the singular gifts of grace bestowed upon you during your life and your gifts of glory after death, I beg you with all my heart to please obtain for me by your intercession the greatest of all blessings—the grace of living a holy life and dying a holy death.

Moreover, I beg you to obtain for me (here mention the favor you desire)

But, if what I ask of you so earnestly does not tend to the glory of God and the good of my soul, obtain for me, I pray, what is more conducive to both. Amen.

SAINT FRANCIS XAVIER

St. Thérèse
of the Child Jesus

O MARVELOUS St. Thérèse of the Child Jesus,
who in your brief mortal career
became a mirror of angelic purity, of daring love,
and wholehearted surrender to Almighty God,
turn your eyes of mercy upon us who trust in you.
Beg for us the grace
to keep our hearts and minds pure and clean
and to abhor in all sincerity whatever is evil.
Dear Thérèse, may we experience in every need
the power of your intercession.
Give us comfort in all the bitterness of this life,
and especially at its end,
that we may be worthy
to share eternal happiness with you in heaven. Amen.

SAINT THÉRÈSE OF LISIEUX

Sacraments in the Home

THE SACRAMENTS are channels through which the riches of Calvary are brought to us in great abundance; they are our guarantee that Christ's blood has not been spilled in vain; they are the visible means by which the invisible good things purchased by Christ's pain and dying and rising up are passed on to us. The words, gestures, and materials (water, bread, oil, etc.) of the sacraments convey to us in an outward, meaningful way the spiritual transformation that takes place within us. The sacraments, finally, are a meeting with the Risen Christ at a definite time and place, under definite circumstances and for a definite, all-important purpose.

In the following section are to be found prayers related to the sacraments sometimes administered in the home. The sacraments are not magical. The great spiritual good to be derived from them depends in large part upon the dispositions of the recipient. Therefore, a person should dispose himself through prayer, both before and after the sacraments, in order to profit by his encounter with Christ.

71

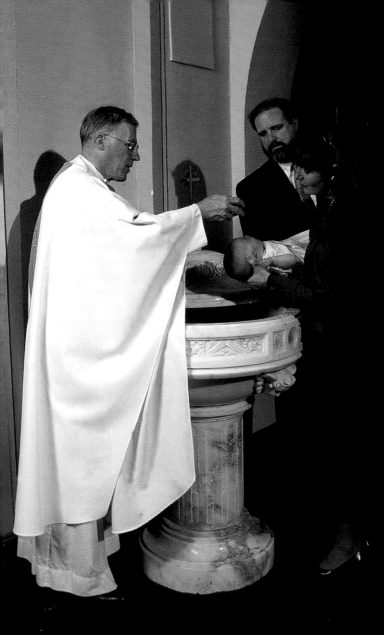

FAMILY PRAYER BEFORE TAKING A CHILD TO CHURCH FOR BAPTISM

> This prayer may be recited by the head of the family as the baptismal party prepares to leave home for the baptism in church.

Heavenly Father, we are about to take our littlest one to be baptized. He (she) is still only our child, but in a very short while, he will also be your child, sharing in your divine life. He will have a right to the riches of your kingdom. Christ, our Brother, will soon also be his Brother. May we so care for him in the coming years that he will never lose the wondrous life that will be given him this day. Help all of us to love one another so that our home, poor as it is, will always be a warm, tender, and healthy harbor for him. May our human failings be so few that, as his eyes begin to open to the world about him, he will be surrounded by goodness. We ask in Christ's name. Amen.

RENEWAL OF BAPTISMAL VOWS

> During the Easter Vigil service, Catholics are called upon to renew, that is, to reaffirm on their own, the vows made on their behalf on the day of baptism by the godparents; nevertheless, it is desirable that each member of the family, on the anniversary of baptism, renew his vows at the evening meal. Indeed, instead of celebrating only the birthdays of each member, the family would do well to celebrate also the anniversary of each one's rebirth in Christ.

I, N., once again renounce Satan, and all his works, and all his pomps. I also solemnly reaffirm on this anniversary of my baptism my Christian faith as expressed in the Apostles' Creed. (Let the individual recite the Apostles' Creed.)

EMERGENCY BAPTISM
IN THE HOME

Ordinarily a newly born child should be taken to the parish church for baptism as soon as possible after birth; but it will sometimes happen that, before this can be done, the child will become sick without warning. If this should occur, someone in the home should baptize the child without delay. A non-Catholic parent should understand that Catholics attach great importance to baptism, believing that an un-baptized child who dies goes into eternity severely handicapped. It will be perfectly happy forever; however, its capacity for happiness will not be nearly as great as it would have been with baptism. This sacrament makes "a new creature" of us, endowing us with the riches of Christ. After a child grows up, he will have to accept Christ as his Savior and live a Christian life in order to be worthy of Heaven, but before he reaches the stage of free choice, Christ is a Savior to him only through baptism.

Anyone in the home may baptize an infant in danger of death, provided he wants to do what the Church does, even though he does not believe in what he is doing. Furthermore, the person baptizing must pour water on the head of the child while at the same time saying the following words:

> "I baptize you in the name of the Father
> and of the Son and of the Holy Spirit."

Later, the infant, if it recovers, should be taken to the parish church for the rest of the baptismal ceremony and in order that the baptism be officially inscribed in the parish records.

It is of great importance to remember that, when there is a miscarriage, the foetus, even though only hours old, should be baptized immediately. This is done by slitting the sack, submerging the foetus in a container of water and lifting it out, saying meanwhile the words, "I baptize you in the name of the Father, and of the Son, and of the Holy Spirit."

PRAYER ON THE ANNIVERSARY
OF CONFIRMATION

It is suggested that, after the family meal, this prayer be said by that member of the family who is celebrating the anniversary of his confirmation.

Holy Spirit, on this anniversary of my confirmation, I thank you again for my sacrament. I am aware of having failed to take full advantage of your being with me. I am sorry. Help me to be a stronger, braver and a more grown-up Christian than I have been so far. Make me more obedient to your inspirations. Let me realize more thoroughly that, because of my confirmation, my life ought to be a proof to others that it is good to walk in the footsteps of Christ. Spirit of love, increase my love for God and my neighbor. Amen.

PRAYER ON THE EVE
OF CONFIRMATION

It is suggested that this prayer be said aloud after the family meal by the one who will be confirmed on the following day.

Holy Spirit, on my Confirmation Day tomorrow, help me

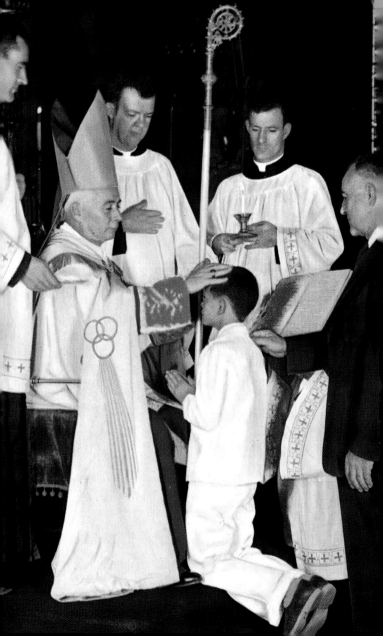

to be fully aware of the riches that will be given to me and let me understand that I am freely taking upon myself a much more active part in Christ's kingdom. May I use well the added strength that will be given to me. The time will not be long in coming when I shall be grown up physically and standing on my own. When that time comes, let me not be ashamed of Christ; let me make it clear to others, by my speech and my way of living, that Christ is everything to me. Amen.

Confession for the Family

THE TIME may not be long in coming when it will be an accepted practice for Catholic families to go as a group to church for confession. Sin is never a purely personal affair. It not only hurts society in general but particularly damages a family and undermines its spiritual well-being. A family therefore should seek as a group to be healed of what is ailing it, otherwise the ill health of some will affect adversely the others. It is suggested that the family, before going to church for confession, gather together for preparatory prayer and for the examination of conscience. (However, no pressure of any kind should be exerted on any member who would be reluctant to join the group.) The head of the family should conduct the entire procedure. If he is not Catholic, he ought, nevertheless, to take as active a part in the religious life of his family as his conscience will permit. If he should remain silent and aloof in religious matters, he would tend to sow doubt in the minds of his children and even perhaps destroy all religious faith in their hearts.

Below will be found a suggested procedure for family preparation for confession.

PREPARATORY PRAYER

To be recited by the Catholic parent.

Christ, our Brother, risen from the dead, we are going now to meet you in the sacrament of penance. You came to the Apostles after they had run out on you and lost faith in you, and you said to them that wonderful word "Peace"!— that word which told them that their cowardice and lack of faith and even Peter's denial of you were all forgiven. Come to us with that infinitely kind word of forgiveness. We have failed you; we have been weak and cowardly and selfish. We wish, all of us, to be deeply sorry for our sins and to be firmly resolved to do better in the future. Help us in this regard.

Holy Spirit, enlighten our minds that we may see ourselves as we really are . . . . that we may know our sins, our weaknesses, our failures to do the good we could have done. May our confession be a source of special grace for us, a healing for the wounds of our soul, a renewal of our desire to love God above all things and our neighbor as ourselves. Give us the courage and the humility to acknowledge in the presence of Christ's representative in the confessional the evil we have done and the good we have failed to do. Help us to understand that only when we have brought ourselves to tell Christ's representative our sins can we be sure that we have owned up to them. Help us with our examination of conscience.

EXAMINATION OF CONSCIENCE

It is suggested here that the head of the family improvise, on the basis of his knowledge of what has gone on in the family since the last confession, a series of questions or remarks. It might sound something like the following: "It seems to me that lately we have had too many critical things to say about the neighbors," and "things aren't too well with this family—a lot of quarreling, thoughtlessness, selfishness, unwillingness to help each other. Disobedience is not good for a family, nor is lying; laziness is sinful; maybe there could be a little more serious study around here. God is our loving Father and we shouldn't use His name irreverently. If anyone has done anything seriously wrong, let him not complicate matters by not telling the sin in confession."

If the head of the house does not feel up to improvisation of this sort, let him simply enumerate the Ten Commandments listed below, pausing after each one so that the members of the family may examine their conscience.

THE TEN COMMANDMENTS

1. I am the Lord, thy God, thou shalt not have strange gods before me.
2. Thou shalt not take the name of the Lord thy God in vain.
3. Remember thou keep holy the Sabbath Day.
4. Honor thy father and thy mother.
5. Thou shalt not kill.
6. Thou shalt not commit adultery.
7. Thou shalt not steal.
8. Thou shalt not bear false witness against thy neighbor.
9. Thou shalt not covet thy neighbor's wife.
10. Thou shalt not covet thy neighbor's goods.

(Then all should make a heart-felt act of contrition together and go to church together for confession.)

ACT OF CONTRITION

Either the following act may be used or one that the entire family would know by heart.

O my God, I am heartily sorry for having offended thee. I detest all my sins because I dread the loss of Heaven and the pains of Hell, but most of all, because I have offended thee, my God, who are so worthy of my love. I firmly resolve with the help of thy grace to confess my sins, to do penance, and to amend my life. Amen.

The following Psalms may be recited here:

Psalm 130

> Out of the depths I cry to you, O Lord;
>> Lord, hear my voice!
> Let your ears be attentive
>> to my voice in supplication:
> If you, O Lord, mark iniquities,
>> Lord, who can stand?
> But with you is forgiveness,
>> that you may be revered.
> I trust in the Lord;
>> my soul trusts in his word.
> My soul waits for the Lord
>> more than sentinels wait for the dawn.
> More than sentinels wait for the dawn,
>> let Israel wait for the Lord,
> For with the Lord is kindness
>> and with him is plenteous redemption;
> And he will redeem Israel
>> from all their iniquities.

Psalm 51

Have mercy on me, O God, in your goodness;
    in the greatness of your compassion wipe out
      my offense.
Thoroughly wash me from my guilt
    and of my sin cleanse me.
For I acknowledge my offense,
    and my sin is before me always:
"Against you only have I sinned,
    and done what is evil in your sight"—
That you may be justified in your sentence,
    vindicated when you condemn.
Indeed, in guilt was I born,
    and in sin my mother conceived me;
Behold, you are pleased with sincerity of heart,
    and in my inmost being you teach me wisdom.
Cleanse me of sin with hyssop, that I may be
      purified;
    wash me, and I shall be whiter than snow.
Let me hear the sounds of joy and gladness;
    the bones you have crushed shall rejoice.
Turn away your face from my sins,
    and blot out all my guilt.
A clean heart create for me, O God,
    and a steadfast spirit renew within me.
Cast me not out from your presence,
    and your holy spirit take not from me.
Give me back the joy of your salvation,
    and a willing spirit sustain in me.

COMMUNION

Communion in the Home

A SICK MEMBER of the family receiving communion in the home is a matter that should concern the whole family; therefore those who are present in the home when the priest arrives should assemble at the door on their knees to greet him and, more importantly, Him whom he brings. One member should have a lighted candle which should not be blown out until after the sick one has received. If, however, the priest has other communion calls to go to, the candle should not be extinguished until he has left the house. All should accompany the priest to the bedside and then retire to a distance if the sick one is to confess. Afterwards, all should return to the bedside and remain on their knees until the service is ended and the priest removes his stole. If he continues to wear his stole, they should not speak to him but rather accompany him quietly to the door. The sick one should be left alone prior to communion and for at least a quarter of an hour afterwards in order to make his preparation for the sacrament and his thanksgiving after receiving it.

Below are to be found some of the traditional private prayers used for this occasion. One may, however, if he wishes, speak from the heart, improvising his own prayers and using what is below only occasionally.

Before Communion

Antiphon. Remember not, O Lord, our offenses nor those of
   our fathers and take not vengeance on our sins.

How lovely is your dwelling place, O Lord of Hosts.
My soul yearns and pines for the courts of the Lord.
My heart and my flesh cry out for the living God.
Even the sparrow finds a home, and the swallow a nest in
   which she puts her young.
Your altars, O Lord of hosts, my king and my God!
Happy they who dwell in your house,
   continually they praise you.
Happy the men whose strength you are!
   their hearts are set upon the pilgrimage.
When they pass through the arid valley,
   they make a spring of it; the early rain clothes it with
   generous growth.
They go from strength to strength;
   they shall see the God of gods in Sion.
O Lord of hosts, hear my prayer, hearken,
   O God of Jacob!
O God, behold our shield, and look upon the face of your
   anointed.
I had rather one day in your courts than a thousand else-
   where;
I had rather lie at the threshold of the house of my God
   than dwell in the tents of the wicked.
For a sun and a shield is the Lord God,
   grace and glory he bestows.

The Lord withholds no good thing from those who walk in
  sincerity.
O Lord of hosts, happy the men who trust in you!
Glory be to the Father, and to the Son, and to the Holy
  Spirit, as it was in the beginning is now and ever shall be,
  world without end. Amen.

You have favored, O Lord, your land;
You have restored the well-being of Jacob.
You have forgiven the guilt of your people;
  you have covered all their sins.
You have withdrawn all your wrath;
  you have revoked your burning anger.
Restore us, O God our savior, and abandon your displea-
  sure against us.
Will you be ever angry with us,
  prolonging your anger to all generations?
Will you not instead give us life;
  and shall not your people rejoice in you?
Show us, O Lord, your kindness and grant us your salva-
  tion.
I will hear what God proclaims;
  the Lord—for he proclaims peace
To his people, and to his faithful ones, and to those who
  put in him their hope.
Near indeed is his salvation to those who fear him, glory
  dwelling in our land.
Kindness and truth shall meet;
  justice and peace shall kiss.
Truth shall spring out of the earth and justice shall look
  down from Heaven.
The Lord himself will give his benefits;
  our land shall yield its increase.

Justice shall walk before him and salvation, along the way
  of his steps.
Glory be to the Father, and to the Son,
    and to the Holy Spirit, as it was in the beginning, is now
    and ever shall be, world without end. Amen.

Incline your ear, O Lord; answer me,
    for I am afflicted and poor.
Keep my life, for I am devoted to you;
    save your servant who trusts in you.
You are my God, have pity on me, O Lord,
    for to you I call all the day.
Gladden the soul of your servant, for to you,
    O Lord, I lift up my soul;
For you, O Lord, are good and forgiving,
    abounding in kindness to all who call upon you.
Hearken, O Lord, to my prayer and attend to the sound of
  my pleading.
In the day of my distress I call upon you,
    for you will answer me.
There is none like you among the gods, O Lord, and there
  are no works like yours.
All the nations you have made shall come and worship you,
    O Lord, and glorify your name.
For you are great, and you do wondrous deeds; you alone
  are God.
Teach me, O Lord, your way that I may walk in your
  truth; direct my heart that it may fear your name.
I will give thanks to you, O Lord my God,
    with all my heart, and I will glorify your name forever.
Great has been your kindness toward me; you have res-
  cued me from the depths of the nether world.
O God, the haughty have risen up against me,

and the company of fierce men seeks my life,
nor do they set you before their eyes.

But you, O Lord, are a God merciful and gracious, slow to anger, abounding in kindness and fidelity.

Turn toward me, and have pity on me; give your strength to your servant and save the son of your handmaid.

Grant me a proof of your favor, that my enemies may see, to their confusion, that you, O Lord, have helped and comforted me.

Glory be to the Father, and to the Son and to the Holy Spirit, as it was in the beginning, is now and ever shall be, world without end. Amen.

I believed, even when I said "I am greatly afflicted,"
I said in my alarm, "No man is dependable."

How shall I make a return to the Lord for all the good he has done for me?

The cup of salvation I will take up, and I will call upon the name of the Lord;

My vows to the Lord I will pay in the presence of all his people.

Precious in the eyes of the Lord is the death of his faithful ones.

O Lord, I am your servant; I am your servant,
the son of your handmaid; you have loosed my bonds.

To you will I offer sacrifice of thanksgiving, and I will call upon the name of the Lord.

My vows to the Lord I will pay in the presence of all his people, in the courts of the house of the Lord, in your midst, O Jerusalem.

Glory be to the Father, and to the Son and to the Holy Spirit, as it was in the beginning, is now and ever shall be, world without end. Amen.

Out of the depths I cry to you, O Lord; Lord, hear my voice!
Let your ears be attentive to my voice in supplication.
If you, O Lord, mark iniquities, Lord, who can stand?
But with you is forgiveness, that you may be revered.
I trust in the Lord; my soul trusts in his word.
My soul waits for the Lord more than sentinels wait for
    the dawn.
More than sentinels wait for the dawn,
    let Israel wait for the Lord,
For with the Lord is kindness and with him is plenteous
    redemption;
And he will redeem Israel from all their iniquities.
Glory be to the Father, and to the Son, and to the Holy
    Spirit, as it was in the beginning, is now and ever shall
    be, world without end. Amen.

Antiphon. Remember not, O Lord, our offenses, nor those
    of our fathers and take not vengeance on our sins.

Lord have mercy on us, Christ have mercy on us, Lord
    have mercy on us.
Our Father, who art in Heaven, hallowed be thy name.
    Thy kingdom come, thy will be done on earth as it is in
    Heaven.
Give us this day our daily bread, and forgive us our tres-
    passes as we forgive those who trespass against us, and
    lead us not into temptation but deliver us from evil.

V. I said, Lord have mercy upon me.
R. Heal my soul for I have sinned against thee.
V. Turn thee, O Lord, a little toward me and be en-
    treated as thy servant.
R. Let thy mercy, O Lord, be upon us as we have hoped
    in thee.

V. Let thy priest be clothed with righteousness.
R. And let thy saints rejoice.
V. From my secret sins, cleanse me, O Lord.
R. And from those that he has not committed spare thy servant.
V. Lord, hear my prayer.
R. And let my cry come unto thee.

Let Us Pray

Incline, O most gracious Lord, your ears of mercy to our prayers, and enlighten our hearts by the grace of the Holy Spirit so that we may merit worthily to receive the sacrament of the Eucharist and to love you with everlasting love.

O God, before whom every heart lies open and to whom every desire speaks, and from whom no secret lies hid, cleanse the thoughts of our hearts by the pouring forth of your Holy Spirit, so that we may merit perfectly to love you and worthily to praise you. Inflame, O Lord, our hearts with the fire of your Holy Spirit so that we may serve you with a chaste heart and please you with a clean heart.

We beseech you, O Lord, that the Holy Spirit who proceeds from you may enlighten our minds and lead us, as your Son has promised, unto all truth. May the power of your Holy Spirit, we beg you, O Lord, be present to us, mercifully to cleanse our hearts and to defend them from all harm.

O God, you teach the hearts of your faithful by the light of the Holy Spirit. Grant that in the same Spirit, we may be truly wise and ever rejoice in His consolation.

Cleanse, we beg you, O Lord, our conscience by your coming, so that when our Lord Jesus Christ, your Son, shall come, He may find in us a mansion prepared for Him, who lives and reigns with you in the unity of the Holy Spirit, God, world without end. Amen.

PRAYER OF ST. AMBROSE

To the table of your banquet, Lord Jesus Christ, I, a sinner, approach with fear and trembling, relying not at all on my own merits, but having confidence in your mercy and goodness. My heart and my body are stained with many sins, my mind and my tongue are not watched over with care; therefore, O loving God, I who am caught in the midst of my excesses turn to you—the fountain of mercy. To you do I hasten to be healed, to your protection I run. I dread to stand before you as my judge; but for you as my Savior I yearn. To you, O Lord, I show my wounds, to you I uncover my shame. I know that my sins are many and great; and I am frightened by them. I hope in your mercies, for of them there is no number.

Therefore look upon me with your eyes of mercy, O Lord Jesus Christ, eternal King, God and man, crucified for man's sake. Graciously hear me who hope in you; you, who are so kind, have pity on me, a sinner. Hail, saving victim, offered upon the cross for me and for all men. Hail, noble and precious blood, flowing from the wounds of my crucified Lord Jesus Christ and washing away the sins of the whole world! Remember, O Lord, your creature whom you have redeemed with your blood.

I repent of having sinned. I desire to amend what I have done. Take from me, therefore, merciful Father, all my iniquities and my sins so that, cleansed in mind and body, I may worthily receive the Holy of Holies. Grant that my receiving of your body and blood which I purpose to take, unworthy though I am, may bring to me pardon for my sins, the perfect cleansing of my faults, the driving out of evil thoughts, the renewal of my efforts to lead a life of genuine love and a most strong protection, both in body and soul, against the wiles of my enemies. Amen.

PRAYER OF ST. THOMAS

Almighty and everlasting God, behold I come to the sacrament of your only begotten Son, Our Lord Jesus Christ. I come as one sick to the physician of life, unclean to the fountain of mercy, blind to the light of eternal brightness, poor and in need to the Lord of heaven and earth. Therefore, I beg you that you would heal my weakness, wash my uncleanness, give light to my blindness, enrich my poverty and cloth my nakedness so that I may receive the bread of angels, the King of kings and the Lord of lords, with such reverence and humility, such contrition and devotion, such purity and faith, such purpose and intention, as shall aid my soul's salvation. Grant that I may not only receive the sacrament of the body and blood of the Lord but also its full reality and power. O most merciful God, give me the privilege of receiving the body of Our Lord Jesus Christ, which he took from the virgin Mary, that I may merit to be incorporated into his mystical body, and to be numbered among his members. O most loving Father, let me behold for all eternity, face to face, your own beloved Son, whom now on my pilgrimage I am about to receive under a veil, who lives and reigns with you in the unity of the Holy Spirit, God, world without end. Amen.

𝔓rayers 𝔄fter 𝔥oly 𝔠ommunion

Antiphon. Let us sing the hymn of the three children which
these holy ones sang of old in the fiery furnace, giving
praise to the Lord.

All ye works of the Lord, bless the Lord;
praise and exalt him above all forever.
O ye angels of the Lord, bless the Lord;
praise and exalt him above all forever.
O all ye waters that are above the heavens,
bless the Lord; praise and exalt him above all forever.
O all ye powers of the Lord, bless the Lord;
praise and exalt him above all forever.
O ye sun and moon, bless the Lord;
praise and exalt him above all forever.
O ye stars of heaven, bless the Lord;
praise and exalt him above all forever.
O every shower and dew, bless ye the Lord;
praise and exalt him above all forever.
O all ye spirits of God, bless the Lord;
praise and exalt him above all forever.
O ye fire and heat, bless the Lord;
praise and exalt him above all forever.
O ye cold and heat, bless the Lord;
praise and exalt him above all forever.
O ye dews and hoar frosts, bless the Lord;
praise and exalt him above all forever.
O ye frost and cold, bless the Lord;
praise and exalt him above all forever.
O ye ice and snow, bless the Lord;
praise and exalt him above all forever.

HEAD OF CHRIST *by Rembrandt*
The Metropolitan Museum of Art, Bequest of Isaac D. Fletcher, 1917

O ye nights and days, bless the Lord;
  praise and exalt him above all forever.
O ye light and darkness, bless the Lord;
  praise and exalt him above all forever.
O ye lightnings and clouds, bless the Lord;
  praise and exalt him above all forever.
O let the earth bless the Lord; let it praise
  and exalt him above all forever.
O ye mountains and hills, bless the Lord;
  praise and exalt him above all forever.
O all ye things that spring up in the earth,
  bless the Lord; praise and exalt him above all forever.
O ye fountains, bless the Lord;
  praise and exalt him above all forever.
O ye seas and rivers, bless the Lord;
  praise and exalt him above all forever.
O ye whales and all that move in the waters,
  bless the Lord; praise and exalt him above all forever.
O all ye fowls of the air, bless the Lord;
  praise and exalt him above all forever.
O all ye beasts and cattle, bless the Lord;
  praise and exalt him above all forever.
O ye sons of men, bless the Lord;
  praise and exalt him above all forever.
O let Israel bless the Lord; let them praise
  and exalt him above all forever.
O ye priests of the Lord, bless the Lord;
  praise and exalt him above all forever.
O ye servants of the Lord, bless the Lord;
  praise and exalt him above all forever.
O ye spirits and souls of the just, bless
  the Lord; praise and exalt him above all forever.

O ye holy and humble of heart, bless the Lord;
praise and exalt him above all forever.
O Ananias, Azarias, and Misael, bless ye
the Lord; praise and exalt him above all forever.
For he hath delivered us from hell, and
saved us out of the hand of death, and
delivered us out of the midst of the burning
flame, and saved us out of the midst of the fire.
Blessed art thou in the firmament of heaven;
and worthy of praise and glorious, exalted above
all forever.

Praise the Lord in his sanctuary,
praise him in the firmament of his strength.
Praise him for his mighty deeds,
praise him for his sovereign majesty.
Praise him with the blast of the trumpet,
praise him with lyre and harp.
Praise him with timbrel and dance,
praise him with strings and pipe.
Praise him with sounding cymbals,
praise him with clanging cymbals.
Let everything that has breath praise the
Lord! Alleluia!

Glory be to the Father, and to the Son and to the
Holy Spirit, as it was in the beginning, is
now and ever shall be, world without end. Amen.

Antiphon. Let us sing the hymn of the three children which
these holy ones sang of old in the fiery furnace, giving
praise to the Lord.
                    Lord, have mercy,

Christ, have mercy,
Lord, have mercy.

Our Father, who art in Heaven, hallowed be thy name, thy kingdom come, thy will be done on earth as it is in Heaven. Give us this day our daily bread and forgive us our trespasses as we forgive those who trespass against us and lead us not into temptation, but deliver us from evil.

Let all your works praise you, O Lord, and let your Saints bless you.

V. The Saints shall rejoice in glory.
R. They shall rejoice in their resting places.
V. Not unto us, O Lord, not unto us.
R. But unto your name give the glory.
V. O Lord, hear my prayer.
R. And let my cry come unto you.

Let Us Pray

O God, who put out the flames of fire for the three children, grant, in your mercy, that the flames of vice may not consume us, your servants. Guide, O Lord, we beg of you, our actions by your inspirations, and promote them by your assistance. Let every prayer and work of ours begin always from you and through you, likewise, be ended. Give us, O Lord, we beg you, to extinguish the flames of our sins, even as you strengthened blessed Lawrence to rise above the fiery torments, through Christ our Lord. Amen.

PRAYER OF ST. THOMAS

I give thanks, O Holy Lord, Father Almighty, Eternal God, who through no merits of my own, but solely through the greatness of your own mercy have nourished me a sinner, and your unworthy servant, with the precious body and blood of your son, Our Lord Jesus Christ. I beg you that this Holy Communion may not be unto me a judgment for punishment, but let it be a saving plea for pardon. Let it be to me the armour of faith and a shield of good will. Let it be the cleansing of all my vices, the destruction of all my evil desires and lust, the increase of love and patience, of humility and obedience and of all virtues. Let my communion be a firm defense against the snares of all enemies, both visible and invisible. Let it be the perfect stilling of all my evil impulses both bodily and spiritual and a firm clinging to you, the one and true God, and the happy fulfillment of my life. And I beg you that you would lead me, a sinner, to that wonderful banquet, where you, together with your Son and the Holy Spirit, are to your saints true life, complete fullness, everlasting joy, supreme delight and perfect happiness. Through the same Christ, our Lord. Amen.

PRAYER TO JESUS CRUCIFIED

To be said before an image of the Crucifix.

Behold, O kind and most sweet Jesus, I cast myself upon my knees in your sight and with the most fervent desire of my soul, I pray and beg you that you will impress upon my heart lively sentiments of faith, hope and love, with true repentance of my sins and a firm desire of amendment, while with deep affection and grief of soul, I ponder within myself and mentally contemplate your five most precious wounds, having before my eyes that which David the prophet put in your own mouth concerning you, O good

Jesus; "They have pierced my hands and feet; they have numbered all my bones."

If said before an image of Christ crucified a partial indulgence; a plenary indulgence under the usual conditions.

SOUL OF CHRIST

> Soul of Christ, sanctify me.
> Body of Christ, save me.
> Blood of Christ, fill my veins.
> Water from the side of Christ, wash me.
> Passion of Christ, strengthen me.
> O Good Jesus, hear me.
> Within your wounds, hide me.
> And never let me be separated from thee.
> From the evil enemy, defend me.
> In the hour of my death, call me.
> And order me to come to you, so that
>   with your saints I may praise you,
> world without end. Amen.

ACT OF SELF-OBLATION

Take, O Lord, all my liberty. Receive my memory, understanding, and entire will. You have given me whatever I have—I give it all back to you, to be entirely subject to your will. Give me only your love and your grace and I am rich enough and ask for nothing more.

A FINAL PRAYER

I beg you, Lord Jesus Christ, that your passion may be to me strength by which I may be guarded, protected and de-

THE CRUCIFIXION *by del Tufo*

THE APPARITION OF PETER THE APOSTLE
TO SAINT PETER NOLASCO
by Francisco de Zurbarán
Museo del Prado, Madrid, Spain

fended; may your wounds be to me food and drink by which I can be fed, strengthened and enlightened; may the shedding of your blood be to me the cleansing of all my faults; may your death be to me life unending and your cross everlasting glory. May these be my refreshment, my joy, my health, and the gladness of my heart. Amen.

*   *   *   *

Jesus therefore said to them, "Amen, amen, I say to you, unless you eat the flesh of the Son of Man, and drink his blood, you shall not have life in you. He who eats my flesh and drinks my blood has life everlasting and I will raise him up on the last day. For my flesh is food indeed, and my blood is drink indeed. He who eats my flesh, and drinks my blood, abides in me and I in him. As the living Father has sent me, and as I live because of the Father, so he who eats me, he also shall live because of me. This is the bread that has come down from heaven; not as your fathers ate the manna, and died. He who eats this bread shall live forever."

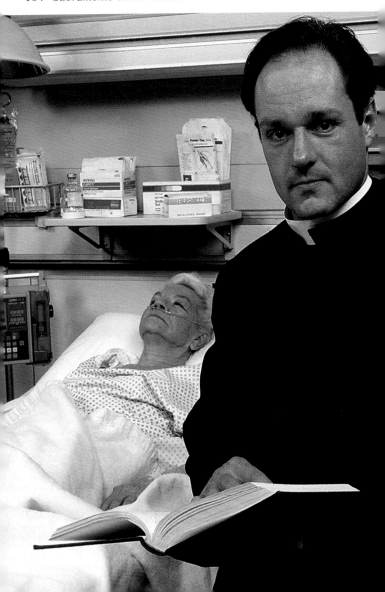

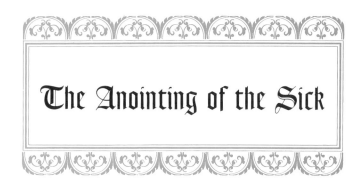

The Anointing of the Sick

THE ANOINTING of the Sick is a sacrament designed to help those who are in danger of death from sickness, accident, or old age. Anyone who senses himself to be seriously ill or who is aware that he is getting well on in years ought to expect that the priest will suggest that he (or she) be anointed. Better still, the person himself under these circumstances ought to indicate his willingness to be anointed if the priest deems it advisable. The anointing does not mean that the person will inevitably die soon after. On the contrary, this sacrament quite often restores the recipient to good health and inspires him to make good use of the years that have been added to his life. If, however, the hour of death is imminent, then Christ will come in this sacrament to lead the sick person from Calvary down into the valley of death, and from there, into the glory of his kingdom. Special graces will be offered to the dying person helping him to make of his death a perfect act of love, that is, the total surrender of himself into the hands of his heavenly Father. If this be the case, he could go straight to Heaven because all that is needed at the end to be fit for the perfect happiness of Heaven is perfect love.

105

The following prayer may be said by the sick person when he knows beforehand that the priest is coming to anoint him, or, if he is incapable of reading the prayer, someone in the family may read it aloud for him.

PRAYER BEFORE THE ANOINTING OF THE SICK

My Brother Christ, I will soon meet you in your sacrament for the sick. Although it is considered that I am in danger of death, let me not be afraid. Let me be aware that, if the Father wants me to come home to him, you will take me by the hand and lead me through the valley of death into the glory of your kingdom. Help me to die the way you died—with your words on my lips, "Father, into your hands I commend my spirit." If I am to leave this life, comfort those whom I leave behind. Help them to realize the great good fortune that is mine—that Christ is coming to take me from this country of exile into the promised land. I ask that my good fortune will one day be theirs also—to die in Christ. Amen.

*   *   *   *

Regarding Prayer in Time of Sickness

To pray when we are sick is difficult. Nevertheless, we ought to try to fill up the long days of sickness with prayer, making good use of time that can be so easily squandered. What many people who are bedridden may well need is some sort of fixed schedule for the day if they are to be faithful in their efforts to pray. Below will be found a suggested schedule. For some it may prove to be too demanding, for others, too lenient, but for all, it will offer some guidance for using the hours of the day profitably. Let it be stressed that it is not very profitable to spend the *whole* day asking *only* for a return to good health; we would do better to pray for growth in God's grace and love and for the good of our neighbor, leaving the question of our health to the will of God

Schedule of Praying During the Day for a Sick Person

Upon Awakening	Morning Prayers (See page 6). Prayers before and after Communion (See page 86, 95).

If the priest is not coming with Communion, the sick one may recite the spiritual Communion on page 229.

Mid-morning	Psalm for the morning (See page 139).
Before lunch	Five decades of the Rosary for a worthy intention. (See page 17 for the Mysteries.)
Mid-afternoon	Scripture Reading for the day (See page 239).
Before the evening meal . . .	Psalm for the afternoon (See page 139).
After dinner	The Rosary (See page 15).
Later in the evening	Psalm for the night (See page 140).
Before going to sleep	Evening Prayers (See page 8).

At any suitable time of the day, the following special prayer may be said.

PRAYER IN TIME OF SICKNESS

Heavenly Father, I firmly believe you watch over us at all times and that you would not allow senseless, needless suffering to come to any of your dear children. I believe, therefore, that my sickness is neither senseless nor needless. I trust you, knowing that you would allow no cross to come my way without at the same time offering me strength sufficient to carry it. Since loving you is essentially a matter of accepting your will, I wish to love you in my acceptance of this sickness. Indeed, I thank you for this precious gift of sickness, because, in some way known to you, it is for my good. Let me not squander this gift. Finally, let me see it as a sharing in the cross of Christ; let me so accept and bear up under my poor health, that it will be for the good health of the body of Christ. If you should want me to go on being an instrument in your hands for the good of others, please restore me to good health. I ask in Christ's name. Amen.

PRAYER FOR A SICK FAMILY MEMBER

> When a member of a family is sick in a hospital, the younger children ordinarily will not be permitted in the room: however in some places the hospital might allow the whole family to gather around the patient's bedside for a brief moment of family prayer. In any event, if the sick one is at home, a family prayer would certainly be feasible and, above all, to be recommended. Each evening after the family meal, the entire family should go to the bedside of the sick one and say the prayer below, or a similar one from other sources, or better still, an improvised prayer. It is suggested that the members take turns saying the prayer each evening.

Heavenly Father, we ask, if it be your will, that our sick one get well as soon as possible. In the meantime, may he (she) understand that the pain and misery of sickness are good for us. May he come out of this sickness with a deeper compassion for all the suffering ones of the world, and be stronger to accept your will when even heavier crosses come his way. May he know the peace and joy of those who suffer willingly in union with the suffering Christ. We ask in His name. Amen.

Regarding Prayer for the Dying

Dying has long since ceased to be the family affair that it used to be. Even in a private room of the hospital we die rather publicly. This is regrettable, if necessary. But when a member of the family is placed on the hospital's critical list, some effort should be made to surround the hours of his dying with family prayer. Certainly when the priest comes for the last rites and, later on, for the prayers of the dying, as many of the family as possible should be present to take part in the liturgy. What is to be done during the rest of the "death watch" should be determined by the head of the household. It is suggested that he (she) quite frankly make known to the sick one his real condition; the last hours of one's life are too precious for one to be the victim of lies, deception, or false assurances; rather, let the whole family convey to the sick one by their attitude and speech their belief that if death does come to him, it should be a joyous going home to his Father in the company of Christ his Savior. All prayers and wishes for his recovery, however ardent, should be conditioned by a desire that God's will be done.

During the long vigil, those of the family who are present may recite five mysteries of the Rosary and, from time to time, appropriate selections from the scriptures may be read. Suggested readings will be found below:

[*Mark 5:22–42*] And there came one of the rulers of the synagogue named Jairus. And seeing Jesus, he fell at his feet, and entreated him much saying, "My daughter is at the point of death; come, lay thy hands upon her, that she may be saved and live."

And he went away with him, and a great crowd was following him and pressing upon him. And there was a woman who for twelve years had had a hemorrhage, and had suffered much at the hands of many physicians, and had spent all that she had, and found no benefit, but rather grew worse. Hearing about Jesus, she came up behind him in the crowd and touched his cloak. For she said, "If I touch but his cloak, I shall be saved." And at once the flow of her blood was dried up, and she felt in her body that she was healed of her affliction.

And Jesus, instantly perceiving in himself that power had gone forth from him, turned to the crowd, and said, "Who touched my cloak?" And his disciples said to him, "Thou seest the crowd pressing upon thee, and dost thou say, 'Who touched me?'" And he was looking round to see her who had done this. But the woman, fearing and trembling, knowing what had happened within her, came and fell down before him, and told him all the truth. But he said to her, "Daughter, thy faith has saved thee. Go in peace, and be thou healed of thy affliction."

While he was yet speaking, there came some from the house of the ruler of the synagogue, saying, "Thy daughter is dead. Why dost thou trouble the Master further?" But Jesus, having heard what was being said, said to the ruler of the synagogue, "Do not be afraid, only have faith." And he allowed no one to follow him except Peter and James, and John the brother of James.

And they came to the house of the ruler of the synagogue and he saw a tumult, people weeping and wailing greatly. And going in he said to them, "Why do you make this din, and weep? The girl is asleep, not dead." And they laughed him to scorn. But he, putting them all out, took the father and mother of the girl and those who were with him, and entered in where the girl was lying. And taking the girl by the hand, he said to her, "Talitha cumi," which is interpreted, "Girl, I say to thee, arise." And the girl rose up immediately and began to walk; she was twelve years old. And they were utterly amazed.

[*Luke 24:1–53*] But on the first day of the week at early dawn, they came to the tomb, taking the spices that they had prepared, and they found the stone rolled back from the tomb. But on entering, they did not find the body of the Lord Jesus. And it came to pass, while they were wondering what to make of this, that, behold, two men stood by them in dazzling raiment. And when the women were struck with fear and bowed their faces to the ground, they said to them, "Why do you seek the living one among the dead? He is not here, but has risen. Remember how he spoke to you while he was yet in Galilee, saying that the Son of Man must be betrayed into the hands of sinful men, and be crucified, and on the third day rise."

And they remembered his words. And having returned from the tomb, they reported all these things to the Eleven, and to all the rest. Now, it was Mary Magdalene and Joanna and Mary, the mother of James, and the other women who were with them, who were telling these things to the apostles. But this tale seemed to them to be nonsense, and they did not believe the women.

But Peter arose and ran to the tomb; and stooping down, he saw the linen cloths laid there; and he went away wondering to himself at what had come to pass.

And behold, two of them were going that very day to a village named Emmaus, which is sixty stadia from Jerusalem. And they were talking to each other about all these things that had happened. And it came to pass, while they were conversing and arguing together, that Jesus himself also drew near and went along with them; but their eyes were held, that they should not recognize him. And he said to them, "What words are these that you are exchanging as you walk and are sad?"

But one of them, named Cleophas, answered and said to him, "Art thou the only stranger in Jerusalem who does not know the things that have happened there in these days?" And he said to them, "What things?"

And they said to him, "Concerning Jesus of Nazareth, who was a prophet, mighty in work and word before God and all the people; and how our chief priests and rulers delivered him up to be sentenced to death, and crucified him. But we were hoping that it was he who should redeem Israel. Yes, and besides all this, today is the third day since these things came to pass. And moreover, certain women of our company, who were at the tomb before it was light, astounded us, and not finding his body, they came, saying that they had also seen a vision of angels, who said that he is alive. So some of our company went to the tomb, and found it even as the women had said, but him they did not see."

But he said to them, "O foolish ones and slow of heart to believe in all that the prophets have spoken! Did not the Christ have to suffer these things before entering into his glory?" And beginning then with Moses and with all the Prophets, he interpreted to them in all the Scriptures the things referring to himself.

And they drew near to the village to which they were going, and he acted as though he were going on. And they urged him, saying, "Stay with us, for it is getting towards evening, and the day is now far spent." And he went in with them. And it came to pass when he reclined at table with them, that he took the bread and blessed and broke and began handing it to them. And their eyes were opened, and they recognized him; and he vanished from their sight. And they said to each other, "Was not our heart burning within us while he was speaking on the road and explaining to us the Scriptures?"

And rising up that very hour, they returned to Jerusalem, where they found the Eleven gathered together and those who were with them, saying, "The Lord has risen indeed, and has appeared to Simon." And they themselves began to relate what had happened on the journey, and how they recognized him in the breaking of the bread.

Now while they were talking of these things, Jesus stood in their midst, and said to them, "Peace to you! It is I, do not be afraid." But they were startled and panic-stricken, and thought that they saw a spirit.

And he said to them, "Why are you disturbed, and why do doubts arise in your hearts? See my hands and feet, that it is I myself. Feel me and see; for a spirit does not have flesh and bones, as you see I have." And having said this, he showed them his hands and his feet. But as they still disbelieved and marvelled for joy, he said, "Have you anything here to eat?" And they offered him a piece of broiled fish and a honeycomb. And when he had eaten in their presence, he took what remained and gave it to them.

And he said to them, "These are the words which I spoke to you while I was yet with you, that all things must be fulfilled that are written in the Law of Moses and the Prophets and the Psalms concerning me." Then he opened their minds, that they might understand the Scriptures. And he said to them, "Thus it is written; and thus the Christ should suffer, and should rise again from the dead on the third day; and that repentance and remission of sins should be preached in his name to all the nations, beginning from Jerusalem. And you yourselves are witnesses of these things. And I send forth upon you the promise of my Father. But wait here in the city, until you are clothed with power from on high."

Now he led them out towards Bethany, and he lifted up his hands and blessed them. And it came to pass as he blessed them, that he parted from them and was carried up into heaven. And they worshipped him, and returned to Jerusalem with great joy. And they were continually in the temple, praising and blessing God. Amen.

[*John 1:1–51*] In the beginning was the Word, and the Word was with God; and the Word was God. He was in the beginning with God. All things were made through him, and without him was made nothing that has been made. In him was life, and the life was the light of men. And the light shines in the darkness; and the darkness grasped it not.

There was a man, one sent from God, whose name was John. This man came as a witness, to bear witness concerning the light, that all might believe through him. He was not himself the light, but was to bear witness to the light. It was the true light that enlightens every man who comes into the world. He was in the world, and the world was made through him, and the world knew him not. He came unto his own, and his own received him not. But to as many as received him he gave the power of becoming sons of God; to those who believe in his name: Who were born not of blood, nor of the will of the flesh, nor of the will of man, but of God.

And the Word was made flesh, and dwelt among us. And we saw his glory—glory as of the only-begotten of the Father—full of grace and of truth. John bore witness concerning him, and cried, "This was he of whom I said, 'He who is to come after me has been set above me, because he was before me.'" And of his fullness we have all received, grace for grace. For the Law was given through Moses; grace and truth came through Jesus Christ. No one has at any time seen God. The only-begotten Son, who is in the bosom of the Father, he has revealed him.

And this is the witness of John, when the Jews sent to him from Jerusalem priests and Levites to ask him, "Who art thou?" And he acknowledged and did not deny; and he acknowledged, "I am not the Christ." And they asked him, "What then? Art thou Elias?" And he said, "I am not." "Art thou the Prophet?" And he answered, "No."

They therefore said to him, "Who art thou? that we may give an answer to those who sent us. What hast thou to say of thyself?" He said, "I am the voice of one crying in the desert, 'Make straight the way of the Lord,' as said Isaias the prophet."

And they who had been sent were from among the Pharisees. And they asked him, and said to him, "Why, then, dost thou baptize, if thou art not the Christ, nor Elias, nor the Prophet?" John said to them in answer, "I baptize with water; but in the midst of you there has stood one whom you do not know. He it is who is to come after me, who has been set above me, the strap of whose sandal I am not worthy to loose."

These things took place at Bethany, beyond the Jordan, where John was baptizing.

The next day John saw Jesus coming to him, and he said, "Behold, the lamb of God, who takes away the sin of the world! This is he of whom I said, 'After me there comes one who has been set above me, because he was before me.' And I did not know him. But that he may be known to Israel, for this reason have I come baptizing with water."

And John bore witness, saying, "I beheld the Spirit descending as a dove from heaven, and it abode upon him. And I did not know him. But he who sent me to baptize with water said to me, 'He upon whom thou wilt see the Spirit descending, and abiding upon him, he it is who baptizes with the Holy Spirit.' And I have seen and have borne witness that this is the Son of God."

Again the next day John was standing there, and two of his disciples. And looking upon Jesus as he walked by, he said, "Behold the Lamb of God!" And the two disciples heard him speak, and they followed Jesus.

But Jesus turned round, and seeing them following him, said to them, "What is it you seek?" They said to him, "Rabbi (which interpreted means Master), where dwellest thou?" He said to them, "Come and see." They came and saw where he was staying; and they stayed with him that day. It was about the tenth hour.

Now Andrew, the brother of Simon Peter, was one of the two who had heard John and had followed him. He found first his brother Simon and said to him, "We have found the Messias (which interpreted is Christ)." And he led him to Jesus. But Jesus, looking upon him, said, "Thou art Simon, the son of John; thou shalt be called Cephas (which interpreted is Peter)."

The next day he was about to leave for Galilee, and he found Philip. And Jesus said to him, "Follow me." Now Philip was from Bethsaida, the town of Andrew and Peter.

Philip found Nathanael, and said to him, "We have found him of whom Moses in the Law and the Prophets wrote, Jesus the son of Joseph of Nazareth." And Nathanael said to him, "Can anything good come out of Nazareth?" Philip said to him, "Come and see."

Jesus saw Nathanael coming to him, and said of him, "Behold a true Israelite in whom there is no guile!" Nathanael said to him, "Whence knowest thou me?" Jesus answered and said to him, "Before Philip called thee, when thou wast under the fig tree, I saw thee." Nathanael answered him and said, "Rabbi, thou art the Son of God, thou art King of Israel."

Answering, Jesus said to him, "Because I said to thee that I saw thee under the fig tree, thou dost believe? Greater things than these shalt thou see." And he said to him, "Amen, amen, I say to you, you shall see heaven opened, and the angels of God ascending and descending upon the Son of Man."

[*John 6:35–70*] But Jesus said to them, "I am the bread of life. He who comes to me shall not hunger, and he who believes in me shall never thirst. But I have told you that you have seen me and you do not believe. All that the Father gives to me shall come to me, and him who comes to me I will not cast out. For I have come down from heaven, not to do my own will, but the will of him who sent me. Now this is the will of him who sent me, the Father, that I should lose nothing of what he has given me, but that I should raise it up on the last day. For this is the will of my Father who sent me, that whoever beholds the Son, and believes in him, shall have everlasting life, and I will raise him up on the last day."

The Jews therefore murmured about him because he had said, "I am the bread that has come down from heaven." And they kept saying, "Is this not Jesus the son of Joseph, whose father and mother we know? How, then, does he say, 'I have come down from heaven'?"

In answer therefore Jesus said to them, "Do not murmur

among yourselves. No one can come to me unless the Father who sent me draw him, and I will raise him up on the last day. It is written in the Prophets, 'And they all shall be taught of God.' Everyone who has listened to the Father, and has learned, comes to me; not that anyone has seen the Father except him who is from God, he has seen the Father. Amen, amen, I say to you, he who believes in me has life everlasting.

"I am the bread of life. Your fathers ate the manna in the desert, and have died. This is the bread that comes down from heaven, so that if anyone eat of it he will not die. I am the living bread that has come down from heaven. If anyone eat of this bread he shall live forever; and the bread that I will give is my flesh for the life of the world."

The Jews on that account argued with one another, saying, "How can this man give us his flesh to eat?"

Jesus therefore said to them, "Amen, amen, I say to you, unless you eat the flesh of the Son of Man, and drink his blood, you shall not have life in you. He who eats my flesh and drinks my blood has life everlasting and I will raise him up on the last day. For my flesh is food indeed, and my blood is drink indeed. He who eats my flesh, and drinks my blood, abides in me and I in him. As the living Father has sent me, and as I live because of the Father, so he who eats me, he also shall live because of me. This is the bread that has come down from heaven; not as your fathers ate the manna, and died. He who eats this bread shall live forever."

These things he said when teaching in the synagogue at Capharnaum.

Many of his disciples therefore, when they heard this, said, "This is a hard saying. Who can listen to it?" But Jesus, knowing in himself that his disciples were murmuring at this, said to them, "Does this scandalize you? What then if you should see the Son of Man ascending where he was before? It is the spirit that gives life; the flesh profits nothing. The words that I have spoken to you are spirit and life. But there are some among you who do not believe." For Jesus knew from the beginning who they were who did not believe, and who it was who should betray him.

And he said, "This is why I have said to you, 'No one can come to me unless he is enabled to do so by my Father'" From this time many of his disciples turned back and no longer went about with him.

Jesus therefore said to the Twelve, "Do you also wish to go away?" Simon Peter therefore answered, "Lord, to whom shall we go? Thou hast words of everlasting life, and we have come to believe and to know that thou art the Christ, the son of God."

[*John 11:1–44*] Now a certain man was sick, Lazarus of Bethany, the village of Mary and her sister Martha. Now it was Mary who anointed the Lord with ointment, and wiped his feet dry with her hair, whose brother Lazarus was sick. The sister therefore sent to him, saying, "Lord, behold, he whom thou lovest is sick."

But when Jesus heard this, he said to them, "This sickness is not unto death, but for the glory of God, that through it the Son of God may be glorified." Now Jesus loved Martha and her sister Mary, and Lazarus. So when he heard that he was sick, he remained two more days in the same place. Then afterwards he said to his disciples, "Let us go again into Judea." The disciples said to him, "Rabbi, just now the Jews were seeking to stone thee; and dost thou go there again?" Jesus answered, "Are there not twelve hours in the day? If a man walks in the day, he does not stumble, because he sees the light of this world. But if he walks in the night, he stumbles, because the light is not in him."

These things he spoke, and after this he said to them, "Lazarus, our friend, sleeps. But I go that I may wake him from sleep." His disciples therefore said, "Lord, if he sleeps, he will be safe." Now Jesus had spoken of his death, but they thought he was speaking of the repose of sleep. So then Jesus said to them plainly, "Lazarus is dead; and I rejoice on your account that I was not there, that you may believe. But let us go to him." Thomas, who is called the Twin, said therefore to his fellow-disciples, "Let us also go, that we may die with him."

Jesus therefore came and found him already four days in the tomb. Now Bethany was close to Jerusalem, some fifteen stadia distant. And many of the Jews had come to Martha and Mary, to comfort them on account of their brother. When, therefore, Martha heard that Jesus was coming, she went to meet him. But Mary remained at home. Martha therefore said to Jesus, "Lord, if thou hadst been here my brother would not have died. But even now I know that whatever thou shalt ask of God, God will give it to thee."

Jesus said to her, "Thy brother shall rise." Martha said to him, "I know that he will rise at the resurrection, on the last day." Jesus said to her, "I am the resurrection and the life; he who believes in me, even if he die, shall live; and whoever lives and believes in me, shall never die. Dost thou believe this?" She said to him, "Yes, Lord, I believe that thou art the Christ, the Son of God, who hast come into the world."

And when she had said this, she went away and quietly called Mary her sister, saying, "The Master is here and calls thee." As soon as she heard this, she rose quickly and came to him, for Jesus had not yet come into the village, but was still at the place where Martha had met him.

When, therefore, the Jews who were with her in the house and were comforting her, saw Mary rise up quickly and go out, they followed her, saying, "She is going to the tomb to weep there."

When, therefore, Mary came where Jesus was, and saw him, she fell at his feet, and said to him, "Lord, if thou hadst been here, my brother would not have died."

When, therefore, Jesus saw her weeping, and the Jews who had come with her weeping, he groaned in spirit and was troubled, and said, "Where have you laid him?" They said to him, "Lord, come and see." And Jesus wept. The Jews therefore said, "See how he loved him." But some of them said, "Could not he who opened the eyes of the blind, have caused that this man should not die?" Jesus therefore, again groaning in himself, came to the tomb. Now it was a cave, and a stone was laid against it. Jesus said, "Take away the stone." Martha, the sister of him who was dead, said to him, "Lord, by this time he is already decayed, for he is dead four days." Jesus said to her, "Have I not told thee that if thou believe thou shalt behold the glory of God?" They therefore removed the stone. And Jesus, raising his eyes, said, "Father, I give thee thanks that thou hast heard me. Yet I knew that thou always hearest me; but because of the people who stand round, I spoke, that they may believe that thou hast sent me." When he had said this, he cried out with a loud voice, "Lazarus, come forth!" And at once he who had been dead came forth, bound feet and hands with bandages, and his face was tied up with a cloth. Jesus said to them, "Unbind him, and let him go."

[*I Corinthians 15:1–58*] Now I recall to your minds, brethren, the gospel that I preached to you, which also you received, wherein also you stand, through which also you are being saved, if you hold it fast, as I preached it to you—unless you have believed to no purpose. For I delivered to you first of all, what I also received, that Christ died for our sins according to the Scriptures, and that he was buried, and that he rose again the third day, according to the Scriptures, and that he appeared to Cephas, and after that to the Eleven. Then he was seen by more than five hundred brethren at one time, many of whom are with us still, but some have fallen asleep. After that he was seen by James, then by all the apostles. And last of all, as by one born out of due time, he was seen also by me. For I am the least of the apostles, and am not worthy to be called an apostle, because I persecuted the Church of God. But by the grace of God I am what I am, and his grace in me has not been fruitless—in fact I have labored more than any of them, yet not I, but the grace of God with me. Whether then it is I or they, so we preach, and so you have believed.

Now if Christ is preached as risen from the dead, how do some among you say that there is no resurrection of the dead? But if there is no resurrection of the dead, neither has Christ risen; and if Christ has not risen, vain then is our preaching, vain too is your faith. Yes, and we are found false witnesses as to God, in that we have borne witness against God that he raised Christ—whom he did not raise, if the dead do not rise. For if the dead do not rise, neither has Christ risen; and if Christ has not risen, vain is your faith, for you are still in your sins. Hence they also who have fallen asleep in Christ, have perished. If with this life only in view we have had hope in Christ, we are of all men the most to be pitied.

But as it is, Christ has risen from the dead, the first-fruits of those who have fallen asleep. For since by a man came death, by a man also comes resurrection of the dead. For as in Adam all die, so in Christ all will be made to live. But each in his own turn, Christ as first-fruits, then they who are Christ's, who have believed, at his coming. Then comes the end, when he delivers the kingdom to God the Father, when he does away with all sovereignty, authority and power. For he must reign, until "he has put all his enemies under his feet." And the last enemy to be destroyed will be death, for "he has put all things under his feet." But when he says all things are subject to him, undoubtedly he is excepted who has subjected all things to him. And when all things are made subject to him, then the Son himself will also be made subject to him who subjected all things to him, that God may be all in all.

Else what shall they do who receive Baptism for the dead? If the dead do not rise at all, why then do people receive Baptism for them? And we, why do we stand in jeopardy every hour? I die daily, I affirm it, by the very pride that I take in you, brethren, in Christ Jesus our Lord. If, as men do, I fought with beasts at Ephesus, what does it profit me? If the dead do not rise, "let us eat and drink for tomorrow we shall die." Do not be led astray, "evil companionships corrupt good morals." Awake as you should, and do not sin; for some have no knowledge of God. To your shame I say so.

But someone will say, "How do the dead rise? Or with what kind of body do they come?" Senseless man, what thou thyself sowest is not brought to life, unless it dies. And when thou sowest, thou dost not sow the body that shall be, but a bare grain, perhaps of wheat or something else. But God gives it a body even as he has willed, and to each of the seeds a body of its own. All flesh is not the same flesh, but there is one flesh of men, another of beasts, another of birds, another of fishes. There are also heavenly bodies and earthly bodies, but of one kind is the glory of the heavenly, of another kind the glory of the earthly. There is one glory of the sun, and another glory of the moon, and another of the stars; for star differs from star in glory. So also with the resurrection of the dead. What is sown in corruption rises in incorruption; what is sown in dishonor rises in glory; what is sown in weakness rises in power; what is sown a natural body rises a spiritual body.

If there is a natural body, there is also a spiritual body. So also it is written, "The first man, Adam, became a living soul"; the last Adam became a life-giving spirit. But it is not the spiritual that comes first, but the physical, and then the spiritual. The first man was of the earth, earthy; the second man is from heaven, heavenly. As was the earthy man, such also are the earthy; and as is the heavenly man, such also are the heavenly. Therefore, even as we have borne the likeness of the earthy, let us bear also the likeness of the heavenly.

Now this I say, brethren, that flesh and blood can obtain no part in the kingdom of God, neither shall corruption have any part in incorruption. Behold, I tell you a mystery: we shall all indeed rise, but we shall not all be changed—in a moment, in the twinkling of an eye, at the last trumpet. For the trumpet shall sound, and the dead shall rise incorruptible and we shall be changed. For this corruptible body must put on incorruption, and this mortal body must put on immortality. But when this mortal body puts on immortality, then shall come to pass the word that is written, "Death is swallowed up in victory! O death, where is thy victory? O death, where is thy sting?"

Now the sting of death is sin, and the power of sin is the Law. But thanks be to God who has given us the victory through our Lord Jesus Christ.

Therefore, my beloved brethren, be steadfast and immovable, always abounding in the work of the Lord, knowing that your labor is not in vain in the Lord.

[*II Corinthians 4:1–18; 5:1–21*] Discharging therefore this ministry in accordance with the mercy shown us, we do not lose heart. On the contrary, we renounce those practices which shame conceals, we avoid unscrupulous conduct, we do not corrupt the word of God; but making known the truth, we commend ourselves to every man's conscience in the sight of God. And if our gospel also is veiled, it is veiled only to those who are perishing. In their case, the god of this world has blinded their unbelieving minds, that they should not see the light of the gospel of the glory of Christ, who is the image of God. For we preach not ourselves, but Jesus Christ as Lord, and ourselves merely as your servants in Jesus. For God, who commanded light to shine out of darkness, has shone in our hearts, to give enlightenment concerning the knowledge of the glory of God, shining on the face of Christ Jesus.

But we carry this treasure in vessels of clay, to show that the abundance of the power is God's and not ours. In all things we suffer tribulation, but we are not distressed; we are sore pressed, but we are not destitute; we endure persecution, but we are not forsaken; we are cast down, but we do not perish; always bearing about in our body the dying of Jesus, so that the life also of Jesus may be made manifest in our bodily frame. For we the living are constantly being handed over to death for Jesus' sake, that the life also of Jesus may be made manifest in our mortal flesh. Thus death is at work in us, but life in you. But since we have the same spirit of faith, as shown in that which is written— "I believed, and so I spoke"—we also believed, wherefore we also speak. For we know that he who raised up Jesus will raise up us also with Jesus, and will place us with you. For all things are for your sakes, so that the grace which abounds through the many may cause thanksgiving to abound, to the glory of God.

Wherefore we do not lose heart. On the contrary, even though our outer man is decaying, yet our inner man is being renewed day by day. For our present light affliction, which is for the moment, prepares for us an eternal weight of glory that is beyond all measure; while we look not at the things that are seen, but at the things that are not seen. For the things that are seen are temporal, but the things that are not seen are eternal.

For we know that if the earthly house in which we dwell be destroyed, we have a building from God, a house not made by human hands, eternal in the heavens. And indeed, in this present state we groan, yearning to be clothed over with that dwelling of ours which is from heaven, if indeed we shall be found clothed, and not naked. For we who are in this tent sigh under our burden, because we do not wish to be unclothed, but rather clothed over, that what is mortal may be swallowed up by life. Now he who made us for this very thing is God, who has given us the Spirit as its pledge.

Always full of courage, then, and knowing that while we are in the body we are exiled from the Lord—for we walk by faith and not by sight—we even have the courage to prefer to be exiled from the body and to be at home with the Lord. And therefore we strive, whether in the body or out of it, to be pleasing to him. For all of us must be made manifest before the tribunal of Christ, so that each one may receive what he has won through the body, according to his works, whether good or evil.

Knowing therefore the fear of the Lord, we try to persuade men; but to God we are manifest. And I hope also that in your consciences we are manifest.

We are not again commending ourselves to you; but we are giving you occasion to boast about us, that you may have an answer for them who glory in appearances and not in heart. For if we were out of our mind, it was for God; if we are sane, it is for you. For the love of Christ impels us, because we have come to the conclusion that, since one died for all, therefore all died; and that Christ died for all, in order that they who are alive may live no longer for themselves, but for him who died for them and rose again.

So that henceforth we know no one according to the flesh. And even though we have known Christ according to the flesh, yet now we know him so no longer. If then any man is in Christ, he is a new creature: the former things have passed away; behold, they are made new! But all things are from God, who has reconciled us to himself through Christ and has given to us the ministry of reconciliation.

For God was truly in Christ, reconciling the world to himself by not reckoning against men their sins and by entrusting to us the message of reconciliation.

On behalf of Christ, therefore, we are acting as ambassadors, God, as it were, appealing through us. We exhort you, for Christ's sake, be reconciled to God. For our sakes he made him to be sin who knew nothing of sin, so that in him we might become the justice of God.

[*Philippians 3:7–14*] But the things that were gain to me, these, for the sake of Christ, I have counted loss. Nay more, I count everything loss because of the excelling knowledge of Jesus Christ, my Lord. For his sake I have suffered the loss of all things, and I count them as dung that I may gain

Christ and be found in him, not having a justice of my own, which is from the Law, but that which is from faith in Christ, the justice from God based upon faith; so that I may know him and the power of his resurrection and the fellowship of his sufferings: become like to him in death, in the hope that somehow I may attain to the resurrection from the dead. Not that I have already obtained this, or already have been made perfect, but I press on hoping that I may lay hold of that for which Christ Jesus has laid hold of me. Brethren, I do not consider that I have laid hold ofit already. But one thing I do: forgetting what is behind, I strain forward to what is before, I press on towards thegoal, to the prize of God's heavenly call in Christ Jesus.

[*Revelation 21:1–27; 22:1–21*] And I saw a new heaven and a new earth. For the first heaven and the first earth passed away, and the sea is no more. And I saw the holy city, the New Jerusalem, coming down out of heaven from God, made ready as a bride adorned for her husband. And I heard a loud voice from the throne saying, "Behold the dwelling of God with men, and he will dwell with them. And they will be his people, and God himself will be with them as their God. And God will wipe away every tear from their eyes. And death shall be no more; neither shall there be mourning, nor crying, nor pain any more, for the former things have passed away."

And he who was sitting on the throne said, "Behold, I make all things new!" And he said, "Write, for these words are trustworthy and true." And he said to me, "It is done! I am the Alpha and the Omega, the beginning and the end. To him who thirsts I will give of the fountain of the water of life freely. He who overcomes shall possess these things, and I will be his God, and he shall be my son. But as for the cowardly and unbelieving, and abominable and murderers, and fornicators and sorcerers, and idolaters and all liars, their portion shall be in the pool that burns with fire and brimstone, which is the second death."

And there came one of the seven angels who had the bowls full of the seven last plagues; and he spoke with me, saying, "Come, I will show thee the bride, the spouse of the Lamb." And he took me up in spirit to a mountain, great and high, and showed me the holy city Jerusalem, coming down out of heaven from God, having the glory of God. Its light was like to a precious stone, as it were a jasperstone, clear as crystal. And it had a wall great and high with twelve gates, and at the gates twelve angels, and names written on them, which are the names of the twelve tribes of the children of Israel. On the east are three gates, and on the north three gates, and on the south three gates, and on the west three gates. And the wall of the city has twelve foundation stones, and on them twelve names of the twelve apostles of the Lamb.

And he who spoke with me had a measure, a golden reed, to measure the city and the gates thereof and the wall. And the city stands foursquare, and its length is as great as its breadth, and he measured the city with the reed, to twelve thousand stadia: the length and the breadth and the height of it are equal. And he measured its wall, of a hundred and forty-four cubits, man's measure, that is, angel's measure. And the material of its wall was jasper; but the city itself was pure gold, like pure glass. And the foundations of the wall of the city were adorned with every precious stone. The first foundation, jasper; the second, sapphire; the third, agate; the fourth, emerald; the fifth, sardonyx; the sixth, sardius; the seventh, chrysolite; the eighth, beryl; the ninth, topaz; the tenth chrysoprase; the eleventh, jacinth; the twelfth, amethyst. And the twelve gates were twelve pearls; that is, each gate was of a single pearl. And the street of the city was pure gold, as it were transparent glass.

And I saw no temple therein. For the Lord God almighty and the Lamb are the temple thereof. And the city has no need of the sun or the moon to shine upon it. For the glory of God lights it up, and the Lamb is the lamp thereof. And the nations shall walk by the light thereof; and the kings of the earth shall bring their glory and honor into it. And its gates shall not be shut by day; for there shall be no night there. And they shall bring the glory and the honor of nations into it. And there shall not enter into it anything defiled, nor he who practises abomination and falsehood, but those only who are written in the book of life of the Lamb.

And he showed me a river of the water of life, clear as crystal, coming forth from the throne of God and of the Lamb. In the midst of the city street, on both sides of the river, was the tree of life, bearing twelve fruits, yielding its fruit according to each month, and the leaves for the healing of the nations.

And there shall be no more any accursed thing; but the throne of God and of the Lamb shall be in it, and his servants shall serve him. And they shall see his face and his name shall be on their foreheads. And night shall be no more, and they shall have no need of light of lamp, or light of sun, for the Lord God will shed light upon them; and they shall reign forever and ever.

And he said to me, "These words are trustworthy and true; and the Lord, the God of the spirits of the prophets, sent his angel to show to his servants what must shortly come to pass. And behold, I come quickly! Blessed is he who keeps the words of the prophecy of this book." And I, John, am he who heard and saw these things. And when I heard and saw, I fell down to worship at the feet of the angel who showed me these things. And he said to me, "Thou must not do that. I am a fellow-servant of thine and of thy brethren the prophets, and of those who keep the words of this book. Worship God!"

And he said to me, "Do not seal up the words of the prophecy of this book; for the time is at hand. He who does wrong, let him do wrong still; and he who is filthy, let him be filthy still; and he who is just, let him be just still; and he who is holy, let him be hallowed still. Behold, I come quickly! And my reward is with me, to render to each one according to his works. I am the Alpha and the Omega, the first and the last, the beginning and the end!" Blessed are they who wash their robes that they may have the right to the tree of life, and that by the gates they may enter into the city. Outside are the dogs, and the sorcerers, and the fornicators, and the murderers, and the idolaters, and everyone who loves and practises falsehood.

"I, Jesus, have sent my angel to testify to you these things concerning the churches. I am the root and the offspring of David, the bright morning star." And the Spirit and the bride say, "Come!" And let him who hears say, "Come!" And let him who thirsts come; and he who wishes, let him receive the water of life freely. I testify to everyone who hears the words of the prophecy of this book. If anyone shall add to them, God will add unto him the plagues that are written in this book. And if anyone shall take away from the words of the book of this prophecy, God will take away his portion from the tree of life, and from the holy city, and from the things that are written in this book. He who testifies to these things says, "It is true, I come

quickly!" Amen! Come, Lord Jesus! The grace of our Lord
Jesus Christ be with all. Amen.

PRAYER FOR THE DYING

> On occasion—when the family group, for example,
> would leave the hospital for the night—a prayer such
> as the following could be said.

Heavenly Father, look down with compassion on this suffering member of our family. May he (she) be strengthened
with your strength in the long hours that lie ahead. May he
accept with serenity the anguish that you have allowed to
come to him. May he be firmly convinced that his Brother,
Christ, who knew far greater pain, will remain here by the
bedside after we have gone.

We ask, if it be your will, that our loved one be brought
back to health. But if you wish to take him home to you, we
will try to accept our loss in humble submission to your
will. (Here let all present recite slowly and devoutly the
Our Father, followed by the Hail Mary.)

> If death comes, the family may say the prayer for the
> deceased on page 182. During the days preceding the
> funeral, let the family follow local prayer customs. If
> the Rosary is recited occasionally, it is desirable that
> the Glorious, rather than the Sorrowful, Mysteries be
> meditated upon.

Prayer When Putting Flowers on a Grave

Father in heaven, you have taken from us one we loved very
much. Because we are human, we cannot help but feel this
loss very keenly. We ask your help in accepting, with deeper submission, your holy will.

We place these flowers upon the grave as a gesture expressing our Christian hope that this one whose remains lie below us in the ground will be raised up unto newness and glory in the power of Christ. We stand here mindful that all of us, one by one, will follow this one into the grave but that we, too, will rise again. We are like these flowers that wither and die in the winter of life; we shall live again in new and eternal beauty under the warm, clear sunlight of Christ's love. May nothing ever separate any of us from Christ so that, when death comes to us, it will be a gentle journey with Him from this life to the far better life of your kingdom. We ask in His name. Amen.

Family Prayer on the Eve of a Wedding

To be recited by the head of the family at the last family meal at which the one about to get married will be present. The feminine pronoun is used throughout the prayer because more often than not a young man about to get married will already be living apart from the family: however a simple change of pronouns will make most of this prayer suitable also for a son in the family about to get married.

Father in heaven, joyfully we accept it as your will that our daughter is about to leave the heart of this family in order to start a family of her own. We ask that she understand the seriousness of the step she is about to take. We ask that she keep in mind that a good marriage demands a high degree of unselfishness. Make her more capable every day of the Christ-like kind of love that will bring real happiness to her marriage. We ask that she be blessed with children and that she be given the wisdom and devotion so necessary for the raising up of true Christians. We love her dearly and will always love her; and because of our love we freely give her to her husband. Help us to resist the temptation to interfere in her marriage or demand that she place us ahead of her new family in her affections.

Finally, may she not fail to invite her Brother Christ to her wedding feast and to trust in him and the power of his sacrament of matrimony all through the years ahead. In Christ's name. Amen.

It is suggested that, at the conclusion of the prayer, each member of the family embrace the daughter as a gesture of farewell and of good wishes for the future.

Private Prayers in the Home

O NE OF THE most beautiful and satisfying ways of acknowledging God to be our Father is to make use of the inspired words of the psalmist. He expresses himself with a high sense of poetry and at the same time speaks a universal language of the heart. The psalter, as Dr. Parsch remarks, is and will remain "the many stringed harp upon which we can sound all the chords of our prayer life, and from which we can draw out all the deep notes of our heart." We ought to revere the psalms if for no other reason than that they formed an integral part of the prayer life of Christ and his Apostles. Furthermore the psalmist is an excellent teacher of prayer for us. So completely does he give tongue to our every aspiration and want, that we need hardly search elsewhere for further expressions of prayer. Finally, a word of caution. We dare not, says Dr. Parsch, "be untruthful in praying the psalms. What we say in a psalm must represent a real experienced need on our part, either in our own soul or in the Church at large; otherwise the words are like 'sounding brass or a tinkling cymbal.'"

Saint Cecilia and the Angel
by Orazio Gentileschi

National Gallery of Art, Washington, D.C.
Samuel H. Kress Collection

"Sing unto the Lord
a new Psalm"

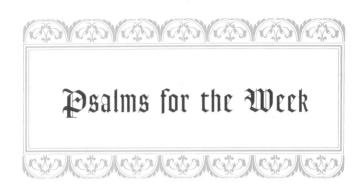

Psalms for the Week

Psalm 119:97-104

How I love your law, O Lord!
It is my meditation all the day.
Your command has made me wiser
   than my enemies,
For it is ever with me.
I have more understanding than all my teachers,
When your decrees are my meditation.
I have more discernment than the elders
Because I observe your precepts.
From every evil way I withhold my feet
   that I may keep your words.
From your ordinances, I turn not away,
   for you have instructed me.
How sweet to my palate are your promises,
Sweeter than honey to my mouth.
Through your precepts,
   I gain discernment;
Therefore I hate every false way.

Glory be to the Father, and to the Son, and to the Holy Spirit, as it was in the beginning, is now and ever shall be, world without end. Amen.

SUNDAY NOON

Psalm 3

O Lord, how many are my adversaries!
Many rise up against me!
Many are saying of me "There is no salvation
    for him in God."
But you, O Lord, are my shield, my glory;
    you lift up my head!
When I call out to the Lord, he answers me
    from his holy mountain.
When I lie down in sleep,
I wake again, for the Lord sustains me.
I fear not the myriads of people
Arrayed against me on every side.
Rise up, O Lord! Save me, my God!
For you strike all my enemies on the cheek,
The teeth of the wicked you break. Salvation is the Lord's!
Upon your people be your blessing!

Glory be to the Father, and to the Son, and to the Holy Spirit, as it was in the beginning, is now and ever shall be, world without end. Amen.

SUNDAY NIGHT

Psalm 91

You who dwell in the shelter of the Most High,
Who abide in the shadow of the Almighty,

Say to the Lord, "My refuge and my fortress,
My God, in whom I trust."
For he will rescue you from the snare of the fowler,
From the destroying pestilence.
With his pinions he will cover you,
And under his wings you shall take refuge;
His faithfulness is a buckler and a shield.
You shall not fear the terror of the night
Nor the arrow that flies by day;
Not the pestilence that roams in darkness
Nor the devastating plague at noon.
Though a thousand fall at your side,
    ten thousand at your right side,
Near you it shall not come.
Rather with your eyes you shall behold
And see the requital of the wicked,
Because you have the Lord for your refuge;
You have made the Most High your stronghold.
No evil shall befall you, nor shall affliction
    come near your tent.
For to his angels he has given command about you,
That they guard you in all your ways.
Upon their hands they shall bear you up,
Lest you dash your foot against a stone.
You shall tread upon the asp and the viper;
You shall trample down the lion and the dragon.
Because he clings to me, I will deliver him;
I will set him on high because he acknowledges my name.
He shall call upon me, and I will answer him;
I will be with him in distress;
I will deliver him and glorify him;
With length of days I will gratify him
And will show him my salvation.

Glory be to the Father, and to the Son, and to the Holy Spirit, as it was in the beginning, is now and ever shall be, world without end. Amen.

MONDAY MORNING

Psalm 20

The Lord answer you in time of distress;
The name of the God of Jacob defend you!
May he send you help from the sanctuary,
From Sion may he sustain you.
May he remember all your offerings
And graciously accept your holocaust.
May he grant you what is in your heart
And fulfill your every plan.
May we shout for joy at your victory
And raise the standards in the name of our God.
The Lord grant all your requests!
Now I know that the Lord has given victory to his anointed,
That he has answered him from his holy heaven
With the strength of his victorious right hand.
Some are strong in chariots; some, in horses;
But we are strong in the name of the Lord, Our God.
Though they bow down and fall, yet we stand
    erect and firm.
O Lord, grant victory to the king, and answer us
    when we call upon you.

Glory be to the Father, and to the Son, and to the Holy Spirit, as it was in the beginning, is now and ever shall be, world without end. Amen.

Psalm 32

Happy is he whose fault is taken away,
Whose sin is covered.
Happy is the man to whom the Lord imputes not guilt,
In whose spirit there is no guile.
As long as I would not speak, my bones wasted away
With my groaning all the day,
For day and night your hand was heavy upon me;
My strength was dried up as by the heat of summer.
Then I acknowledged my sin to you, my guilt I covered not.
I said, "I confess my faults to the Lord,"
And you took away the guilt of my sin.
For this shall every faithful man pray to you in time of stress.
Though deep waters overflow, they shall not reach him.
You are my shelter; from distress you will preserve me;
With glad cries of freedom you will ring me round.
I will instruct you and show you the way you should walk;
I will counsel you, keeping my eye on you.
Be not senseless like horses or mules:
With bit and bridle their temper must be curbed,
Else they will not come near you.
Many are the sorrows of the wicked,
But kindness surrounds him who trusts in the Lord.
Be glad in the Lord and rejoice, you just; exult, all you
upright of heart.

Glory be to the Father, and to the Son, and to the Holy Spirit,
as it was in the beginning, is now and ever shall be, world
without end. Amen.

MONDAY NIGHT

Psalm 121

I lift up my eyes toward the mountains;
Whence shall help come to me?
My help is from the Lord,
Who made heaven and earth.
May he not suffer your foot to slip;
May he slumber not who guards you:
Indeed he neither slumbers nor sleeps,
The guardian of Israel.
The Lord is your guardian; the Lord is your shade,
He is beside you at your right hand.
The sun shall not harm you by day,
Nor the moon by night.
The Lord will guard you from all evil:
He will guard your life.
The Lord will guard your coming and your going,
Both now and forever.

Glory be to the Father, and to the Son, and to the Holy Spirit,
as it was in the beginning, is now and ever shall be, world
without end. Amen.

TUESDAY MORNING

Psalm 37:30-40

The mouth of the just man tells of wisdom
And his tongue utters what is right.
The law of his God is in his heart,
And his steps do not falter.
The wicked man spies on the just,
And seeks to slay him.

The Lord will not leave him in his power
Nor let him be condemned when he is on trial.
Wait for the Lord, and keep his way;
He will promote you to ownership of the land;
When the wicked are destroyed, you shall look on.
I saw a wicked man, fierce, and stalwart as a
    flourishing, age-old tree.
Yet as I passed by, lo! he was no more;
I sought him, but he could not be found.
Watch the wholehearted man, and mark the upright;
For there is a future for the man of peace.
Sinners shall all alike be destroyed;
The future of the wicked shall be cut off.
The salvation of the just is from the Lord;
He is their refuge in time of distress.
And the Lord helps them and delivers them;
He delivers them from the wicked and saves them,
Because they take refuge in him.

Glory be to the Father, and to the Son, and to the Holy Spirit,
as it was in the beginning, is now and ever shall be, world
without end. Amen.

TUESDAY NOON

Psalm 41

Happy is he who has regard for the lowly and the poor;
In the day of misfortune the Lord will deliver him.
The Lord will keep and preserve him;
He will make him happy on the earth,
And not give him over to the will of his enemies.
The Lord will help him on his sickbed,
He will take away all his ailment when he is ill.

Once I said "O Lord, have pity on me;
Heal me, though I have sinned against you.
My enemies say the worst of me;
   'When will he die and his name perish?'
When one comes to see me,
   he speaks without sincerity;
His heart stores up malice;
When he leaves he gives voice to it outside.
All my foes whisper together against me; against me
   they imagine the worst;
'A malignant disease fills his frame';
   and 'Now that he lies ill, he will not rise again.'
Even my friend who had my trust and partook of my bread,
   has raised his heel against me.
But you, O Lord, have pity on me, and raise me up,
   that I may repay them."
That you love me I know by this,
That my enemy does not triumph over me,
But because of my integrity you sustain me
And let me stand before you forever.
Blessed be the Lord, the God of Israel,
From all eternity and forever. Amen. Amen.

Glory be to the Father, and to the Son, and to the Holy Spirit,
as it was in the beginning, is now and ever shall be, world
without end. Amen.

TUESDAY NIGHT

Psalm 16

Keep me, O God, for in you I take refuge;
I say to the Lord, "My Lord are you. Apart from you
   I have no good."

How wonderfully has he made me cherish the holy ones
    who are in his land!
They multiply their sorrows who court other gods.
Blood libations to them I will not pour out,
Nor will I take their names upon my lips.
O Lord, my allotted portion and my cup,
You it is who holds fast my lot.
For me the measuring lines have fallen on pleasant sites.
Fair to me indeed is my inheritance.
I bless the Lord who counsels me;
Even in the night my heart exhorts me.
I set the Lord ever before me;
With him at my right hand I shall not be disturbed.
Therefore my heart is glad and my soul rejoices,
My body, too, abides in confidence;
Because you will not abandon my soul to the nether world,
Nor will you suffer your faithful one to undergo corruption.
You will show me the path to life,
Fulness of joys in your presense,
The delights at your right hand forever.

Glory be to the Father, and to the Son, and to the Holy Spirit,
as it was in the beginning, is now and ever shall be, world
without end. Amen.

WEDNESDAY MORNING

Psalm 46

God is our refuge and our strength,
An ever-present help in distress.
Therefore we fear not, though the earth be shaken
And mountains plunge into the depths of the sea;
Though its waters rage and foam

And the mountains quake at its surging.
The Lord of hosts is with us;
Our stronghold is the God of Jacob.
There is a stream whose runlets gladden the city of God,
The holy dwelling of the Most High.
God is in its midst; it shall not be disturbed;
God will help it at the break of dawn.
Though nations are in turmoil, kingdoms totter,
His voice resounds, the earth melts away,
The Lord of hosts is with us;
Our stronghold is the God of Jacob.
Come! behold the deeds of the Lord,
The astounding things he has wrought on earth:
He has stopped wars to the end of the earth:
The bow he breaks; he splinters the spears;
    he burns the shields with fire.
Desist! and confess that I am God,
Exalted among the nations, exalted upon the earth.
The Lord of hosts is with us;
Our stronghold is the God of Jacob.

Glory be to the Father, and to the Son, and to the Holy Spirit,
as it was in the beginning, is now and ever shall be, world
without end. Amen.

WEDNESDAY NOON

Psalm 57

Have pity on me, O God; have pity on me,
For in you I take refuge.
In the shadow of your wings I take refuge,
Till harm pass by.
I call to God the Most High, to God, my benefactor.

May he send from heaven and save me;
May he make those a reproach who trample upon me;
May God send his kindness and his faithfulness.
I lie prostrate in the midst of lions
Which devour men;
Their teeth are spears and arrows, their tongue is a sharp
    sword.
Be exalted above the heavens, O God;
Above all the earth be your glory!
They have prepared a net for my feet; they have bowed
    me down;
They have dug a pit before me, but they fall into it.
My heart is steadfast, O God; my heart is steadfast;
I will sing and chant praise.
Awake, O my soul; awake, lyre and harp!
I will wake the dawn.
I will give thanks to you among the peoples, O Lord,
I will chant your praise among the nations,
For your kindness towers to the heavens,
    and your faithfulness to the skies.
Be exalted above the heavens, O God;
Above all the earth be your glory!

Glory be to the Father, and to the Son, and to the Holy Spirit,
as it was in the beginning, is now and ever shall be, world
without end. Amen.

WEDNESDAY NIGHT

Psalm 34

I will bless the Lord at all times;
His praise shall be ever in my mouth.
Let my soul glory in the Lord;

The lowly will hear me and be glad.

Glorify the Lord with me, let us together extol his name.

I sought the Lord, and he answered me and delivered me
from all my fears.

Look to him that you may be radiant with joy,

And your faces may not blush with shame.

When the afflicted man called out, the Lord heard him,

And from all his distress he saved him.

The angel of the Lord encamps around those who fear
him, and delivers them.

Taste and see how good the Lord is;

Happy the man who takes refuge in him.

Fear the Lord, you his holy ones,

For naught is lacking to those who fear him.

The great grow poor and hungry;

But those who seek the Lord want for no good thing.

Come, children, hear me; I will teach you the fear of
the Lord.

Which of you desires life, and takes delight in
prosperous days?

Keep your tongue from evil and your lips from
speaking guile;

Turn from evil, and do good; seek peace, and follow after it.

The Lord has eyes for the just, and ears for their cry.

The Lord confronts the evildoers, to destroy remembrance
of them from the earth.

When the just cry out, the Lord hears them,

And from all their distress he rescues them.

The Lord is close to the brokenhearted;

And those who are crushed in spirit he saves.

Many are the troubles of the just man,

But out of them all the Lord delivers him;

He watches over all his bones;
Not one of them shall be broken.
Vice slays the wicked, and the enemies of the just
    pay for their guilt.
But the Lord redeems the lives of his servants;
No one incurs guilt who takes refuge in him.

Glory be to the Father, and to the Son and to the Holy Spirit,
as it was in the beginning, is now and ever shall be, world
without end. Amen.

THURSDAY MORNING

Psalm 62

Only in God is my soul at rest;
From him comes my salvation.
He only is my rock and my salvation,
My stronghold; I shall not be disturbed at all.
How long will you set upon a man and all together beat
    him down
As though he were a sagging fence, a battered wall?
Truly from my place on high they plan to dislodge me;
They delight in lies;
They bless with their mouths, but inwardly they curse.
Only in God be at rest, my soul,
For from him comes my hope.
He only is my rock and my salvation,
My stronghold; I shall not be disturbed.
With God is my safety and my glory,
He is the rock of my strength; my refuge is in God.
Trust in him at all times, O my people!
Pour out your hearts before him; God is our refuge!
Only a breath are mortal men; an illusion are men of rank.

In a balance they prove lighter, all together, than a breath.
Trust not in extortion; in plunder take no empty pride;
Though wealth abound, set not your heart upon it.
One thing God said; these two things which I heard: that
 power belongs to God, and yours, O Lord, is kindness;
 and that you render to everyone according to his deeds.

Glory be to the Father, and to the Son, and to the Holy Spirit,
as it was in the beginning, is now and ever shall be, world
without end. Amen.

THURSDAY NOON

Psalm 72:8-19

May he rule from sea to sea,
And from the River to the ends of the earth.
His foes shall bow before him, and his enemies shall lick
 the dust.
The kings of Tharis and the Isles shall offer gifts;
The kings of Arabia and Saba shall bring tribute.
All kings shall pay him homage, all nations shall serve him.
For he shall rescue the poor man when he cries out,
And the afflicted when he has no one to help him.
He shall have pity for the lowly and poor;
The lives of the poor he shall save.
From fraud and violence he shall redeem them,
And precious shall their blood be in his sight.
May he live to be given the gold of Arabia,
 and to be prayed for continually;
Day by day shall they bless him.
May there be an abundance of grain upon the earth;
On the tops of the mountains the crops shall rustle like
 Lebanon;

The city dwellers shall flourish like the verdure of the fields.
May his name be blessed forever;
As long as the sun his name shall remain.
In him shall all the tribes of the earth be blessed;
All the nations shall proclaim his happiness.
Blessed be the Lord, the God of Israel,
    who alone does wondrous deeds.
And blessed forever be his glorious name;
May the whole earth be filled with his glory. Amen. Amen.

Glory be to the Father, and to the Son, and to the Holy Spirit,
as it was in the beginning, is now and ever shall be, world
without end. Amen.

THURSDAY NIGHT

Psalm 138

I will give thanks to you, O Lord, with all my heart,
For you have heard the words of my mouth;
In the presence of the angels I will sing your praise;
I will worship at your holy temple and give thanks to
    your name,
Because of your kindness and your truth;
For you have made great above all things
    your name and your promise.
When I called, you answered me;
You built up strength within me.
All the kings of the earth shall give thanks to you,
    O Lord,
When they hear the words of your mouth;
And they shall sing of the ways of the Lord:
    "Great is the glory of the Lord."
The Lord is exalted, yet the lowly he sees,

And the proud he knows from afar.
Though I walk amid distress, you preserve me;
Against the anger of my enemies you raise your hand;
Your right hand saves me.
The Lord will complete what he has done for me;
Your kindness, O Lord, endures forever;
Forsake not the work of your hands.

Glory be to the Father, and to the Son, and to the Holy
Spirit, as it was in the beginning, is now and ever shall be,
world without end. Amen.

FRIDAY MORNING

Psalm 22

My God, my God, why have you forsaken me,
Far from my prayer, from the words of my cry?
O my God, I cry out by day, and you answer not;
By night, and there is no relief for me.
Yet you are enthroned in the holy place,
O glory of Israel!
In you our fathers trusted;
They trusted, and you delivered them.
To you they cried, and they escaped;
In you they trusted, and they were not put to shame.
But I am a worm, not a man;
The scorn of men, despised by the people.
All who see me scoff at me;
They mock me with parted lips, they wag their heads:
"He relied on the Lord; let him deliver him,
    let him rescue him, if he loves him."
You have been my guide since I was first formed,
My security at my mother's breast.

To you I was committed at birth, from my mother's womb
  you are my God.
Be not far from me, for I am in distress;
Be near, for I have no one to help me.
Many bullocks surround me;
The strong bulls of Basan encircle me.
They open their mouths against me
  like ravening and roaring lions.
I am like water poured out; all my bones are racked.
My heart has become like wax
Melting away within my bosom.
My throat is dried up like baked clay,
My tongue cleaves to my jaws;
To the dust of death you have brought me down.
Indeed, many dogs surround me,
A pack of evildoers closes in upon me;
They have pierced my hands and my feet;
I can count all my bones.
They look on and gloat over me;
They divide my garments among them,
And for my vesture they cast lots.
But you, O Lord, be not far from me;
O my help, hasten to aid me.
Rescue my soul from the sword, my loneliness from
  the grip of the dog.
Save me from the lion's mouth; from the horns of the wild
  bulls, my wretched life.
I will proclaim your name to my brethren;
In the midst of the assembly I will praise you: "You who
  fear the Lord, praise him; all you descendents of Jacob,
  give glory to him;
Revere him, all you descendents of Israel! For he has not
  spurned or disdained the wretched man in his misery.

Nor did he turn his face away from him, but when he
    cried out to him, he heard him."
So by your gift will I utter praise in the vast assembly;
I will fulfill my vows before those who fear him.
The lowly shall eat their fill;
They who seek the Lord shall praise him:
"May your hearts be ever merry!"
All the ends of the earth shall remember and turn to
    the Lord;
All the families of the nations shall bow down before him.
For dominion is the Lord's, and he rules the nations.
To him alone shall bow down all who sleep in the earth;
Before him shall bend all who go down into the dust.
And to him my soul shall live; my descendants shall
    serve him.
Let the coming generation be told of the Lord
That they may proclaim to people yet to be born
    the justice he has shown.

Glory be to the Father, and to the Son, and to the Holy Spirit,
as it was in the beginning, is now and ever shall be, world
without end. Amen.

FRIDAY NOON

Psalm 23

The Lord is my Shepherd; I shall not want.
In verdant pastures he gives me repose;
Beside restful waters he leads me; he refreshes my soul.
He guides me in right paths for his name's sake.
Even though I walk in the dark valley I fear no evil;
For you are at my side
With your rod and your staff that give me courage.

You spread the table before me in the sight of my foes;
You anoint my head with oil; my cup overflows.
Only goodness and kindness follow me all the days of
   my life;
And I shall dwell in the house of the Lord for years to come.

Glory be to the Father, and to the Son, and to the Holy Spirit,
as it was in the beginning, is now and ever shall be, world
without end. Amen.

FRIDAY NIGHT

Psalm 141

O Lord, to you I call; hasten to me;
Harken to my voice when I call upon you.
Let my prayer come like incense before you;
The lifting up of my hands like the evening sacrifice.
O Lord, set a watch before my mouth,
   a guard at the door of my lips.
Let not my heart incline to the evil of engaging
   in deeds of wickedness
With men who are evildoers;
And let me not partake of their dainties.
Let the just man strike me; that is kindness;
Let him reprove me; it is oil for the head,
   Which my head shall not refuse,
But I will still pray under these afflictions.
Their judges were cast down over the crag,
And they heard how pleasant were my words.
As when a plowman breaks furrows in the field,
   so their bones are strewn by the edge of the nether world.
For toward you, O God, my Lord, my eyes are turned;
In you I take refuge; strip me not of life.

Keep me from the trap they have set for me,
    and from the snares of evildoers.
Let all the wicked fall, each into his own net,
    while I escape.

Glory be to the Father, and to the Son, and to the Holy Spirit,
as it was in the beginning, is now and ever shall be, world
without end. Amen.

SATURDAY MORNING

Psalm 92

It is good to give thanks to the Lord,
To sing praise to your name, Most High,
To proclaim your kindness at dawn
And your faithfulness throughout the night,
With ten-stringed instrument and lyre,
With melody upon the harp.
For you make me glad, O Lord, by your deeds;
At the works of your hands I rejoice.
How great are your works, O Lord!
How very deep are your thoughts!
A senseless man knows not, nor does a fool understand this.
Though the wicked flourish like grass
And all evildoers thrive,
They are destined for eternal destruction;
While you, O Lord, are the Most High forever.
For behold, your enemies, O Lord,
For behold, your enemies shall perish;
All evildoers shall be scattered.
You have exalted my horn like the wild bull's;
You have anointed me with rich oil.
And my eye has looked down upon my foes,

and my ears have heard of the fall of my
    wicked adversaries.
The just man shall flourish like the palm tree,
Like a cedar of Lebanon shall he grow.
They that are planted in the house of the Lord
    shall flourish in the courts of our God.
They shall bear fruit even in old age;
Vigorous and sturdy shall they be,
Declaring how just is the Lord, my Rock in whom there is
    no wrong.

Glory be to the Father, and to the Son, and to the Holy Spirit,
as it was in the beginning, is now and ever shall be, world
without end. Amen.

Psalm 104:1-12

Bless the Lord, O my soul!
O Lord, my God, you are great indeed!
You are clothed with majesty and glory,
Robed in light as with a cloak.
You have spread out the heavens like a tentcloth;
You have constructed your palace upon the waters.
You make the clouds your chariot;
You travel on the wings of the wind.
You make the winds your messengers,
And flaming fire your ministers.
You fixed the earth upon its foundation,
Not to be moved forever;
With the ocean, as with a garment, you covered it;
Above the mountains the waters stood.
At your rebuke they fled,
At the sound of your thunder they took flight;

As the mountains rose, they went down the valleys to the
place you had fixed for them.
You set a limit they may not pass, nor shall they cover the
earth again.
You send forth springs into the watercourses
That wind among the mountains, and give drink to
every beast of the field,
Till the wild asses quench their thirst.
Beside them the birds of heaven dwell;
From among the branches they send forth their song.

Glory be to the Father, and to the Son, and to the Holy Spirit,
as it was in the beginning, is now and ever shall be, world
without end. Amen.

SATURDAY NIGHT

Psalm 145:10-21

Let all your works give you thanks, O Lord,
And let your faithful ones bless you.
Let them discourse on the glory of your kingdom
And speak of your might, making known to men
your might
And the glorious splendor of your kingdom.
Your kingdom is a kingdom for all ages,
And your dominion endures through all generations.
The Lord is faithful in all his words and holy in all
his works.
The Lord lifts up all who are falling and raises up
all who are bowed down.
The eyes of all look hopefully to you, and you give them
their food in due season;
You open your hand and satisfy the desire of every
living thing.

The Lord is just in all his ways and holy in all his works.
The Lord is near to all who call upon him,
To all who call upon him in truth.
He fulfills the desire of those who fear him, he hears their
cry and saves them.
The Lord keeps all who love him, but all the wicked
he will destroy.
May my mouth speak the praise of the Lord, and may all
flesh bless his holy name forever and ever.

Glory be to the Father, and to the Son, and to the Holy Spirit,
as it was in the beginning, is now and ever shall be, world
without end. Amen.

The Magnificat

My soul magnifies the Lord,
and my spirit rejoices in God my Savior;
Because he has regarded the lowliness of his handmaid;
For, behold, henceforth all generations shall call me blessed;
Because he who is mighty has done great things for me, and
holy is his name;
And his mercy is from generation to generation on those
who fear him.
He has shown might with his arm, he has scattered the
proud in the conceit of their heart.
He has put down the mighty from their thrones, and has
exalted the lowly.
He has filled the hungry with good things, and the rich he
has sent away empty.
He has given help to Israel, his servant, mindful of his
mercy—
Even as he spoke to our fathers—
To Abraham and to his posterity forever.

SAINT MONICA
by Luis Tristán
Museo del Prado, Madrid, Spain

Prayers to Various Saints

PRAYER TO ONE'S PATRON SAINT

O HEAVENLY PATRON, whose name I bear, pray continually to God for me. Strengthen me in my faith, help me be good, guard me in the conflict that I may defeat the devil and attain to glory everlasting. Amen.

A PARENT'S PRAYER TO ST. MONICA
FOR A WAYWARD SON
OR DAUGHTER

DEAR ST. MONICA, sainted mother of Augustine the sinner, the Lord Jesus mercifully regarded your tears. The conversion of your son to a genuinely holy life was the fruit of your prayers. From the heights of your heavenly home, happy mother of your saintly son, pray for those who wander far from God and add your prayers to those of all parents who sorrow over the straying souls of their sons or daughters. Pray for us that, following your example, and that of all God's children, we may at length enjoy the eternal vision of our Father in Heaven. Amen.

PRAYER TO ST. GERARD FOR A MARRIED WOMAN WISHING TO HAVE CHILDREN

O GOOD ST. GERARD, powerful intercessor before God and wonder worker of our day, I call upon you and seek your help. You always tried to do God's will in life; help me also to do the holy will of God. Beg the Lord of life from whom all fatherhood proceeds to render me fruitful in offspring that I may raise up children to serve God in this life and to inherit the kingdom of his glory in the world to come. Amen.

PRAYER TO ST. GERARD MAJELLA FOR A MARRIED WOMAN NOT WISHING, FOR THE MOMENT AND FOR GRAVE REASONS, TO BECOME PREGNANT

DEAR ST. GERARD, you know our case, I am sure. My husband and I believe another child right now would be a disaster. If we are wrong about this, pray for us that we will be given the light to see that we are wrong and the strength to accept the will of God. But since we feel we are right in our judgment, pray that our act of love may help to deepen our love for each other without, for the time being, resulting in a pregnancy. Above all, pray that our problems will be resolved quickly so that soon again our love can become fruitful with children. Amen.

PRAYER TO ST. TÉRÈSE FOR THOSE IN THE MISSION FIELD

DEAR ST. TÉRÈSE, chosen by the church as the Heavenly Patroness of the Missions, we ask you to take under your

SAINT FRANCIS

by Cosimo Tura

National Gallery of Art,
Washington, D.C.
Samuel H. Kress Collection

special protection those valiant souls who have left family, home, friends—all that the human heart holds dear—in order to spread the kingdom of Christ.

When you lived on earth, your soul reached out to those soldiers of the Cross. Day after day you prayed for them, you suffered for them, you made them and their work the core of your whole life. Today you are in Heaven; today you see Jesus face to face. Since you understand the needs of our modern missionaries, remember them to Christ their Lord. Beg Jesus to give them courage to fight even when they can see no reward, to rely on him for their comfort and peace. Beg him to bless their work that they might spread everywhere his Kingdom, for that is their life, their joy and their goal. St. Térèse, we trust in you. Amen.

PRAYER IN HONOR OF
ST. FRANCIS OF ASSISI

WHEN THE WORLD was growing cold, Lord Jesus, you renewed in the flesh of Blessed Francis the sacred marks of your passion in order to inflame our hearts with the fire of your love. Grant in your kindness that, by his merits and prayers, we may always willingly carry the Cross and bring forth fruits worthy of repentance, you who live and reign for ever and ever. Amen.

THE ANNUNCIATION *by Cosimo Tura*

National Gallery of Art, Washington, D.C.
Samuel H. Kress Collection

LITANY OF THE SAINTS

> It is suggested that this Litany be recited by the family during the Forty Hours devotion in the parish when they have not been able to go to church. The head of the household should lead the litany and those present make the responses.

Lord, have mercy on us.
Christ, have mercy on us.
Lord, have mercy on us.
Christ, hear us.
Christ, graciously hear us.
God, the Father of Heaven, have mercy on us.
God, the Son, the Redeemer of the world, have mercy on us.
God, the Holy Ghost, have mercy on us.
Holy Trinity, one God, have mercy on us.
Holy Mary,   pray for us.
Holy Mother of God,
Holy Virgin of Virgins,
St. Michael,
St. Gabriel,
St. Raphael,
All you Holy Angels and Archangels,
All you Holy Orders of Blessed Spirits,   pray
St. John the Baptist,   for
St. Joseph,   us.
All you Holy Patriarchs and Prophets,
St. Peter,
St. Paul,
St. Andrew,
St. James,
St. John,
St. Thomas,

ST. HELENA *by Cima da Conegliano*

National Gallery of Art, Washington, D.C.
Samuel H. Kress Collection

St. James,   pray for us.
St. Philip,
St. Bartholomew,
St. Matthew,
St. Simon,
St. Thaddeus,
St. Matthias,
St. Barnabas,
St. Luke,
St. Mark,
All you holy Apostles and Evangelists,
All you Holy Disciples of the Lord,
All you Holy Innocents,
St. Stephen,
St. Laurence,
St. Vincent,   pray
Sts. Fabian and Sebastian,   for
Sts. John and Paul,   us.
Sts. Cosmas and Damian,
Sts. Gervase and Protase,
All you Holy Martyrs,
St. Sylvester,
St. Gregory,
St. Ambrose,
St. Agustine,
St. Jerome,
St. Martin,
St. Nicholas,
All you holy Bishops and Confessors,
All you holy doctors,
St. Anthony,
St. Benedict,
St. Bernard,

THE DREAM OF ST. CATHERINE OF ALEXANDRIA

by Lodovico Carracci

National Gallery of Art, Washington, D.C.
Samuel H. Kress Collection

St. Dominic,   pray for us.
St. Francis,
All you holy priests and levites,
All you holy monks and hermits,
St. Mary Magdalene,
St. Agatha,   pray
St. Lucy,   for
St. Agnes,   us.
St. Cecilia,
St. Catherine,
St. Anastasia,
All you holy virgins and widows,
All you holy men and women, saints of God,
   intercede for us.
Be merciful, spare us, O Lord.
Be merciful, graciously hear us, O Lord.
From all evil,   deliver us, O Lord.
From all sin,
From your wrath,
From sudden and unprovided death,
From the snares of the devil,
From anger, and hatred, and all ill-will,
From the spirit of fornication,
From the scourge of earthquake,   deliver
From plague, famine, and war,   us, O
From lightning and tempest,   Lord.
From everlasting death,
Through the mystery of your holy Incarnation,
Through your coming,
Through your birth,
Through your baptism and holy fasting,
Through the institution of the Most Blessed
   Sacrament,

Through your holy cross and passion,
Through your death and burial,
Through your holy resurrection,   deliver
Through your admirable ascension,   us, O
Through the coming of the Holy Ghost, the   Lord.
    Paraclete,
In the day of judgment,
We sinners,   we beg you, hear us.
That you would spare us,
That you would pardon us,
That you would bring us to true penance,
That you would govern and preserve your
    Holy Church,
That you would preserve our Apostolic Pre-
    late and all orders of the Church in holy   we beg
    religion,   you,
That you would humble the enemies of the   hear us.
    Holy Church,
That you would give peace and true concord
    to Christian kings and princes,
That you would bring back to the unity of
    the Church all those who have strayed
    away and lead to the light of the gospel all
    unbelievers,
That you would strengthen and preserve us
    in your holy service,
That you would lift up our minds to heavenly
    desires,
That you would give eternal blessings to all
    our benefactors,

SAINT MARTIN AND THE BEGGAR *by El Greco*
National Gallery of Art, Washington, D.C., Widener Collection

That you would deliver our souls and the
    souls of our brothers, relatives, and bene-
    factors from eternal damnation,

That you would make available and preserve
    for us the fruits of the earth,

That you would grant eternal rest to all the
    faithful departed,

That you would graciously hear us,

Son of God,

we beg
you,
hear us.

Lamb of God, you take away the sins of the
    world; spare us O Lord.

Lamb of God, you take away the sins of the
    world; graciously hear us O Lord.

Lamb of God, you take away the sins of the
    world; have mercy on us.

Let Us Pray

Almighty, everlasting God, you have dominion over both
the living and the dead and are merciful to all who you
already know to be yours by faith and good works; we
humbly beg you that they for whom we pray, whether they
still be in this world or have already gone into the next,
may, by the grace of your fatherly love and the true intercession of all the saints, obtain the remission of all their
sins. Through our Lord Jesus Christ, your son, who with
you in the unity of the Holy Spirit, lives and reigns, God,
world without end. Amen.

SAINT ILDEFONSO
by El Greco
National Gallery of Art, Washington, D.C.
Andrew Mellon Collection

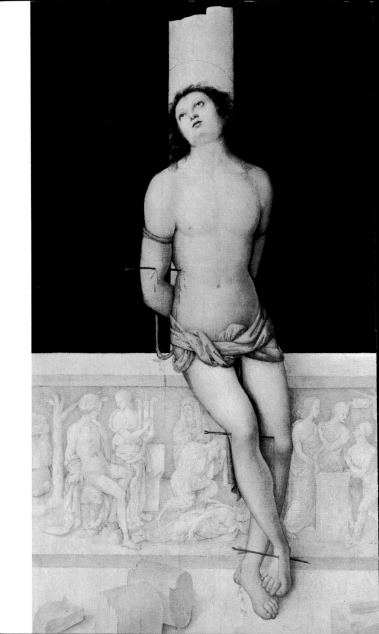

Prayers for Various Needs and Occasions

PRAYER FOR NEW YEAR'S EVE

This prayer may be said by the family before the family meal on New Year's Eve.

GOOD AND KIND FATHER, we commend our family and all that is ours to your fatherly protection. We confide all to your love. Fill our house with your blessings, even as you filled the Holy House of Nazareth with your presence. Above all else, keep sin far from it. Reign by your law and by your holy love over this household. Let each one of us obey you, love you, and study how to copy in his own life the example of Christ, of Mary, our Mother, and of St. Joseph.

Keep far from our home during this coming year all evils and misfortunes; but grant that we may ever be resigned to your divine will even in the sorrows which may come to us in this New Year.

Finally, grant all of us the grace to live in love for one another and in love for our neighbor. We ask in Christ's name. Amen.

PRAYER FOR THE PRESIDENT

It is suggested that this prayer be said by the family on Inauguration Day.

GOD OF MIGHT AND WISDOM, through your authority justice is rightly administered, laws are enacted and judgments decreed. We ask you to assist, with your Holy Spirit of council and fortitude, the President of these United States, that he may conduct his administration in righteousness and be eminently useful to your people over whom he presides. May he encourage due respect for virtue and religion by the faithful execution of the law with justice and mercy, and by restraining vice and immorality.

PRAYER BEFORE PAYING TAXES

LORD, tomorrow as the head of this family, I will mail my tax returns to our government. May all of us here understand that we are making a contribution to the common good of our great country and of the world. Let us never be bitter or selfish over paying our taxes. Guide our law-makers that they may use our tax money wisely and fairly for the spread of justice and peace among all nations. May they carry out our desires that other peoples share in the great abundance of good things you have given our country.

PRAYER FOR STUDENTS

To be said after family meal on the eve of examinations by all the family members attending school.

GIVE US, LORD, a mind that learns when it is taught. Help us use our intellect for something better than ourselves alone. Make us want knowledge so that we may know you better, so that we can love and defend your kingdom, so that we can become complete, fully developed human beings. Let us carry our learning humbly. Make us realize that it is a gift from you and must be returned to you. Send your Holy Spirit to help us see clearly, to judge wisely, to love what is true, to direct our minds to all that is good and noble and beautiful in heaven and on earth. Use us as your special instruments, intelligent instruments, in spreading your kingdom throughout the whole world until all the world knows you as we know you, and knowing you, loves you with a deep and lasting love.

PRAYER FOR PRIESTS

> This prayer may be said by the family on the day of diocesan ordinations.

TAKE CARE of your priests, Lord, for they are yours. Watch over them that they be not led astray by the world, the flesh, or the devil. Keep them because they must live in the world, yet apart from it. Strengthen them in their loneliness, cheer them up when they become discouraged. Make them worthy and effective instruments in your hands for our eternal good.

PRAYER FOR NUNS

BLESS, O LORD, all the nuns throughout the world. People of every kind—the ignorant, the penniless, the sick and dying, the homeless, the aged, the young,—all have experienced the generous help, the smiling kindness of a nun. As Veronica of Jerusalem consoled you on the Way of the Cross, so these selfless women today console you in the needy souls of every walk of life. In gratitude for what they have done for the world and for me in particular, I ask you to bless them always with your peace and joy and grace. Amen.

PRAYER BEFORE STARTING VACATION TRIP OR OTHER JOURNEYS

MAY THE GOOD LORD guide us on the road of peace and well-being, and may the Angel Raphael accompany us along the way so that we may return safely again to our home.

Let Us Pray

God, you enabled the children of Israel to pass with dry feet through the midst of the sea, and, by the guidance of a star, opened up to the three Wise Men the way that leads to you. Grant, we beg you, a safe and pleasant journey so that, in company with your holy angel, we may arrive in good shape not only at our present destination but finally at the snug harbor of your eternal City. Through Christ, our Lord. Amen.

PRAYER FOR NOVEMBER 2nd

This prayer may be said by the family at the family meal on November 2, and may also be used on the occasion of the death, or anniversary of the death, of a relative or friend.

Let Us Pray

LORD, you desire to pardon and to save us. We ask your mercy for our brothers, our relatives, and our benefactors who have departed from this world (especially N. . . . .).

Grant, through the intercession of the Virgin Mary and of all the Saints, that they may have a share in your eternal happiness. Give us, the living, strength to accept your will in our loss. This we ask of you through our Lord Jesus Christ, your Son, who lives and reigns with you in the unity of the Holy Spirit, God, forever. Amen.

Eternal rest grant unto them, O Lord, and let perpetual light shine upon them. May they rest in peace. Amen.

PRAYER FOR ELECTION DAY EVE

This prayer may be recited by the head of the family at the evening meal on the day before elections.

LORD, tomorrow we exercise our right to vote. Grant that we may do so wisely and in good conscience, choosing the candidates whom we sincerely feel will work with selfless dedication for the common good. We thank you, Lord, for the great blessing of living in a free country. (We ask that those present here who are not yet old enough to vote will grow up with a keen appreciation of their freedoms and with the desire to be citizens worthy of the greatness of our country). We ask in Christ's name. Amen.

PRAYER FOR FATHER'S DAY

This prayer may be said by the oldest child in the family at the evening meal on Father's Day, or on the birthday of the father of the family.

WE THANK YOU, dear God, for giving us our father. Enlighten us so that we may realize the depth of his love for us and the greatness of his sacrifices for us. His fatherly care reflects your goodness, his manliness your strength, his understanding your wisdom. He is your faithful servant and image. Bless him with peace of soul, health of body, and success in his work. Amen.

PRAYER FOR MOTHER'S DAY

This prayer may be said by the oldest child in the family at the evening meal on Mother's Day, or on the birthday of the mother of the family.

LORD JESUS, look with love and mercy upon our mother. Reward her untiring generosity, her love and care for us. We ask for her a share in the riches you conferred upon your Mother—health of body, peace of soul, happiness of family, and the bountiful grace of God. Give her the rich joy of a mother's heart that her children may grow in wisdom and grace before God and men. Amen.

PRAYER FOR VETERAN'S DAY

This prayer may be recited by the family on Veterans Day or Armed Forces Day.

DEAR LORD, we ask you to watch over those exposed to the horrors of war and the spiritual dangers of military life. We pray that the members of our Armed Forces gain faith in you—a faith so deep and so strong that it will sustain them through times of adversity By your grace, strengthen them against the contagion of bad example that, being preserved from wrong doing and serving you faithfully, they may be ready to meet death whenever it may happen. If they must deal out death to our enemies, may it not be out of hatred.

PRAYER FOR
THANKSGIVING DAY

As loyal Americans, we should heed the wishes of our president, expressed in his annual Thanksgiving proclamation, to thank God for His blessings and to ask His continued protection. The following prayer may he said by the head of the family at the Thanksgiving Dinner.

CONTINUE to smile down upon our country, Lord; show us your love and your solicitude, bless our nation's leaders—the president, the congress, the courts. Enlighten them to govern wisely, to protect the interests of all citizens with justice and true charity, and to respect and love your law. Give all Americans a deep and lasting faith in you. Fire our hearts with the desire to spread your spirit and life in the hearts of our fellow-countrymen, so that your charity will overflow the land. Inspire us with a true patriotism for this earthly home and then, after a life of faithful service to you and to our country, may we come as a nation safely back to our eternal home. Amen.

FIRST SUNDAY OF ADVENT

To be recited by the family at the evening meal on the first Sunday of Advent.

OUR BROTHER CHRIST, make us mindful in these days before Christmas of your threefold coming. You came to make yourself one with us on that cold night in Bethlehem so that we could become one with you. You come each Christmas Day with an abundance of your grace so that we may be more closely united to you. You'll come again

surely on the last day to take those of us who love you into
your eternal kingdom. Give us serenity in this mad pre-
Christmas rush so as not to forget what Christmas is all
about. Help us to make our hearts receptive to an abundance of Christmas grace by an Advent filled with prayer,
penance, and good works. And may we be ready when you
come back again at the end. Amen.

PRAYER FOR ASH WEDNESDAY

> This prayer may be recited by the head of the family
> at the evening meal on Ash Wednesday.

LORD, now that the penitential season of Lent is beginning, help us to realize how much we stand in need of
penance. We have grown selfish; we need to curb our selfish
desires by acts of self-restraint. May we be able to see, Lord,
that Lent is all about love, that not eating between meals,
doing without meat occasionally, and perhaps giving up
television and movies and other pleasant things are what
we need to get over being selfish. But may our program also
be positive, in that we make a special effort to be kind and
thoughtful of others. We ask this in Christ's name. Amen.

A PRAYER FOR
A FAMILY DECISION

HOLY SPIRIT of counsel and understanding; I pray, as head
of this family, that you enlighten my mind concerning the
problems which confront us. Guide me to make those decisions which will be to your glory and for our spiritual good.
Do not permit mere feelings, selfish preferences or senseless fears to influence my judgment. May each decision be

made according your will. May all of my choices proclaim my faith and trust in you. Amen.

A PRAYER FOR CHOOSING THE RIGHT PARTNER IN MARRIAGE

> Choosing the right partner in marriage is a very important matter; therefore it is something that the individual should contemplate in prayer. He or she may use his or her own words. The following prayer is simply a suggestion as to the form that this prayer might take.

MY JESUS, I KNOW that you are calling me to serve you in the married state. I know, too, that it is a life that calls for self-sacrifice, courage and the guidance of the Holy Spirit. It will not be easy to live as a true Christian parent, to put the interests of you and your kingdom before those of my sometimes selfish heart. But, my Brother, I know you will give me all the graces needed to live as a holy and happily married Christian. Of all these graces, Lord, the greatest for which I can ask is the right partner who will share with me all I have, all I am, and all I will be. Guide me in my choice. Help me to fall in love with the one person you know will be best for me. Give me the person who will strengthen me through life's hardships and inspire me to see all the goodness and happiness of two people living their life together, with you, their God, in their midst. Amen.

PRAYER FOR AN UNMARRIED PERSON

DEAR GOD, I AM not called to be one of your religious or priests, yet I know I can still live my life for you. I am not drawn to the married state, still I realize I have a place in the larger family of mankind. Help me fulfill both these obligations. To you I confide my chastity; guard it that I might live with a pure heart and a clean body in the midst of the world. Teach me to do all my work out of love for you. Help me to turn to you more and more, to make the interests of your kingdom my interests. Teach me, too, to live for others. Please never allow me to become selfish. Let me, by trying to live a Christ-like life, bear witness to those about me to the goodness of Christ. Amen.

FAMILY PRAYER IN TIME OF DANGER

MAY the strength of God lead us. May the power of God preserve us. May the wisdom of God instruct us. May the hand of God protect us. May the way of God direct us. May the shield of God defend us. May an army of God's angels guard us against the snares of the evil ones, against the temptations of the world. Amen.

PRAYER FOR APOSTOLIC ZEAL

JESUS, give us the spirit of apostles. Let us be filled with the desire to influence others for your sake. May our goal in life be not merely to keep the treasure of the faith, but to bring it to others. Help us to remember that no one lives his life alone, but always helps others either to heaven or to hell. Let us so live, Lord, that the world may be a better place for our having lived in it. Dear Jesus, give us a world view of things. Keep us from getting confined to ourselves and our own little problems. Enlarge our horizon with your greatness and your vision. Let us see it as you saw it, hanging from the cross, dying for all men. Amen.

A PARENT'S PRAYER FOR CHILDREN

O JESUS, friend of little children, you who from your youth grew in wisdom and grace before God and men, who although the God of your parents, subjected yourself to them in everything, watch with special care, we beg you, these children whom we have helped you create. Enable them to control the new powers which will come to them; their understanding that they may clearly know your will; their will that they may courageously follow it. Grant that they may grow in wisdom, understanding the world, its tricks and deceits, its beauty and its transcience, finally desiring, as you did, nothing but the will of your and their Father. Above all, most gentle Savior, let them grow in grace, never for a minute of their lives living in the darkness of sin, outside of the warmth and light of your friendship. O Christ, who grew as any other child, you know the trials they face; fill their minds with knowledge, fill their hearts with courage, fill their lives with your love. Amen.

PRAYER TO MARY FOR A GIRL THINKING OF BECOMING A SISTER

DEAREST MOTHER, my Mother, I come to you today with a mind and a heart full of need. Tell me, Mary, what does God want of me? As you once called yourself his handmaid and he made his will known to you, so too do I call myself today his handmaid. Will you beg him, then, to make his will clear for me as well? Is he really asking me to become his bride, to assist in the spreading of his kingdom? If so, then I want to follow him. Please, dear Mother, ask him to clear my mind of doubt and hesitation so that I may be able to

walk along the path he points out for me. I know well that
if mine is the grace of a special vocation, it will cost; but I
am willing to do everything I ought to pay the price. He
may be asking me to give up many things that a woman
holds dear, but I know that in return I will receive a
hundredfold. I will have him; I will have the house of God
for my own. I will have children of the spirit; those children
whom I will teach, counsel and encourage; all those for
whom I will pray and for whom I will spend my life. I
pray now for only this, Mother; give me insight to know his
will, the will to accept it and then the strength to live always
as one who has given herself—body and soul, heart and
mind—to her Lord, her God, to her Jesus and yours. Amen.

PRAYER FOR THOSE LOOKING FORWARD
TO MARRIAGE

LORD, you know that we are fond of each other; but fond-
ness is not enough. If marriage is in our future, we must
truly love each other; we must be capable of the total gift
of ourselves to each other, of living our lives for each
other. Help us to find out during our dates together whether
we are capable of this kind of love. And let us not confuse
the issue by excessive demonstrations of our affection for
each other. Let us constantly realize that this sort of thing
can easily lead to the tragic mistake of giving ourselves to
each other physically before we have done so spiritually in
your sight and before your altar. If it be your will that we
marry, make our love for each other grow in intensity during these months; but if it becomes clear that we are not
suited to each other, give us the courage to terminate our
relationship quickly but with deep kindness toward each
other. In Christ's name, Amen.

A PRAYER FOR CHOOSING
A STATE OF LIFE

O MY GOD, who are the God of wisdom and of counsel, who reads in my heart the sincere will to please you alone, and who knows my desire to govern myself with regard to my choice of a state of life entirely in accordance with your most holy will; grant me, by the intercession of the most Holy Virgin, my Mother, and of my Holy Patrons, the grace to know what state I ought to choose and, when known, embrace it, so that in it, I may be able to pursue and increase your glory, work out my salvation, and merit that heavenly reward you have promised to those who do your holy will. Amen.

PRAYER TO GET OVER BROODING
ABOUT INJURIES

LORD, help me to forgive and forget. Let me see that brooding over real or imaginary injuries is poison to the soul. I know from experience that at the moment I suffer adversity or some injustice, I am not much affected, but later on, when I recall the annoyance, I become irritated and resentful and tempted to revenge. Help me, dear Jesus, not to keep thinking about past offenses. Help me to forget them and get on to something else. Amen.

PRAYER FOR A TEACHER

DEAR LORD, give me the grace to go about my job conscientiously. Let me be able to communicate effectively with my students. Let me not be ruled by personal preferences, but let my concern for my students be measured by the real needs of each one. May I be able to give of myself totally every day for the sake of my students, so that I will teach them by example what true Christian living is. Amen.

PRAYER FOR RESIGNATION AFTER HAVING BEEN TREATED WITH CONTEMPT BY OTHERS

I HAVE been treated with contempt, dear Lord, and I ask for courage to benefit from what has happened to me. Teach me to know that great graces cannot be obtained without humility. Those who are to have them must be humiliated —to be made worthy by humility to receive the blessings that you withhold from the proud. Having experienced the present humiliation, may I treasure and look upon it as a sure sign that you have some special grace in store for me. Amen.

A PRAYER FOR OVERCOMING A DISLIKE FOR SOMEONE

LORD, I am aware that this is senseless of me. After all, you like this person very much and I, in my blindness and stupidity, am simply unable to see the immense amount of good in him (her) that you see. Help me to get over my dislike. But if, because of some sort of emotional block, my dislike persists, help me to be especially kind to him. Amen.

PRAYER FOR THOSE WE DO NOT LIKE OR HAVE HARMED

It frequently happens even in the best of families that members will criticize neighbors or relatives at the dinner table. When this happens, it would be a good idea for the head of the family after the meal to say the following prayer.

IN THE PERFECT PRAYER, merciful Jesus, you taught us to pray: "forgive us our debts as we forgive our debtors." We are deeply in your debt, yet again and again you forgive us. How can we be other than forgiving when we see your mercy to sinners and when—even more amazing—we have known times without number your mercy and forgiveness? We nailed you to the cross, affronted you with apathy and ingratitude, yet you forgive us again and again and take us back into your love. How can we dislike anyone when you are so merciful to everyone? Bless those for whom we feel dislike and resentment; bless those whom we have criticized or spoken unkindly of. Where we have done anything wrong, undo the harm by your grace, and by another miracle of mercy, give us the grace at least to love those whom we now find difficult or unattractive. Give us some of your all-embracing love. Amen.

PRAYER IN TIME OF SICKNESS

HELP ME, LORD, to profit by this illness that you have allowed to come to me. May I see that sickness can be a help to me in becoming less selfish and in growing in love. In my present helplessness may I learn more profoundly how much I depend upon you. May this sickness also help me to realize that the things of this world in themselves are of little or no value to me. And finally, may this sickness remind me that life can be brief and that, therefore, I ought to strive harder to do your holy will as perfectly as possible so that in the next life where there is no sickness or pain, but only joy, I may be with you for all eternity. Amen.

PRAYER TO MARY FOR A HAPPY DEATH

O MARY, conceived without sin, pray for us who have recourse to you. O refuge of sinners, Mother of the dying, forsake us not at the hour of our death. Obtain for us the grace of perfect sorrow, sincere contrition, the pardon and remission of our sins, a worthy receiving of Holy Viaticum, and the comfort of the sacrament of the Anointing of the Sick in order that we may appear with greater security before the throne of the just but merciful judge, Our God and Our Redeemer. Amen.

PRAYER FOR PEACE

GIVE US PEACE in our times, O Lord, because there is none other that fights for us, but only you, our God.

V. Peace be within your walls,
R. And abundance within your towers.

Let us Pray

O God, from whom all holy desires, all right counsels and all just works proceed, give to your servants that peace which the world cannot give. May our hearts be set to obey your commandments and may we, being delivered from the fear of our enemies, pass our time under your protection in blessed quietness. Through Christ our Lord. Amen.

Private Prayers at Church

The Way of the Cross

For private devotion in church

MY BROTHER CHRIST, I was there two thousand years ago. It was I who dragged you before Annas and Caiphas, and on to Herod and Pilate. It was I who whipped you with the cruel lash and crowned you with thorns. I placed the heavy cross on your bleeding shoulders and drove you up the hill of death. It was I, Lord, I and my sins of yesterday, today and always.

I prepared for you a hillside parade of blood and death—this road of the cross. I have walked this way behind you, sneering and laughing. I have walked in the trail of your blood. I am sorry.

Today I wish to travel this road again with you, not now as a murderer but as a friend.

195

Jesus Condemned to Death

Jesus Condemned to Death

It had to be this way. You had said and done a lot of things that we didn't like. Don't think you were going to get away with it. You had called us Pharisees and whited sepulchres, full of rottenness within. You had the nerve to say that the poor were fortunate. You said it was going to be difficult for the rich to get into heaven. You said it was wrong to lust after another man's wife. You told us we would have to love our enemies. You said and did many things that were offensive to important people. You were friendly with the poor, the foreigners, and destitute old widows. You didn't ask for a recommendation from anybody, you didn't use influence, you didn't cultivate the right people. Well, it had to be, that's all. The world just had to condemn you. They condemned you then and we would condemn you now. In fact, every day we condemn you because we simply don't like your commandments, nor your advice, nor your self-sacrificing ways, nor even your style. It had to be this way— you condemned to die. You asked for it. O, my Brother! I already know that if I follow in your footsteps, I also will be condemned. They will notice me right away; they will snicker at me, they will call me a sanctimonious hypocrite. Or, they will consider me a damned fool. Nevertheless, I know that you are right. Christ, give me the strength to go on with you, even though they think I am crazy. Even though they condemn me along with you. I can't help it, I know you are right.

Jesus Takes Up His Cross

Jesus Takes Up His Cross

No, not you, my Brother, that Cross belongs to me. Please don't insist. I tell you it is made out of my sins; I'm the one who should carry it. Alright, Lord, it's no use fighting with you. You are God, you always win. Shoulder the cross, Lord, only you can carry it anyway. All of us together couldn't carry it. The Cross of our rebirth. None of us can do anything about it. Not even your Mother, who carried you, could carry it. Carry it, please, we ask it of you. You know very well how to take hold of it. You were a carpenter from your childhood, you know how to grasp a heavy piece of wood, how to get it up on your shoulder. You did it many times in Nazareth. You would take up wood, put it on your shoulders and go wherever you had to go. You had been in training for this all your short life—to know how to carry wood. As an expert carpenter, you've always known and liked good wood. So you are the only one who knows the secret of the wood of the Cross. Embrace it, Christ, and walk, please. We will walk behind you to learn how to take hold of and carry a Cross. We don't know . . . and we need so much to know.

Jesus Falls the First Time

Jesus Falls the First Time

I see, my Brother, how you get back on your feet after you fall. Your nerves and muscles become taut; through a supreme effort of will you pick yourself up; you spread your feet apart for a firmer stand; you reach down and resolutely take hold of the Cross which lies on the ground. You determine to carry the Cross again and again as often as need be. Your arms strain and the Cross is once more lifted. You have fallen so that we may know how to stand up from a fall and how to carry, over and over again, with Christ-like nobility and firmness our own crosses. You want us to forget about falling. You want us to concentrate upon being brave; upon getting up after a fall and lifting the cross and continuing forward. To remain stretched out in the mud is for cowards. To get up, to shoulder the cross, to continue on—this is the example you have set. This is what your true followers must therefore do.

Jesus Meets His Mother

Jesus Meets His Mother

Mother, you can't carry the Cross for him. He has got to do it alone. You can't die for him either. He must do the dying, Mother. Be careful, Mary; these barbarians are going to notice right away that you are the mother of the condemned one. Don't you see how much you look like him? He has your eyes, your gestures; he is so much like you. It stands to reason that if he had no earthly father, he would have to look very much like you. It's enough to look at the two of you for a moment to see that you are Mother and Son. You are both so much alike. He carries the Cross and you carry it, too. He embraces it. You will also, as much as he will let you. He has loved us unto death and you have, too. He wanted to be our Brother and you wanted to be our Mother. It's enough to look at the two of you for a moment to see that you are Mother and Son. You are both so much alike.

Simon of Cyrene Helps Jesus to Carry the Cross

Simon of Cyrene Helps Jesus to Carry the Cross

Simon didn't want to. Of course not. He was just like us. He didn't want to carry the Cross. They *made* him carry it, and it's that way with us. The cross is inescapable, something we will find wherever we will go. Simon reached for the Cross, disgustedly. Nevertheless, little by little—he didn't know why—his hand began to caress and cling to the wood. That wood had something. There was a moment when Jesus, in an effort to get a better grip on the Cross, got his hand beneath Simon's and lifted his hand and the Cross together. In one instant, Simon understood what it takes us so long to understand—that it's Christ who carries not only his own Cross, but a large share of ours. Why, my brother, did you want Simon to help you? You wanted us to help you so that we could share your task with you. So that we would know our crosses have great value—are an extension of your cross. A lot of people around me can't carry their cross. You have put them in my path so that I would help them, but I . . . Well, I forget that it would be really you I would be helping.

Veronica Wipes the Face of Jesus

Veronica Wipes the Face of Jesus

It was a woman who dared break the enemy ranks. There were enough men there on Christ's side; the apostles and others, but they didn't dare; prudence, human respect, plain fear. So it's we men who hang behind. Behind in sacrifice, behind in total commitment to Christ. We men are very chivalrous, even in the field of religion; we let the women go ahead. We are very polite. Let Christ and the women go on ahead. We'll come along behind making up the rear guard of Christianity, a solid, compact rear guard; everybody standing up, hardly a man on his knees. Up ahead we allow Christ to be dragged along with the Cross on his shoulders and some few women by his side—the three Marys and Veronica. We are very courteous—we have allowed the women to be the ones closest to the Cross of Christ.

Jesus Falls the Second Time

Jesus Falls the Second Time

It was a shove, Christ—you know it very well and we know it, too. It was a shove that we gave you cleverly and from behind. Some of us who looked like we were going along very sorrowfully behind you. Or, perhaps it was a shove from one of the weeping daughters of Jerusalem, who will meet me in the next Station, all broken up with weeping. There are some women who have the facility of sinning and continuing to look contrite, angelic, devout. On the other hand, in such a crowd of good and bad people who follow Christ, it is so easy to give him a shove without anybody else noticing it. And Christ falls, brought down by the shove of the sins of the "good." Of us who know how to do just what we want and still seem like good people; we throw the blame for evil in the world on the pagans, the atheists, the non-Christians, on Caiphas, on Judas. Christ sprawled on the ground because of the sins of the "good" people. This fall pained you more, my Brother, because you were shoved from behind.

Jesus Speaks to the Daughters of Jerusalem

Jesus Speaks to the Daughters of Jerusalem

They are good women, Christ; they weep because they feel sorry for you. They weep because of what *others* have done to you, because of how badly *others* have treated you. It is easy for us to weep for the evil that *others* do, to deplore the filth and corruption we find everywhere in the world. Oh, how well do we weep, dear Christ, for the sins of others! For this we have the skill of professional mourners. We are terribly sorry that there is so much evil—that so many offend you. We are terribly sorry about everything—except our own sins. This is something else again. I sit in judgment on everyone—except myself. "Weep for yourselves." Christ, it is true. It hadn't occurred to me. I see very well the defects of others, how much they make you suffer, how much they offend you, but as for me . . . Lord, give me a little honesty and the light to see and to admit that *I* am a great sinner, that *I* have treated you so badly. Christ, grant that I may learn to weep for *myself*, for my *sins*.

Jesus Falls the Third Time

212

Jesus Falls the Third Time

Is he dead? No, Christ, you can't die there; you have to die up on the hill, nailed to a Cross. You have to rescue us by suffering more, much more! This is the reason why Christ did not allow himself to die right then and there. A supreme effort of the will; the will to go on living in order to suffer more. Christ, if you had allowed yourself to die there at the third fall, it would still have been a glorious death; we would all have been very grateful to you for having suffered so much for us. You had already done enough to become immensely famous and you would have gotten out of dying, nailed to a Cross. The best of us, Christ, do this very thing so often. We struggle for awhile, but then we say we have done enough. It's alright, we say, we can rest now. Some of us do even less. We stay down after the first or second fall. We, the weak, the tired of every age. We who stay down in the mud of our sins and the mud of our self-defeat and the mud of our luke-warmness. Get up, Christ, please, so that all of us may know how to get up with you. All of us sinners, weaklings, pessimists, and hopeless ones. We can make it, Christ, we can make it!

Jesus Is Stripped of His Clothing

Jesus Is Stripped of His Clothing

Jesus, you were the one who said it, "Blessed are the poor." Now you are really going to get a taste of poverty. They are going to leave you with nothing. Those who want more rob you of the little you have. They have always done this and still do. They are experts at it. Without pity they rip off everything you have on, even though in doing so, they lacerate your body. The trouble is Jesus, that you just don't know that "business is business." They will divide up what you have and gamble for what can't be divided. You, Christ, stripped of everything, that's how you are going to redeem us—with all of what is left to you—your body and blood. We, on the other hand, are dressed to the hilt—with lies and hypocrisy and deceit. We are wrapped in, choked by, appearances. This way it's impossible for us to mount the Cross. Come, Christ, strip me of ill-directed desires of the flesh and of the eyes; strip me of my damnable pride. Above all, dear Christ, strip away my disguise.

Jesus Is Nailed to the Cross

Jesus Is Nailed to the Cross

Your hands lie open, Christ, more open than ever before, to forgive. Your nailed feet are still, Christ, more still than ever before so that we can always come to you. Your body, Christ, which adjusts itself so admirably to the cross was made by God in the form of a cross, was destined for the Cross. Your body and ours, surprisingly, are designed in the form of a Cross, as though God wished all of us to embrace it. The Cross is our task and our triumph. O, yes, the Cross for which we were made and from which we foolishly run. Because of your hands being nailed and open and because of mine being quick and sensual, talented for injustice, closed for hatred and injury to others, forgive us Lord, because we *knew* what we were doing. Because of your feet which are still and twisted and bleeding and because of mine which have wandered down filthy roads and are covered now with dirt, forgive us, Lord, for we *knew* what we were doing. For all of our misdeeds; for all acts of cruelty, for all slovenliness, for every injustice to others, for each refusal to do your will forgive us, Christ.

Twelfth Station

Jesus Dies on the Cross

Jesus Dies on the Cross

Jesus, our God, dies. Yes, my Brother, death came also to you. You, dead, like my father, who in his last moments was squeezing my hand, and then came the moment when he stopped squeezing. He was gone from us, gone from his chair at the head of the table. You, Jesus, dead, just as my husband died, with his eyes wide open and such a look of pity in them for me, that even now I cry when I think of it. You, Jesus, dead, like the man in the concentration camp, abandoned and emaciated. You, Jesus, dead, like those who died in war, like those who died at sea. You, Jesus, who should not have died, dead like all the dead in the world. You, dead, as I will die one day. Thank you, Christ, my Brother in death. Thank you for having wanted to die. Now the death of loved ones isn't going to be so hard for me, nor my own death, for that matter. You are really my Brother, Jesus, because you have died, too.

Jesus Is Removed from the Cross

Jesus Is Removed from the Cross

Take him, Mother, it's all over. We give him back to you. There, Mother, you hold him in your arms as you did in Bethlehem. Remember? You gave him to us in Bethlehem, all of us. Look what we have done to him. Forgive us, Mother, you were afraid that we wouldn't know how to care for a God. Today we give him back to you. It's still him; we know that in spite of everything, you will recognize him . . . *you are* his Mother. He is the same one you sang to sleep in Bethlehem, rocking him in your arms. Now also he is asleep. We have taken care of that. He has been in our criminal hands. We have sung him to sleep with a song of sin and death. He is asleep, Mother, and we simply don't know what to do about him. We come also to ask you something . . . forgive us, and ask his forgiveness for us. Another thing, Mother, give him a kiss from you and from us. Just as you did in Bethlehem.

Jesus Is Buried

Jesus Is Buried

They have taken you away. They have buried you in a cave; they have covered you with clothes; they have sealed your burial place with a rock; the suffering is over. Everything is over. No! Your way of the Cross, Christ, is not over. Your Mystical Body will continue to walk the road to Calvary, until the end of time. You go on suffering in all the people we meet on our way of the Cross. Christ, you still walk the streets of the world with the crosses of all men,

> of those who do not wish to carry their Cross,
>
> of those who can't,
>
> of those of us who fall so many times,
>
> of those of us who do not help our brother carry his cross
>
> of those of us who place our cross on the shoulders of others.

We know that behind the Cross and behind death there is victory, but alone we can't make it. Lord, we ask you to come again, to walk the road of the Cross. This time, our road. Christ, our Brother, come again with us.

Fifteenth Station

[*I Corinthians*] Now this I say, brethren, that flesh and blood can obtain no part in the kingdom of God, neither shall corruption have any part in incorruption. Behold, I tell you a mystery: we shall all indeed rise, but we shall not all be changed—in a moment, in the twinkling of an eye, at the last trumpet. For the trumpet shall sound, and the dead shall rise incorruptible and we shall be changed. For this corruptible body must put on incorruption, and this mortal body must put on immortality. But when this mortal body puts on immortality, then shall come to pass the word that is written, "Death is swallowed up in victory! O death, where is thy victory? O death, where is thy sting?" Now the sting of death is sin, and the power of sin is the Law. But thanks be to God who has given us the victory through our Lord Jesus Christ. Therefore, my beloved brethren, be steadfast and immovable, always abounding in the work of the Lord, knowing that your labor is not in vain in the Lord.

THE RESURRECTION
by Cecco del Caravaggio
The Art Institute of Chicago

Visits to the Blessed Sacrament

W E BELIEVE that Christ is present in a unique way in the tabernacles of our churches. When the priest at Mass leads the family of God in proclaiming anew the death of Christ on Calvary and His passing from this world to the Father, he brings down upon the altar the presence of the risen Christ as the wounded (but glorified) victim of His sacrifice. After the Mass is over, Christ the Victim continues to be present in the Sacrament.

Thus, a visit paid to a church where He is sacramentally present enables us to share, in a limited, but nevertheless real and fruitful way, in the benefits of the Mass. People discover that, when they stop by and visit with Him in a quiet church, they experience a deep peace, a relaxation of their tensions, and refreshment for their souls—a literal fulfillment of the promise of Christ "Come to me, all of you who labour and are burdened, and I will refresh you." While some find it enough merely to be in the sacramental presence of Christ, others spend the moments in "heart" talk with Christ. Still others find formal prayers of great help.

In the following pages will be found suggested forms for

SAINT PASCHAL BAYLON *by Tiepolo*
Museo del Prado, Madrid, Spain

visiting the Blessed Sacrament for each day of the week. The language of these prayers is often unabashedly affectionate, having been put down in the spirit—and indeed, often in the very words of—St. Alphonsus Liguori. Men who, like St. Alphonsus, are capable of a virile, natural, and deep affection for their brother Christ will not be ill at ease with these prayers. Others would perhaps do better to put their feelings for Christ in words of their own that would come more naturally to them.

INTRODUCTORY PRAYER

> To be said every day.

MY BROTHER JESUS, because you love us, you remain night and day in this Sacrament, awaiting, calling, and welcoming all who come to visit you. I believe you are really present here in the tabernacle. I acknowledge that you are my King and my Savior. I thank you for everything you have done for me, especially for the gift of your sacramental presence. My Jesus, I wish to make the gift of myself to you by doing your will as perfectly as possible. I am sorry I haven't always done too well about this in the past, but, weak and helpless as I am, I will try with your help to do better in the future. No matter what you have in store for me, I will try to go along with it. All I want in return is to be with you, now and always, and to have the strength to walk in your footsteps.

VISIT FOR SUNDAY

HERE I AM, my brother Jesus, before this altar on which you dwell day and night for my sake. You are the source of every good, you are the healer of every ill, you are the treasure of every poor creature. Here I am now at your feet, a sinner who is, of all others, the poorest and the sickest and who asks your mercy. Have pity upon me. Now that I see you in the Sacrament, come down from heaven upon earth only to do good to me, I will not be disheartened at the sight of my misery. I praise you, I thank you, I love you, and if you want me to ask you for something—I will ask for this—listen to me—I want to stop offending you and start pleasing you. Lord, I do love you. Grant that I may speak the truth, and that I may speak in the same way during life and through all eternity. Most Holy Virgin Mary, my Patron Saints, you angels, all you wonderful people of Paradise, help me to love my most lovable God. O Good Shepherd, True Bread, Jesus, have mercy on us, feed us, guard us, show us good things in the land of the living.

SPIRITUAL COMMUNION

To be said every day of the visit.

MY JESUS, I believe that you are present in the most Holy Sacrament. I love you above all things and I desire to receive you into my soul. Since I cannot receive you now sacramentally, come at least spiritually into my heart. I want to be wholly united to you; never let me become separated from you.

Hail Holy Queen, etc.

VISIT FOR MONDAY

LET US UNDERSTAND that as Jesus Christ in Heaven is, as St. Paul said, "always living to make intercession for us," so in the Sacrament of the Altar, he is continually, both night and day, exercising the compassionate office of our advocate; offering himself as the glorified victim for us to the eternal Father, thus to obtain for us his mercies and innumerable graces. Therefore, we ought to approach and converse with Jesus in the Blessed Sacrament without fear of punishment and unrestrained, as with a dear friend who loves us with an eternal love.

Since then you gave me permission, let me, O My King and Lord, now open my heart to you with confidence and say; O My Jesus, I well know the injustice that men do you. You love them, and they do not love you. You offer them every good thing and they offer you nothing but contempt. You want them to listen to you and they pay no attention. You hold out to them your graces and they refuse them. Christ, is it true that I also at one time was just as contemptuous of you? O God, it is but too true; but I am determined to make amends and to try, during the time I still have to live, to make up for all the wasted years by doing all that I possibly can to please you.

Tell me, Lord, what you ask of me. I will try to do it unreservedly. Make known to me your desires and I will do the best I can.

My Brother, I now firmly promise that I will try from this day forward never to fail to do anything I know will be pleasing to you, even should I lose thereby parents, friends, esteem, health, or even life. Let it all go, provided it's you I please. I want to be totally committed to you the way men have been known to commit themselves to a political leader. In your presence I want to feel what men feel in the presence of a great and good man they admire. Call it enthusiasm, devotion, affection, love—whatever it is, I want to feel that I would go to the end of the world with you.

(*Spiritual Communion*, page 229)
Hail Holy Queen, etc.

VISIT FOR TUESDAY

MY BROTHER JESUS, you are present here on the Altar. When you come to me in Communion, you are present in a very special way; you become my food. You unite yourself entirely to me, you give your whole self to me, so that I can then say with truth, my Jesus, you are now all mine. Since then you give yourself all to me, it is reasonable that I should give myself all to you. I'm nobody and you are God. O God of love, when shall I find myself all yours in deeds and not only in words? You can do it by the merits of your great sacrifice. Increase my confidence that I may at once obtain this grace of you, and that I may live my life not for myself but for you. You, O Lord, hear the prayers of all; hear now the prayers of a person who indeed really wants to love you. I want to love you with all my strength. But help me to understand this word "love"; help me to see that it does not mean being filled up with gushy, exaggeratedly sentimental feelings toward you; rather, that it does mean wanting to obey you in everything you will without self-interest, without any emotional satisfaction, without any reward. I want to love you, to serve you through love. Christ Jesus, since love ultimately is the gift of self, take possession of my liberty, my will, of all that I have.

(*Spiritual Communion*, page 229)
Hail Holy Queen, etc.

VISIT FOR WEDNESDAY

MY JESUS, I will try not to complain of what you have planned for me. I know that it is all for my good. It is enough for me to know that you want things this way and I will try to want them this way also, now and forever. Do anything you want with me. I unite myself entirely to your will, which is holy, good, beautiful, perfect, loving. O will of My God, how dear you are to me! My will is ever to live and die united and bound up with you. Your pleasure is my pleasure. I want your desires to be my desires. My God, my God, help me. Make me live from now on for you alone. Make me want only what you want and make me live only to love your will. Grant that I may die for your love since you died for me. I curse those days in which I did my own will so much to your displeasure. I love you, will of God, as much as I love God, since you are one with him. I love you, then, with my whole heart and give my whole self to you. O will of God, you are my love.

(*Spiritual Communion*, page 229)

Hail Holy Queen, etc.

VISIT FOR THURSDAY

MY LORD, why do I kneel here with such an emptiness in my heart? I think I know the answer. I am in the presence of one whose life was an act of total self-giving. Is not the very way that you are present here a vivid reminder of this fact? You held a piece of bread in your hands the night before you died. You said "This is my body which is given for you." You are present here in the same way as that night.

I find your presence comforting. It is nice to be here with you in this quiet church. But I am also ill at ease when I start to compare your life with mine. I am such a failure when it comes to love. I can kneel here and tell you that I love you, but what always happens when I leave here? The same cowardice and lukewarmness as before. The same careful concern for my own pleasure and comfort, the same unwillingness to spend myself for others. I simply am not like you. Oh, but I want to be; please, please help me. I keep saying I love you. But five minutes later, I can walk right by you in the street and refuse to have anything to do with you because—well, you're dressed rather poorly, your skin often is too dark (or too light) for my liking. You look as though you belong in jail. I come back later and tell you how sorry I am about all this. But do I really mean it? Will I go out of here now and really begin to love you in your brothers? I will, I will. But you must help me.

(*Spiritual Communion*, page 229)

Hail Holy Queen, etc.

VISIT FOR FRIDAY

MY DEAR BROTHER, Jesus, I hear you say from this Tabernacle in which you are present, "This is my rest for ever and ever: here I will dwell because I have chosen it." Since then you have chosen your dwelling on our altars in the midst of us, remaining there in the most Holy Sacrament, and since your love for us makes you there find your rest, it is but just that our hearts also should ever dwell with you in affection and should find all pleasure and rest in you. Fortunate are those who can find no nicer rest in the world than in remaining near to you. And fortunate should I be, my Lord, did I from this time forward find no greater delight than in remaining always in your presence or in always thinking of you, who in the most Holy Sacrament are always thinking of me and my welfare. O my Lord, why have I lost so many years in which I have not loved you? O miserable years, I curse you and I bless you, O infinite patience of my God, for having for so many years put up with me, though so ungrateful for your love; and still, notwithstanding this ingratitude, you wait for me, and why, my God, why? It is that one day, overcome by your mercy and by your love, I may yield wholly to you. Lord, I will no longer resist, I will no longer be ungrateful. It is but just that I should consecrate to you the time, be it long or short, that I still have to live. I hope for your help, my Jesus, to become entirely yours. You were good to me when I fled from you and despised your love. How much more so, now that I seek and desire to love you! Give me then the grace to love you, O God, worthy of infinite love. I want to love you with my whole heart, above all things, more than myself, more than my life. I am sorry for having turned away from you; forgive me and, with your forgiveness, grant me the grace to love you much in this life until death and in the next life for all eternity. O almighty God, show the world the greatness of your power in the wonder of a soul, ungrateful as mine has been, becoming one of your greatest lovers. Do this by your merits, my Jesus. It is my ardent desire; and I resolve thus to love you during my whole life. You inspire me with this desire; give me also the strength to accomplish it. My Jesus, I thank you for having waited for me until now.

(*Spiritual Communion*, page 229)

Hail Holy Queen, etc.

VISIT FOR SATURDAY

O DIVINE WORD, O my own Jesus, I see you sacrificed and victimized on the altar for my love. It is then but right that as you sacrifice yourself as a victim of love for me, I at least should consecrate myself wholly to you. Yes, my Brother, I now sacrifice to you my whole soul, my entire self, my whole will and my whole life. I unite this poor sacrifice of mine, my Father in Heaven, with the infinite sacrifice your Son once offered to you on the Cross, and which he now offers to you so many times every day on our altars. Accept my sacrifice, then, through the merits of Jesus and grant me the grace to renew it every day of my life, and to die sacrificing my whole self to your honor. I desire the grace granted to so many martyrs to die for your love; but if I am unworthy of so great a grace, grant at least, my Lord, that I may sacrifice my life to you, together with my entire will, by accepting whatever death you send me. Lord, I desire this grace; I desire to die with the intention of honoring and pleasing you thereby; and from this moment I sacrifice my life to you and I offer you my death when or wherever it may take place. My Jesus, I want my death to be like yours—the total surrender of myself into the hands of the Father.

(*Spiritual Communion*, page 229)

Hail Holy Queen, etc.

BIBLE READING

Family Reading of the Bible

IN HOMES where the reading of the Bible has become an accepted and successful family practice, one will consequently and inevitably find a true and deep Christian faith. But serious difficulties lie in the path of the parent who is trying to start this practice. If they are not avoided, the practice will be rejected by the family and will be unsuccessful in obtaining the desired results.

For one thing, it is self-defeating to plow indiscriminately through the books of the Bible. Selections must be made that will hold the interest of the children, if you wish them to persevere in studying the word of God. The parent must also familiarize himself with the text beforehand in order to be able to read it in an interesting and meaningful way, to be able to put into his own words how the reading is related to family life and to be able to answer questions that would be raised by the children. In the following pages will be found selections from the Bible for each day of the year together with appropriate explanatory material. The selections, however, are not intended to be a final and unchangeable guide for family reading; a parent might well prefer other selections from time to time. Nor must the parent feel obligated to adhere to the dates cited for the various selections; they are set down merely as a convenient answer to the question, "What shall we read tonight"?

When should the reading take place? Here may be stressed once again the importance of having the family eat together in the evening. Where this is achieved, it should not be difficult to delay the clean-up after the meal for the ten or fifteen minutes the reading would require; however, some families may find it more convenient to hold the reading at some other time.

The head of the household should always do the reading, or, in his (or her) absence, the next in charge. No one should be forced to remain at the table after the first few weeks of reading; nothing more quickly kills a child's interest in the word of God than to have it read to him against his will. Indeed, if nearly all members of the family soon find excuses for absenting themselves, the fault would lie with the way in which the reading is done.

Even with the best will in the world and under ideal circumstances, family Bible reading will be a difficult project to put over. Because of the great good to be achieved however, parents should not give up too easily. Helpful literature on this subject is easily available at your local Catholic book store.

The parent should start his preparation by reading the Encyclical Letter found in the beginning of the Bible. He should also read the explanatory notes at the beginning of each book as well as the footnotes that would pertain to the text he will be reading to the family on any given night.

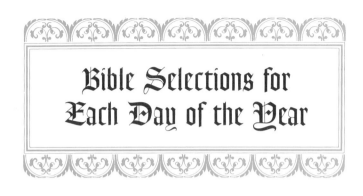

Bible Selections for Each Day of the Year

Prayer to be said before each reading.

COME HOLY SPIRIT, fill the hearts of your faithful and fire them with the fire of your love.
   V. Send forth your spirit and they shall be created;
   R. And you shall renew the face of the earth.

Let Us Pray

GOD, YOU TEACH your faithful by the light of the Holy Spirit; through this same spirit, grant us right judgment in all things and joy in His comforting presence.
We ask in Christ's name. Amen.

Suggested daily readings, with an occasional commentary, are indicated in the following pages. However, no commentary on New Testament selections is given since it is felt that the average Christian family will understand enough of the New Testament material to profit greatly from the reading. Indeed, much that is obscure in the Gospels and Epistles will become more clear to the family once it has a deeper acquaintance with the Old Testament.

The Book of Genesis

GENESIS MEANS the beginning. The first chapters tell in story form how the world began. It is neither a scientific nor even a historical account. Only when we come to the figure of Abraham do we enter the realm of history. Unquestionably though, the first chapters deal with substantial fact. God *did* create the world and man out of nothing; man *did* reject God, thereby bringing chaos to the world; God did *not* reject man but promised that someone would come to repair all the harm done; man *does* have an enemy in Satan (whether or not he took the form of a serpent matters little); Noah and the flood may or may not have been a matter of history, but the inspired fact that stands out in the narrative about Noah is that sin has tragic consequences.

With Abraham we have the beginning of our recorded history. He was to be the father of the people with whom God was to deal directly over the next eighteen centuries. God made a covenant (agreement, pact, testament) with Abraham that was in effect until the coming of Christ, whereupon there was to be a New Testament and the birth of a new people of God in Christ. It helps our understanding of the Old Testament to bear in mind that the history we are reading is an account of how this agreement worked out over the centuries, the Jews prospering during periods of fidelity to God and suffering great misfortune during periods of infidelity. Isaac is born of Abraham and in turn begets Jacob and Esau. The story of how Jacob wrested from

Esau the latter's birthright presents moral difficulties to the reader. However, God had plans for Jacob; he re-made with Jacob the agreement made with Abraham. God changed Jacob's name to Israel. God blessed Israel with twelve sons who became the heads of the twelve tribes of Israel.

January	**1**	Genesis 1, 2, 3
	2	John 1
	3	Genesis 4, 5, 6
	4	John 2
	5	Genesis 7, 8, 9
	6	John 3
	7	Genesis 11 (omit verses 10-26), 12, 13
	8	John 4
	9	Genesis 14, 15, 16
	10	John 5
	11	Genesis 17, 18, 19 (omit verse 8, 30-38)
	12	John 6
	13	Genesis 20, 21, 22 (omit verses 20-24)
	14	John 7
	15	Genesis 24
	16	John 8
	17	Genesis 25, 26, 27
	18	John 9
	19	Genesis 28, 29, 30
	20	John 10
	21	Genesis 31, 32, 33
	22	John 11
	23	Genesis 37, 39, 40

January	24	John 12
	25	Genesis 41, 42, 43
	26	John 13, 14
	27	Genesis 44, 45, 46:1-7, 26-34
	28	John 15, 16, 17
	29	Genesis 47, 48, 49, 50
	30	John 18, 19

The Book of Exodus

THIS BOOK is the clue and key to all that will come later. Just as Christ, in an infinitely more important way, is the essential figure of the New Testament, so is Moses the central figure of the Old Testament. We see in the turbulent story of Moses leading his people to freedom a shadowy but real pre-figuring of Christ leading his people to eternal freedom in the kingdom of Heaven. Exodus means a going out, an escape to freedom; in the miraculous, cliff-hanging escape of the Jews under Moses, God shows forth in a remarkable way his loving concern for his children. God will give a greater and more loving proof of his concern when he sends His Son to liberate his new people in Christ from the far more perilous tyranny of Satan.

January	31	Exodus 1, 2, 3
February	1	John 20, 21
	2	Exodus 4, 5, 6
	3	Matthew 1
	4	Exodus 7, 8, 9
	5	Matthew 2

The Book of Leviticus

MUCH OF THIS BOOK does not lend itself to family reading. It contains chapter after chapter of laws governing the daily life of the Jewish people. It gets its name from the tribe of Levi, who was one of Jacob's twelve sons and whose descendants were to be the priests of Israel. We have made a brief selection from this book that will be of interest to the family.

The Book of Numbers

THE TITLE REFERS to the two censuses of the Hebrews that were taken. In general, though, this book is a continuation of Jewish history and, specifically, of their arrival at the Jordan at last after forty years of wandering.

February	**18**	Summarize Numbers 1 to 3. Read 6:22-27, 9:1-5, 10:1-12, 33-36, 12.
	19	Matthew 9
	20	Numbers 14, 16, 17
	21	Matthew 10
	22	Numbers 20, 21:1-9, 22, 27:12-23
	23	Matthew 11

The Book of Joshua

IN THIS BOOK we follow still further the fortunes of the Hebrews under their great leader, Joshua. If the children ask "How come all this slaughter?", perhaps the only acceptable answer is that the Lord had to take these people as they were. They were free men and men conditioned by the brutal times in which they lived. Christ had not yet come to deliver His message of perfect love.

February	**24**	Joshua 1, 2, 3, 4
	25	Matthew 12
	26	Joshua 5, 6, 7, 8
	27	Matthew 13
	28	Joshua 9, 10:1-14 , 23, 24
March	**1**	Matthew 14

The Book of Judges

THE ACTION described in this book covers the history of the Jewish people during the 12th and 11th centuries B.C. Their wanderings were over and they were settling down to a more stable way of life on their farms. Their leaders during these crucial decades were called Judges. These leaders had their hands full leading the people to victory over ever-present enemies and getting them to repent of their frequent lapses into idolatry. The Judges were not always admirable men but they were effective instruments in preserving the Jewish nation for their part in our redemption.

March	**2**	Judges 2:6-22, 6, 7, 8:1-28
	3	Matthew 14
	4	Judges 11, 13
	5	Matthew 15
	6	Judges 14, 15, 16
	7	Matthew 16

The Book of Ruth

A LOVABLE, readable story, the point of which may be missed unless we note that in Chapter 4:17, Ruth, a gentile and a convert, gives birth to Obed who would be David's grandfather. Christ would be a descendant of David. In the story of Ruth we already have an indication that the kingdom of God will later include the gentile as well as the Jew. Although God did not specify to His people that the *Christ* would come from the house of David, He did say that *salvation* would.

March	**8**	Ruth
	9	Matthew 17

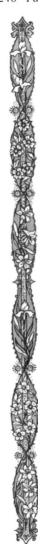

I and II Samuel

THESE BOOKS are a continuation of Jewish History from the close of the period of Judges to the rise and establishment of the monarchy in Israel. David is the key figure in these two books. He brings Israel to unprecedented prosperity and greatness; but the people will begin to consider greatness and prosperity as the only purpose of life, forgetting that we are made by God and for God. They will consequently come upon hard times again.

March 10	I Samuel 1, 2
11	Matthew 18
12	I Samuel 3, 4, 5, 6
13	Matthew 19
14	I Samuel 7, 8, 9
15	Matthew 20
16	I Samuel 10, 11, 12
17	Matthew 21
18	I Samuel 13, 14
19	Matthew 22
20	I Samuel 15, 16
21	Matthew 23
22	I Samuel 17, 18
23	Matthew 24
24	I Samuel 19, 20
25	Matthew 25
26	I Samuel 21, 22, 23
27	Matthew 26, 27, 28
28	I Samuel 24, 25
29	Mark 1, 2

March 30	I Samuel 26, 27, 28
31	Mark 3, 4
April 1	I Samuel 29, 30, 31
2	Mark 5
3	II Samuel 1, 2
4	Mark 6
5	II Samuel 3, 4, 5
6	Mark 6
7	II Samuel 6, 7, 8, 9
8	Mark 7
9	II Samuel 10, 11, 12:1-25
10	Mark 8:1-21
11	II Samuel 15, 16
12	Mark 8:22-39
13	II Samuel 17, 18
14	Mark 9

I and II Kings

UNDER SOLOMON, Israel was to achieve its greatest glory. But the Lord had chosen his people to prepare the world for a great spiritual kingdom under Christ. Consequently, as we learn in these two books, Israel's greatness did not last long. She became a divided nation. Only the prophets, raised up by God to call their people to repentance, prevented Israel from disappearing as a nation from the vital history of mankind.

April 15	I Kings 1:5-53, 2
16	Mark 10
17	I Kings 3, 4:1, 4:20-34
18	Mark 11

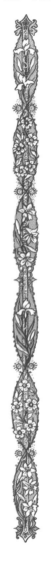

19	I Kings 8
20	Mark 12
21	I Kings 9, 10, 11:1-13, 11:41-43
22	Mark 13
23	I Kings 17, 18
24	I Kings 19, 20
25	Mark 14
26	I Kings 21, 22
27	Mark 15, 16
28	II Kings, 1, 2
29	Luke 1
30	II Kings 3, 4
May 1	Luke 2
2	II Kings 5, 6:1-26
3	Luke 3
4	II Kings 7, 8
5	Luke 4
6	II Kings 9, 10
7	Luke 5
8	II Kings 11, 12
9	Luke 6
10	II Kings 13, 14
11	Luke 7
12	II Kings 15, 16
13	Luke 8
14	II Kings 17, 18, 19
15	Luke 9
16	II Kings 20, 21, 22
17	Luke 10
18	II Kings 23, 24, 25
19	Luke 11

The Book of Tobit

WHETHER THIS story is fiction or history matters little. What does matter is the inspired lesson it teaches of confidence in God and the rewards of a virtuous life.

The Book of Judith

JUDITH IS ONE of the great heroines in Jewish history. It should be explained to young children that her solution to the extremely critical problems facing her people was born out of necessity. She was a woman of her times and she rescued her people from complete destruction in a way that seemed fitting to her. The positive aspects of her character ought to be stressed—her bravery, patriotism, prudence, and love of God.

June 1 Judith 1, 2, 3
2 Luke 18
3 Judith 4, 5
4 Luke 19
5 Judith 6, 7
6 Luke 20
7 Judith 8, 9
8 Luke 21
9 Judith 10, 11, 12
10 Luke 22, 23
11 Judith 13, 14
12 Luke 24
13 Judith 15, 16
14 Acts 1

The Book of Esther

A QUEEN of great humility, faith, and courage, Esther reminds us of our Queen Mary, and the latter's role in the salvation of the new people of God in Christ.

June 15 Esther 11:2-12, 12
16 Acts 2
17 Esther 1, 2, 3:1-13
18 Acts 3
19 Esther 13:1-7, 4:1-8, 15:1-3, 4:9-17
20 Acts 4
21 Esther 14, 5:1-2, 15:4-19
22 Acts 5
23 Esther 5:3-14, 6, 7, 8:1-12
24 Acts 6

June	25	Esther 6, 8:13-17, 9, 10
	26	Acts 7

The Book of Job

THIS BOOK, although one of the great classics of the world's literature, is much too deep for the children in the family and indeed for many grown-ups. However the basic story can be gleaned from the selections listed below. They tell of Job's unflinching confidence in God despite incredible hardships and sufferings.

June	27	Job 1, 2
	28	Acts 8
	29	Job 3:1-6, 24-26, 4:1-9, 6:22-26, 8:1-7, 10:1-3
	30	Acts 9
July	1	Job 11:1-6, 13-16, 13:13-19, 31:5-8, 32
	2	Acts 10
	3	Job 38, 39
	4	Acts 11
	5	Job 40, 41
	6	Acts 12

The Prophets, Isaiah, Jeremiah, Baruch, etc.

THE BOOKS of the Prophets, generally speaking, make difficult reading for the average family. But their importance for understanding the total meaning of the scripture is much too great for them to be

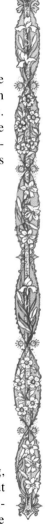

skipped over entirely. Thus we have listed below selections from their books for family reading.

The Prophets were not raised up by God simply to prophesy the coming of Christ; rather they were to be prophets more in the sense of *witnesses*, reminding their people in forceful and dramatic ways of their relationship with God, preaching repentance to their people when they had wandered far from God, pointing out that their people had been chosen by God for a very special work which they were neglecting. Because of man's tendency to drift from God, the world will always be in need of Prophets, or witnesses, who will stand before the people and cry out the good news of salvation. We Christians, through our sacrament of confirmation, are also called, in varying degrees, to be witnesses to the world that Christ is our saviour and, just as it was wrong for Jonas not to want to preach to the Ninivites, so it would be wrong for us Christians to remain silent in a world that has not accepted Christ. To understand the Prophets, we must understand that their problems are also our problems, their mission our mission, their responsibilities our responsibilities.

July	**7**	Isaiah 6:1-10, 1:11-20, 3:13-26, 5:1-7
	8	Acts 13
	9	Isaiah 5:20-30, 10:16-22, 11:1-5
	10	Acts 14
	11	Isaiah 40:1-5, 45:1-6, 49:14-18

July	**12**	Acts 15
	13	Isaiah 51:1-3, 52:13-15, 53:1-12
	14	Acts 16
	15	Isaiah 55:1-2, 56:6-8, 56:18-23
	16	Acts 17
	17	Jeremiah 1, 2
	18	Acts 18
	19	Jeremiah 3, 4
	20	Acts 19
	21	Baruch 1, 2
	22	Acts 20
	23	Baruch 3, 4, 5
	24	Acts 21
	25	Baruch 6
	26	Acts 22
	27	Ezekiel 1:1-20
	28	Acts 23
	29	Ezekiel 34:1-34
	30	Acts 24
	31	Ezekiel 37:1-14
August	**1**	Acts 25
	2	Daniel 1
	3	Acts 26
	4	Daniel 2
	5	Acts 27
	6	Daniel 3:1-45
	7	Acts 28
	8	Daniel 3:46-100
	9	Romans 1:1-23, 28-32
	10	Daniel 5
	11	Romans 2:1-11

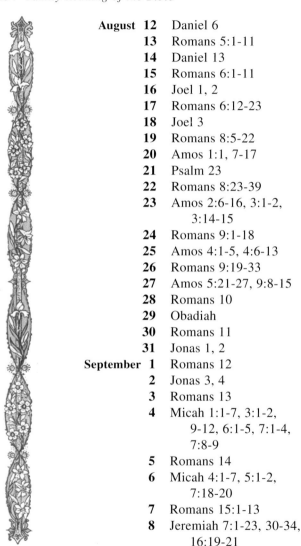

September	**9**	Romans 15:14-33
	10	Jeremiah 18, 19
	11	Romans 16
	12	Habakkuk 1, 2:1-4
	13	I Corinthians 1
	14	Jeremiah 37
	15	I Corinthians 2
	16	Jeremiah 38
	17	I Corinthians 3
	18	Jeremiah 39
	19	I Corinthians 4
	20	Jeremiah 40
	21	I Corinthians 5
	22	Jeremiah 42
	23	I Corinthians 10:-13
	24	Jeremiah 43
	25	I Corinthians 10:14-33
	26	Jeremiah 44
	27	I Corinthians 11:1-16
	28	Zephaniah 1
	29	I Corinthians 11:17-34
	30	Zephaniah 2, 3
October	**1**	I Corinthians 12
	2	Haggai
	3	I Corinthians 13
	4	Malachi 1
	5	I Corinthians 14:1-19
	6	Malachi 2
	7	I Corinthians 14:20-40
	8	Malachi 3, 4
	9	I Corinthians 15:1-19
	10	Zechariah 9
	11	I Corinthians 15:20-34

I and II Maccabees

THESE TWO BOOKS tell the same story from different viewpoints. The first book is a straight-forward and quite military account of an impassioned struggle for freedom to worship the Lord and to keep his law. The second book, telling less of the story, is more of an inspirational sermon on the courage and fidelity of the Maccabees. The issue is clearly laid down in verses 58 to 60 of Chapter 3 of the first book; "And Judas said: Gird yourselves, and be valiant men, and be ready against the morning, that you may fight with these nations that are assembled against us to destroy us and our sanctuary. For it is better for us to die in battle, than to see the evils of our nation and of the holies; never-

theless as it shall be the will of God in heaven, so
be it done."

October	**25**	Psalm 50
	26	II Corinthians 4
	27	I Maccabees 2
	28	II Corinthians 5
	29	I Maccabees 3
	30	II Corinthians 6
	31	I Maccabees 4
November	**1**	II Corinthians 7
	2	I Maccabees 5
	3	II Corinthians 8
	4	I Maccabees 6
	5	II Corinthians 9
	6	I Maccabees 7
	7	II Corinthians 10
	8	I Maccabees 8
	9	II Corinthians 11
	10	I Maccabees 9
	11	II Corinthians 12
	12	I Maccabees 10
	13	II Corinthians 13
	14	I Maccabees 11
	15	Galatians 1
	16	I Maccabees 12
	17	Galatians 2
	18	I Maccabees 13
	19	Galatians 5:13-26
	20	I Maccabees 14
	21	Galatians 6
	22	I Maccabees 15
	23	Ephesians 1

November	**24**	I Maccabees 16
	25	Ephesians 2
	26	II Maccabees 1
	27	Ephesians 3
	28	II Maccabees 2
	29	Ephesians 4
	30	II Maccabees 3
December	**1**	Ephesians 5
	2	II Maccabees 4
	3	Ephesians 6
	4	II Maccabees 5
	5	Phillipians 1
	6	II Maccabees 6
	7	Phillipians 2:1-18
	8	II Maccabees 7
	9	Phillipians 3
	10	II Maccabees 8
	11	Phillipians 4
	12	II Maccabees 9
	13	Colossians 1
	14	II Maccabees 10
	15	Colossians 3
	16	II Maccabees 11
	17	I Thessalonians 4, 5
	18	II Maccabees 12
	19	James 1, 2
	20	II Maccabees 13
	21	I Peter 3:8-22, 4
	22	II Maccabees 14, 15
	23	Luke 1
	24	Luke 2
	25	Matthew 1
	26	Matthew 2:1-12

To this Our most merciful Redeemer we must therefore bring all back by every means in our power; for He is the divine consoler of the afflicted; He it is Who teaches all, whether they be invested with public authority or are bound in duty to obey and submit, true honesty, absolute justice and generous charity; it is He in fine, and He alone, Who can be the firm foundation and support of peace and tranquility: "For other foundation no man can lay, but that which is laid: which is Christ Jesus." This the author of salvation, Christ, will men more fully know, more ardently love and more faithfully imitate in proportion as they are more assiduously urged to know and meditate the Sacred Letters, especially the New Testament, for, as St. Jerome the Doctor of Stridon says: "To ignore the Scripture is to ignore Christ"; and again: "If there is anything in this life which sustains a wise man and induces him to maintain his serenity amidst the tribulations and adversities of the world, it is in the first place, I consider, the meditation and knowledge of the Scriptures."   Pius XII

Family Practices

THE FAMILY PRACTICES suggested below are designed to help children (and grown-ups) to be more aware of the glorious fact of our salvation in Christ Jesus. It is difficult for all of us to remember this fact from Sunday to Sunday. But if we tie it in with the things about us—water, trees, winter, spring, food, flowers—we will be surrounded by constant reminders of our great good fortune in Christ. Rather than let the world take us from God, we should use the world and the good things in it to bring us to God.

The practices explained below are by no means the only ones a family may use. They are set down as suggestions or guidelines. It should be noticed, however, that they have been used for years by many families who have found them immensely helpful in creating in children a spontaneous, uninhibited, joyful awareness of their splendid destiny as children of their Father in Heaven. Through these practices the saving action of Christ, their Brother, becomes a vibrant reality for them. The Mass, for example, which can be at times

CHRIST BLESSING CHILDREN *by Pacecco de Rosa*
The Metropolitan Museum of Art, Gift of Eugene Boross, 1927

confusing to children, becomes for them a thing of deeper meaning and beauty, an integral part of their lives. Parents may pick and choose among these suggestions. Better still, they may invent their own family practices. It is important, however, that they make some effort to bring Christ into the daily lives of their children. Since children like doing things, these practices are designed to give them something Christian to do—something that will be interesting and fun and at the same time, highlight for them the mysteries of our salvation.

ADVENT PRACTICES

ADVENT'S FIRST Sunday has been named Stirring-up Sunday. The prayer of the day is "Stir up your power, we ask you, O Lord, and COME!" So, Mother, roll up your sleeves and start stirring together ingredients of the traditional fruit cake for the holiday feast. You may know all sorts of recipes, but will this one do?

> 1 lb. each of
>   currants
>   seedless raisins
>   prunes
> Cut with scissors into small pieces.
> Mix and stir in, soaking for 3 days:
>   1 pt. light rum
>   1 pt. white table wine
> Stir together:
>   6 cups flour
>   4 tsp. baking powder
>   1 tsp. each nutmeg, cinnamon
> Cream:
>   1 lb. butter
>   2 cups sugar

Add: 8 beaten eggs,
             1 tsp. vanilla

Mix well, then add flour mixture gradually. Lastly, fold in fruit and liquor, and 1 cup walnuts, if desired. Grease and line with wax paper 4 bread pans or 2 tube pans. (1) Place cakes on rack in middle of oven; (2) bake 3 hours; (3) place shallow pan of water (hot) on bottom of slow oven (300°). Remove water last 30 minutes of baking. Cool the cake and wrap in aluminum foil. Store in an air-tight container in a cool place. Allow at least two weeks, preferably longer, for aging.

The first Sunday of Advent is also the time to put the Advent Wreath into service. Not only is this practice logical, but the wreath attractive and handsome. It makes its symbolic point without too much trouble and definitely hints at the coming of Christmas by its fragrant greenness. The wreath, as a symbol, is a circle showing eternity, and is made of evergreen, the symbol of undying life. Four candles are placed in the circle for the four Advent Weeks and the purple ribbon tied around the candles tells of the need for penance spoken of in the Advent Gospels. The greens can be of any variety, the most common perhaps being pine or balsam, or even laurel. Cones, moss and berries can be added as decoration; the frame for the wreath can be made from any number of fixtures—coat hangers bent into shape, or a tube mold filled with sand to anchor the greens.

A very important part of the wreath is the blessing that the father of the house prays over it.

> Father: Our help is in the name of the Lord,
>
> All: Who made heaven and earth.
>
> Father: Let us pray. O God, by whose word all things are made holy, pour forth Your blessings upon this wreath, and grant that we who use it may prepare our hearts for

THE ADVENT WREATH

the coming of Christ and may receive from You abundant graces. Through Christ, our Lord.

All: Amen.

It should be noted here the important place a father's blessing has in a home. It's not a poetic expression or a "nice" gesture, but the actual prerogative given him by God, our common Father, who lets the heads of families share in his own great power. Thus, as a baptized Christian sharing in Christ's priesthood, the father blesses his children at night, for example, or when they're sick; or he blesses the food at meals, and, at various times during the year, blesses special things which the family is using to enliven their Christian spirit. Hence, he now blesses the Advent wreath, with all joining in as a family awaiting their Lord.

Starting on the first Sunday of Advent, one candle is lit each week and evening prayers are said by it. An interesting part of this will be to watch the young children vying with each other to be the first at the table for the lighting of the wreath, and the first to blow out the candle at the end of the meal. A good chance for a little restraint?

Advent is, indeed, the time for restraint and penance. We've got to wake up from sleep, shake off the "old" man (or woman) in us, and start remembering again all our Father has done for us. The spirit of Advent penance, however, is different. It's not a painful mortification as in Lent, but a yearning, an eager desire for salvation to come. Penance during this season should take the form of gifts to the Risen King Christ whose birthday we again celebrate. These gifts need not be great, for who of us can do really great things? Reading to the youngsters an extra story, mother fixing daughter's hair if she usually doesn't, one of the children drying dishes a bit less resentfully, restraining a sharp word, or letting a brother or sister have a book he or she usually clings to—all of these are little gifts, but their seed blooms into rare beauty.

As the Fruit Cake and Wreath are traditional customs, being an "angel" is another. Angels, after all, have the glorious task of praising God and giving him honor, so each one of the family can give our Saving God trumpet blasts of praise by doing little things for each other all during Advent time. This practice creates a longing in itself and a curious suspense, especially for the children, who really seem to sense the coming of their God. Each member writes his name on a piece of paper, all the papers are pooled and stirred up, then each person in the family picks a name, careful not to let anyone else know for whom he is to be an angel. That lucky person will then have an angel who will do all sorts of good things for him on the sly; and the angel himself (or herself) will see the importance of going about doing good—all as a gift of praise for the coming Lord.

As Christmas approaches, each angel, disguising his handwriting, writes a little note telling his charge the things done for him—prayers for a test, a "sneak" shoe-shine, an extra candy bar left mysteriously in a drawer, and so forth. Then on Christmas Eve, as all sit down to eat, there might be a Christmas card in each one's place signed by his angel, another suspenseful moment for all. But how much more will the father's blessing, "Bless us Lord and these your *gifts*...." mean when each finds that a thorn in his side has been doing so much for him!

The days and weeks of our waiting will pass quickly. Mother will be busy with other cooking, and so why not have Father bless it all and trace it with the sign of the cross?

Blessing of the Bread and Cakes

Lord Jesus Christ, bread of angels, the living bread of eternal life, please bless this bread as You blessed the five loaves in the desert, that all who partake of it may have health of body and soul. Who live and reign forever. Amen.

It is reported that one family really got the picture of how the Lord came into this world. They took the children to a farm where there was a stable for animals. By just saying, "It was like this, but maybe a little worse," they made the children realize that the King of Creation was not born in an antiseptic hospital. Granted, this will not be very easy to do if a family lives five stories high in an apartment house of a crowded city, but a trip to the poverty-filled slums might do just as well.

The "Come, Lord Jesus" of a few weeks back soon changes to the gasp that "Christmas is here already?!" Of course, it couldn't come quickly enough for the children, but *they* didn't do all the baking and cleaning! Advent abruptly ends and Christmas begins. The Lord has come. The purple ribbons of the wreath are taken off and brighter decorations are fixed to the circular symbol—perhaps even one white candle can be fixed in the middle of it showing that Christ, *the* perfect light, is here.

The Christmas tree is up by now and brightly shining as a fitting sign of Christian joy. And the crib scene has found its prominent place once more in the family circle. One way to arrange the crib would be to place it *in* the tree—perhaps half way up and in plain view of all. This makes the connection of the Christ-coming and the tree (evergreen, eternal life) a bit more obvious. The figures are placed in it as usual on Christmas Eve.

A VISIT TO THE STABLE

When the Eve of Christmas finally comes, the father of the house blesses both crib and tree.

Blessing of the Crib

Bless, we ask you, Almighty God, this crib which we have prepared in honor of the new birth in the flesh of your only-begotten Son, that all who devotedly think about this scene and see the mystery of his incarnation, may be filled with the light of his glory. Who lives and reigns with you forever. Amen.

Blessing of the Tree

Father: O God, come to my assistance.
O Lord, make haste to help me.
Glory be to the Father and to the Son and to the Holy Ghost.

All: As it was in the beginning, is now and ever shall be, world without end. Amen.

Father: Then shall all the trees of the forest exult before the Lord, for he comes;
Sing to the Lord a new song; sing to the Lord, all you lands.
Sing to the Lord; bless his name; announce his salvation, day after day.
Tell his glory among the nations; among all peoples, his wondrous deeds.
For great is the Lord and highly to be praised; awesome is he, beyond all gods.
Splendor and majesty go before him; praise and grandeur are in his sanctuary.
Give to the Lord, you families of nations,

give to the Lord glory and praise; give to the Lord the glory due his name!

Bring gifts, and enter his courts; worship the Lord in holy attire.

Tremble before him, all the earth; say among the nations: The Lord is King.

Let the heavens be glad and the earth rejoice; let the sea and what fills it resound; let the plains be joyful and all that is in them.

Then shall all the trees of the forest exult before the Lord, for he comes; for he comes to rule the earth.

He shall rule the world with justice and the peoples with his constancy.

Glory be to the Father and to the Son and to the Holy Spirit.

All: As it was in the beginning, is now and ever shall be, world without end. Amen.

Oldest child: Lesson from Isaiah, the Prophet:

Thus says the Lord: The land that was desolate and impassable shall be glad, and the wilderness shall be glad, and the wilderness shall rejoice and shall flourish like the lily. It shall bud forth and blossom, and shall rejoice with joy and praise; the glory of Lebanon is given to it; the beauty of Carmel and Sharon, they shall see the glory of the Lord and the beauty of Our God.

All: Thanks be to God.

Father: And there shall come forth a rod out of the root of Jesse.

And a flower shall rise up out of his root.
O Lord, hear my prayers.

All: And let my cry come to you.

Father: Let us pray. O God, who made this most holy night to shine forth with the brightness of the true light, please bless this tree which we adorn with lights in honor of him who has come to enlighten us who sit in darkness and in the shadow of death. And grant that we upon whom shines the new light of your Word made flesh, may show forth in our actions that which by faith shines in our minds. Through the same Christ our Lord.

All: Amen.

There is no need here to list various cooking treats for the family since magazines are filled with them at Christmas time. But one that has a Christian twist and is a good medium for instruction is the dessert for the feast of the Holy Innocents after Christmas, on December 28. It is Angel Food Cake, topped with ice cream and frozen strawberries or cherries. This is always a favorite, but the martyr red decorations will give added meaning.

God has become a man and pitched his tent with us here. But he came to his own and his own did not recognize him. So he revealed himself to us, the Nations, the Gentiles. On January 6, the feast of Epiphany, we celebrate this great, good news. We should keep our Christmas tree up and bright until this date. Our stress on this day is the star atop of the tree—a star we must always follow. Our Advent Wreath turned Christ Wreath could now be turned into the Star Wreath. By taking out the candle, we could place a

PALM SUNDAY PRACTICE

large star on the wreath helping us to remember that we have seen a great light and must never leave its course, but always walk in its rays.

At the family meal on Epiphany evening, there could be an exchange of gifts. One Christmas gift for each member of the family could be kept for this night. The meaning is obvious, and besides, no one objects to another present!

The dessert to top the day off might be appealing; you could call it Epiphany Cake. Any kind will do. Mother could place a coin in it and whoever would get the hidden money would be "King for the Night." Not only will the children like the idea of a cake but they'll all be itching to see if they'll be king for a few hours.

The final day of the Christmas Season is February 2nd, the Feast of Lights, Candlemas. In the evening, with the blest candle you received at Church that day, you pray:

> Now thou dost dismiss thy servant, O Lord,
> According to thy word in peace;
> Because my eyes have seen thy salvation,
> Which thou hast prepared before the face of all
>   peoples;
> A light to the revelation of the Gentiles.
> And the glory of thy people Israel.

The candle is obviously a sign of life and light—a reminder to the Christian his life should be a light obvious to all. He must not hide his good works, but show by his light-filled goodness that Christ is light unto us all.

It isn't long before we can see an end to winter and the coming of spring. But nature still must go through its birth pangs, the seed must die before it blooms, and the Christian must turn again to his Lord—but this time in sorrow, in deep penance for the way he has turned away from his Lord, the firstborn of the dead, now the Risen Savior.

Before we know it, a day called Septuagesima has arrived. On this day (or rather, the day before it) the joyous word-hymn of praise is put away—The *Alleluia*. Our attention to the joyous coming of Christ, his glory in heaven will stop for a while. We concentrate on all he had to go through for us, his death at an early age and the things we've done to cause it. So, instead of Alleluia, we pray "Help us," "Save us," "I'm sorry."

One little thing you could have the children do is to make an elaborately decorated sign saying "Alleluia." On Septuagesima, let the mother hide it in some dark place; then on Easter, when the light of the Risen Lord overwhelms us, have them find it and place it prominently on your Easter table. This hiding of the Alleluia will be the start of serious attention to the penances of the coming days. The finding will mark the end of their penances and the opening up of candy boxes.

Lent's first day comes. And one thing we should ask for on that day is the earnestness to live out these days in a truly Christ-like way—not making them a series of "do nots" or on the other hand a series of how to get around the demands of lenten penances. And the first concrete sign of Lent is Ash Wednesday. This day will bring with it the fret of how to prepare meatless meals, or the dread of the season lasting so long, but it can be balanced off with a few moment's thought on the meaning of ashes. They simply and directly mean that all material things will one day end —house, car, clothes, toys, pets, money, foods—all will fall into dust. So at this grace-appointed time, we fix our eyes of faith on some bigger issues—namely our salvation, our heavenly health, and life with Our Father in Heaven.

But to begin this season, our palms of last year can be burned, and the ashes put on our plants, or if we have a garden, sprinkled over the sleeping earth. Also a center piece of thorny branches or some prickly plant can adorn the table; this clearly shows us the pain involved in our salvation, not only by Christ, but the pain it takes us to find salvation.

Since we are all acquainted with various forms of lenten penance, we need not dwell on them here. But there is a need to find symbolic ways of making these practices both practical and evident for the children of the home. Have them take dried beans or peas (a sign of dormant life ready to blossom) and string them one each time a little sacrifice has been done for the Lord. At the end of Lent, for Easter, perhaps these dried beans or peas could be made into a delicious soup. You will find that once this sort of practice is encouraged, the family as a whole will find other little ways of enlivening a meaningful season of grace with other personal practices. Consciousness of God and his saving actions work many marvels—especially the marvel of changing the "inner" self or spirit. We don't stress obser-vances for themselves, but acting out these customs does manage to make us more aware of our needs—hence we want to *do* more! When spring is about to make its entry, and the mid-point of Lent has passed, the most profound and solemn of times comes—Passion Sunday. The last throes of winter will cede to life-giving spring. Not only does natural life bud forth, but God's life bursts upon us.

But as the immediate prelude, Passion Sunday, arrives, the children will perhaps want to "imitate" the parish church by covering with purple cloth any statues at home. This reminder is obvious enough.

And on the second Sunday of the Passion, Palm Sunday,

HOLY THURSDAY READING

blessed palms are again placed on the crucifix, reminding us that the cross is a sign of victory, not defeat.

The first of the three big days of holy week is Holy Thursday. No doubt the family will join the parish family to celebrate that day's saving actions, but at home, the family could perhaps gather for a few minutes to read aloud some account of Christ's Last Supper and the beginning of his sufferings. A reading from the Family Bible is most appropriate for this purpose. Alternatively, a passage could be read from a classic spiritual work that reflects on the suffering of Christ. Appropriate passages from the Imitation of Christ by Thomas à Kempis or the Spiritual Exercises by St. Ignatius of Loyola would be excellent for this purpose.

To enact a Paschal Meal (the Jewish meal celebrated by Christ at the Last Supper) could propose some difficulty, though there is no more impressive way than this to experience within one's own home and with one's own family just what a sacrificial meal is.

All of us sense that Good Friday is a day set apart. But to begin the day on the right foot perhaps Mother could serve Hot Cross buns for breakfast. The simplicity of this basic food and its modest topping make us stop for a minute and think of our redemption.

Holy Saturday is the day for the final preparations at home and church. No doubt in your home it is the exciting time to color eggs, a sign of life in themselves—hence the great stress on eggs at this season. Everyone ought to take a hand in coloring eggs, but there should be one egg done up more beautifully than the others, and it could be called the "Alleluia egg." This is hidden along with all the others, but whoever finds this one should get a special prize.

Then of course, if the children have made an Alleluia sign, and have hidden it weeks before, on Easter Morning itself, or after the Easter Vigil, have them scurry to find it, and place it in a prominent place somewhere in the house. The great Alleluia is now the praise of Easter, and for the weeks to come should be added to all meal prayers.

Joyful Easter is here. Christ is Risen! Christ is risen indeed, Alleluia. The fast is over and the feast begins. Here are some special meal prayers that ring with the reason of our Easter Joy.

Leader:	Christ is risen, Alleluia.
All:	He is risen indeed, Alleluia.
Leader:	This is the day which the Lord has made.
All:	Let us rejoice and be glad in it.
Leader:	Our Father, etc
All:	Give us this day, etc.
Leader:	Let us pray. Pour forth upon us, Lord, the spirit of thy love, that those whom thou hast nourished with the Easter sacraments may, because of thy love, dwell together in peace. Through Christ our Lord.
All:	Amen.
Leader:	Bless us, O Lord, and these thy gifts, which we are about to receive from thy bounty. Through Christ our Lord.
All:	Amen.

After the Meal

Leader:	All you who are baptized, Alleluia.
All:	Have put on Christ, Alleluia.
Oldest Child:	From St. Paul the Apostle: Beloved, if you have risen with Christ, seek the things that are above, where Christ is seated at the right hand of God. For you have died and

	your life is hidden with Christ in God. When Christ, your life, shall appear, then you too will appear with Him in glory.
All:	Thanks be to God.
Leader:	We give thee thanks, Almighty God, for these and all thy gifts which we have received from thy bounty. Through Christ our Lord.
All:	Amen.

Our new Easter clothes remind us of the newness we put on from the life given us by our Risen Savior. The Church that day is glorious, as is everyone in it. And the morning breakfast should be glorious, too, and very special.

Besides the Alleluia sign, the all important home decoration should be the Christ candle. Try to buy the tallest and fattest of white candles, and let everyone have a hand in decorating it with gold paper or stars or letters of Christ's name. This should burn at the big meal of each day during the Easter Season; this, together with the Easter Feast prayers above, is a daily reminder of the happy newness that has once again come to God's people, washed once more in the blood of God's lamb, who is Christ.

Easter is welded to its complement, Pentecost—an Old Covenant celebration now changed by the coming of God's Spirit of love. Pentecost means that we now have God's help in spreading the kingdom Christ brought with his Risen life. Pentecost stresses action—the action of a Christian in the world—to clamor, yell to all he meets that Christ is our hope for salvation.

God's Spirit brings many gifts, but to emphasize the seven most powerful ones, we can come back to our use of candles. These also are arranged in a circle, but this time some

FINDING THE ALLELUIA CARD

decorative label could be attached showing which each represents. On each of the seven days before Pentecost, one could be lit, and a prayer offered requesting the Spirit to increase our Piety, Wisdom, Reverence for God, Understanding, Counsel, Courage or Knowledge. Or you could use the Pentecost Novena found on page 53.

Since this holy time is a brilliant one, what better place to show this than at the table. Numerous suggestions have been given through the years for festive desserts for Pentecost. One is to top cherry pie with pastry doves. To decorate a light above the table, you could have the children make white doves out of paper.

Being a witness for the Lord is the thing to be stressed on this grace-filled day. So at dinner, perhaps each could give suggestions as to some apostolic thing he would do during the coming week, and if possible, something that would be for a person outside of the family circle. This can show that we must *go out* to spread the good news of Christ and not be content with confining our Christian life *only* to our family. We are the mouth, and feet, and hands of Christ. Let's use them!

Pentecost time fans out to include the rest of the church's year of grace. What to do as reminders for the rest of the year? Well, you're on your own, parents. You'll think of something if you think long and hard enough.

We do not go to our Father in heaven alone. The Lord has come to save a people; he lives in his people, he makes his people holy, yet he knits himself to each individual soul closer than our little minds can imagine. All the customs or practices that have been concentrated in these few pages are but signs; signs to us of how important it is to remember our relationship to Christ, signs to us how serious we must take this relationship while we are here on earth. We must see that we are never to stop learning about our God and all he has done for us. He is the rainbow with all its hues, he is the diamond-like light with infinitely varied colors. He loves us, not more than he can say, but more than we could ever understand—it is this love which we must penetrate ever more deeply through the smallest action or practice. Our family traditions take their force from the table of the Lord at the parish church and it is to that table that they return—fuller and richer. If a parent can get the point of small family customs across, then the whole family can run with Christ to the Father at a speed they had never dreamed of. Be it fast or feast, the family, knowing God is with them, will never want just the water which quenches thirst for the moment; they will want to have rivers of water flowing from Jesus which will fill them forever.

Spiritual Readings

I N THIS SECTION will be found selections from the sermons of the Fathers of the Church. They are masterpieces of spiritual writing and required reading for priests and religious in the recitation of the breviary. Sermons such as these were a major factor in the splendid spiritual formation of the early Christians and should be of great help to Christians of our day.

Although the selections are short, they are not to be read hurriedly but rather, slowly and meditatively. Like the Scriptures, these writings are rich food for the mind and must be digested slowly. They can be read and re-read many times over. They are especially recommended for those who are unable to hear the Word of God at Mass on Sunday. For this reason, the selections are arranged according to the seasons of the Church year.

The Fathers of the Church all through the centuries have been the inspiration for great works of art. Some of these masterpieces are reproduced in full color in the following pages.

Readings for Advent

WHEN our Savior was instructing His disciples about the coming of the kingdom of God and about the end of the world and of time, teaching His entire Church in the person of the apostles, He said, "Beware lest perhaps your hearts be weighed down by gluttony and drunkenness and worldly thoughts." Indeed, we know that that command pertains more especially to us, to whom the foretold day, even though it be hidden, cannot be doubted to be close at hand.

It behooves every man to be prepared for its coming lest he be found either given up to gluttony or entangled in the cares of the world. For, most dearly beloved, it is proved by daily experience that keenness of mind is dulled by drunkenness, and that the strength of the heart is weakened by over-eating, so that the pleasure of eating is injurious to the health of the body unless the principle of temperance resists the enticement, and, because it would become a burden, withdraws from the pleasure.

For although the flesh desires nothing without the soul, and gets its feelings from the same source as it takes its movements, it is nevertheless the duty of the same soul to

THE ANNUNCIATION *by Master of Moulins*
The Art Institute of Chicago

deny certain things to the substance subject to itself and by an interior judgment to restrain the exterior from unbecoming things, that being more often free from bodily desires, it may devote itself to divine wisdom in the chamber of the mind where, all noise of earthly cares being silenced, the soul may rejoice in holy meditations and eternal delights.

But although in this life it is difficult that such a state be continuous, it can nevertheless be frequently taken up anew, that we may be occupied oftener and for longer periods with spiritual matters rather than with carnal. And while we give more time to better pursuits, even temporal actions are changed into incorruptible riches.   St. Leo, *Pope*

Having seen so many signs and such great wonders, one should not have been easily moved to take offense, but to admire. Yet the mind of unbelievers did take grave scandal at Him, when, after such miracles, they saw Him die. Wherefore Paul says: "But we preach Christ crucified, to the Jews a stumbling-block indeed, but to the Gentiles foolishness."

It seemed foolish indeed to men that for men the very Author of life should die. And hence man took scandal against Him from the very circumstance whence he ought to have become more a debtor. For the more God suffered disgraceful things for men, so much the more worthily ought He to be honored by men.

Why did He say, "Blessed is he who is not scandalized in Me," except to designate in clear words the abjection and humility of His death? As if He would openly say: "I do indeed wonderful things, but I do not disdain to suffer indignities. Thus, because I am like to you in death, men must take care that they, who reverence My miracles, do not despise death in Me."   St. Gregory, *Pope*

SINCE the season of the year and the custom of our devotion advises, dearly beloved, we announce to you with pastoral solicitude that the fast of the tenth month is to be celebrated, by which, for the plentiful harvest of all the fruits, a libation of continence is most fittingly offered to God, their donor.

For what can be more efficacious than fasting, by the practice of which we draw near to God, and, resisting the devil, overcome seductive vices? For fasting has always been food for the strong.

Moreover, from abstinence proceed chaste thoughts, rational desires, and sound counsels; and by voluntary afflictions the flesh dies to its concupiscences and the spirit is renewed in strength.

But because the salvation of our souls is not acquired by fasting alone, let us supplement our fasting with works of mercy towards the poor. Let us spend for virtue what we have subtracted from pleasure. Let the abstinence of the one fasting be food for the poor. Let us be zealous for the defense of widows, for the assistance of orphans, for the consolation of those who mourn, for the peace of dissenters. Let the stranger be taken in, the oppressed helped, the naked clothed, the sick cared for, so that whoever of us shall have offered of his good works a sacrifice of such piety to God, the Author of all good things, may deserve to receive the reward of the heavenly kingdom from the same God.

On Wednesday and Friday, therefore, let us fast; on Saturday, however, let us celebrate the vigil at the tomb of the Apostle Peter, by whose merits may we be able to obtain what we ask through our Lord Jesus Christ, who with the Father and the Holy Spirit liveth and reigneth forever and ever. Amen.   ST. LEO, *Pope*

THE DIVINE MYSTERIES are truly hidden, nor can any man easily know the counsel of God, according to the saying of the prophet; nevertheless, from other acts and mandates of the Lord our Savior we are able to understand that it was of even more deliberate design that she who was espoused to a man was especially chosen to give birth to our Lord. But why was she not made pregnant before she was espoused? Perhaps it was lest it be said that she had conceived in adultery.

"And the angel being come in." Study the virgin in her manners; study her in her modest reserve; study her in her conversation; study her in this mystery. It is proper for virgins to tremble and to be afraid at every approach of a man, to fear all conversations with a man. Let woman strive to imitate this example of self-respect. She is alone in her chamber; only the angel shall find her whom no man shall behold; she, alone without companion, alone without witness, is saluted by the angel so that she be not dishonored by any shameful greeting.

For the mystery of such a great message was not to be uttered by the mouth of a man, but of an angel. It is first heard today: "The Holy Ghost shall come upon thee." It is both heard and believed. To conclude—"Behold the handmaid of the Lord," she says, "be it done unto me according to thy word."

See her humility; behold her devotion. She, who is chosen as Mother of God, calls herself "the handmaid of the Lord," nor is she suddenly elated by the promise.

ST. AMBROSE

ALL WHO ASK to be believed are expected to give reasons why they should be believed. Therefore, when the angel had announced what should come to pass, he made known to the Virgin Mary, as a reason for believing in him, that an aged and sterile woman had conceived. This he did to assure her that whatever was pleasing to God was also possible. When Mary heard this, she set out for the hill country, not because she did not believe the announcement, or was incredulous of the messenger, or doubted the example of Elizabeth, but cheerfully, as if to fulfill a vow; with devotion, as to a religious duty, in haste for very joy. Whither, indeed, if not to greater heights, should she who was now full of God make her way with haste? The grace of the Holy Spirit knows no languid efforts.

Do you also, O holy women, learn what attention you ought to bestow on your kinsfolk when they are with child. The virgin modesty of Mary did not hold her back from mixing with the crowd, though till then she had lived alone in strictest privacy; nor did the roughness of the mountain ways abate her zeal, nor the length of the journey keep her back from doing a kindness. The Virgin set out in haste into the hill country, a Virgin mindful of her duty, unmindful of mishaps, urged on by affection, heedless of the delicacy of her sex, leaving her home behind her. Learn, O virgins, not to run about to the houses of strangers, not to loiter in the streets, not to spend time talking with others in public.

Mary, who moved quietly about her own home, in haste only on the public roads, abode three months with her kinswoman.

You have learned, O virgins, the modesty of Mary; learn also her humility. She went as a relative to her relative, the younger to the elder; and not only did she come, but she first saluted Elizabeth. For the more chaste a virgin is, the more humble she should be. She will know how to submit to her elders. She who professes chastity should be mistress of humility. For humility is the root of piety, and the very rule of its teaching. It is to be noted that the superior comes to the inferior that the inferior may be assisted. Mary comes to Elizabeth, Christ to John.   ST. AMBROSE

IF WE, dearly beloved, with faith and prudence understand the beginning of our creation, we shall find that man was formed to the likeness of God in order that he might be an imitator of his Maker, and that this is a dignity natural to our race that the form of the Divine Majesty shines in us as in a kind of mirror. To which dignity daily the grace of the Savior truly restores us, since what fell in the first Adam is raised up in the second.

There is no cause for our restoration, however, except the mercy of God, whom we would not love unless He first loved us and scattered the darkness of our ignorance by the light of His truth.

Foretelling this through the holy Isaias, the Lord said: "I will lead the blind into the way which they know not, and in the paths of which they were ignorant I will make them walk; I will make darkness light before them, and crooked things straight. These things have I done to them, and have not forsaken them." And again: "I was found by them that did not seek me: I appeared openly to those who made no inquiry of me."

How this is accomplished the Apostle John teaches, saying: "We know that the Son of God is come, and he hath given us understanding that we may know the true God, and may be in his true Son." And again: "Let us therefore love God, because God first hath loved us."

So, by loving us God reforms us to His own likeness, and, in order to find the image of His own goodness in us, He grants us that by which we ourselves may work what He works, namely, lighting the lamps of our minds, and inflaming us with the fire of His love, so that we may love not only Him, but likewise what He loves.   St. Leo, *Pope*

John said to the multitudes that went forth to be baptized by him: "Ye offspring of vipers, who hath showed you to flee from the wrath to come?" The *wrath to come* is a reference to the last judgment which the sinner will not be able to escape then if he does not have recourse now to expressions of penance. Now it must be noted that wicked children who imitate the actions of their evil parents are called the offspring of vipers for this reason, because they envy the good and persecute them; because they render evil to some and seek to injure their neighbors; for in all these actions they follow the paths of their carnal-minded forebears, as poisoned children born of poisoned parents.

But because we have already sinned and have become involved in evil practices, let John tell us what we must do that we may be able to flee the wrath to come. Here is what he tells us: "Bring forth therefore fruits worthy of penance." It must be observed in these words that the friend of the Spouse not only admonishes us to bring forth fruits of penance, but fruits *worthy* of penance. For it is one thing to bring forth fruits of penance; quite another to bring forth fruits worthy of penance.

Speaking of fruits worthy of penance, it ought to be known that whoever has commited no illicit acts, to him is it rightly permitted to use licit things, and so to perform works of piety without giving up the things of this world. But if anyone has fallen into the sin of fornication—or what is worse, adultery—he must so much the more abstain from licit things, the more he is conscious of having done that which is illicit.

Nor should the fruit of good works be equal in one who has sinned less and in one who has sinned more; likewise in him who has never fallen and in him who has fallen a few times and in him who has fallen many times. By this saying, then, "Bring forth fruits worthy of penance," the conscience of each one is bound to acquire through penance so much the greater riches of good works the more serious the losses it has brought upon itself through its own fault.

St. Gregory, *Pope*

Why was He not conceived of a simple virgin, but of a virgin who was espoused? First, in order that through Joseph's lineage the descent of Mary might be shown; secondly, lest she be stoned as an adulteress by the Jews; thirdly, so that when fleeing into Egypt, she might have a companion. The martyr Ignatius has also added a fourth reason why He was conceived of one espoused, saying: "In order that His birth might be hidden from Satan, since the latter thought that Jesus was begotten not of a virgin, but of one in wedlock."

"Before they came together she was found with child of the Holy Ghost." She was not found by any other except Joseph, who already possessed a husband's privilege to know all that concerned her. But because it is said here, "*Before* they came together," it does not follow that they came together afterwards; the Scripture shows that this did not happen.

"Whereupon, Joseph, her husband, being a just man and not willing to expose her publicly, was minded to put her away privately." If anyone be joined to one guilty of fornication, he is made one body with the fornicator, and it is commanded in the law that not only those guilty, but also those having knowledge of the crime are liable to the punishment of the sin. How can Joseph, since he concealed the crime of his wife, be described as a just man? But this testimony is Mary's—that Joseph, *knowing* her chastity and marvelling at what had happened, kept secret the mystery of which he was ignorant.

"Joseph, son of David, fear not to take unto thee Mary thy wife." We have already stated above that spouses are called wives, as our book against Helvidius more fully sets forth. Indeed, in the attitude of one paying respect the angel speaks to Joseph in a dream in order to confirm the justice of his silence. And at the same time it is to be noted that Joseph is said to be the son of David so that Mary, too, might be shown to be from the family of David.

ST. JEROME

Readings for Christmas

OUR SAVIOR is born today, dearly beloved, let us rejoice! For it is not right that place be given to sadness when it is the birthday of life, which, having taken away the fear of death, fills us with joy by reason of the eternal life which it promises. No one is shut out from a share in this happiness. All have one common cause of joy, for, as our Lord, the destroyer of sin and death, finds no one free from guilt, so He comes to liberate everyone.

Let the just man exult, for he draws near to the palm; let the sinner rejoice, for he is invited to forgiveness; let all take courage for all are called to life. For the Son of God, according to the fullness of time, which the inscrutable depth of the divine counsel ordained, took upon Himself the nature of the human race in order to reconcile it to its Maker, so that the inventor of death, the devil, might be overcome through that very nature which he had conquered.

In this conflict, entered into for our sakes, He fights with a great and admirable insistence on fairness, since the Almighty Lord meets the most terrible enemy not in His own majesty, but in our lowliness, pitting against the same form,

THE ADORATION OF THE SHEPHERDS *by Natale Schiavoni*

the same nature, partaker in every way of our mortality, yet free from all sin. Truly incongruous with this birth is that which is declared of all men: "No man is clean from stain, neither an infant whose life upon earth is but one day!" Nothing, then, of the concupiscence of the flesh found place in this singular nativity, nothing of the law of sin. A royal virgin from the root of David is chosen, who, about to be made pregnant with the Sacred Offspring, conceives the Child, divine and human, first in her mind rather than in her body. And lest, unaware of the divine plan, she be frightened at the unusual tidings, she learns from the words of an angel what is to be effected in her by the Holy Spirit; nor does she believe it to be a loss of her virginity that she is about to become the Mother of God.

Therefore, dearly beloved, let us give thanks to God the Father through His Son, in the Holy Spirit, who, because of His great charity with which He hath loved us, has had mercy on us; and, when we were dead in our sins, He re-vivified us in Christ so that we might be in Him a new creature and a new image. So let us put off the old man with his works, and having obtained a participation in the generation of Christ, let us renounce the works of the flesh. Recognize, O Christian, thy dignity! And being made partaker of the divine nature, do not return to thy old wretchedness by an evil manner of life. Be mindful of whose head and body thou art a member! Remember that, being torn from the power of darkness, thou hast been born into the light and kingdom of God.   St. Leo, *Pope*

Behold the beginning of the newborn Church. Christ is born, and the shepherds began to watch, in order to gather into the sheepfold of the Lord the flocks of the nations who were formerly living after the manner of wild beasts, lest they suffer from the attacks of any spiritual beasts during the overshadowing darkness of the nights. And well do those shepherds whom the Lord instructs keep watch. For the flock is the people; the night is the world; and the shepherds are the priests. Or perchance he also may be signified by the shepherd to whom it was said: "Be watchful and strengthen." For the Lord not only appointed bishops, but He also destined angels to guard His flock.   St. Ambrose

Yesterday we celebrated the temporal birth of our Eternal King; today we celebrate the triumphant passion of His soldier. For yesterday our King, clothed in the garb of our flesh and coming from the palace of the virginal womb, deigned to visit the world; today the soldier, leaving the tent of the body, has gone to heaven in triumph. The One, while preserving the majesty of the Everlasting God, putting on the servile girdle of flesh, entered into the field of this world for the fray. The other, laying aside the perishable garment of the body, ascended to the palace of heaven to reign eternally. The One descended, veiled in flesh; the other ascended, crowned with blood.

The latter ascended while the Jews were stoning him, because the former descended while the angels were rejoicing. "Glory to God in the highest," sang the exulting Angels yesterday; today, rejoicing, they received Stephen into their company! Yesterday the Lord came forth from the womb of the Virgin; today the soldier of Christ has passed from the prison of the flesh.

Yesterday Christ was wrapped in swathing bands for our sake; today Stephen is clothed by Him in the robe of immortality. Yesterday the narrow confines of the crib held the Infant Christ; today the immensity of heaven has received the triumphant Stephen. The Lord descended alone that He might raise up many; our King has humbled Himself that He might exalt His soldiers. It is necessary for us, nevertheless, brethren, to acknowledge with what arms Stephen was girded and able to overcome the cruelty of the Jews that thus he merited so happily to triumph.

Stephen, therefore, that he might merit to obtain the *crown* his name signifies, had as his weapon charity, and by means of that he was completely victorious. Because of love for God, he did not flee the raging Jews; because of his love of neighbor, he interceded for those stoning him. Because of love he convinced the erring of their errors that they might be corrected; because of love, he prayed for those stoning him that they might not be punished. Supported by the strength of charity, he overcame Saul who was so cruelly raging against him; and him whom he had as a persecutor on earth, he deserved to have as a companion in heaven.   St. Fulgentius

The church is acquainted with two different lives divinely preached and commended to her: one is the life of faith, the other the life of vision; one the life of this pilgrimage, the other the life of the eternal mansions: one the life of labor, the other the life of rest; one the life of the journey, the other the life of home; one the life of action, the other the life of contemplation.

The one avoids evil and does good, the other has no evil from which to turn away; but only a great good to enjoy. The one fights against the foe; the other reigns, having no foe. One comes to the aid of the needy; the other is there where no needy are found. One forgives the sins of others that its own may be forgiven; the other suffers nothing it could forgive, nor does anything that calls for forgiveness.

One is scourged with evils lest it be lifted up by prosperity; the other enjoys such a fullness of grace that it is free from every evil, and cleaves so firmly to the Highest Good that it has no temptation to pride. Hence the one life is good, but yet full of sorrows; the other is better and perfectly blessed. Of the first of these lives the Apostle Peter is the type; of the other, John.

The one labors here even to the end, and finds its end hereafter; the other reaches out into the hereafter and in eternity finds no end. Therefore to Peter it is said, "Follow me," but of John, "If I wish him to remain until I come, what is it to thee? Do thou follow me." But what is this? How little do I understand, how little do I grasp it! What is the meaning of this? Is it "Follow me, imitating me in bearing earthly sorrow; let him remain until I come to bestow everlasting rewards"?   St. Augustine

With happy joy, indeed, did these shepherds hasten to see that which they had heard, and because they instantly sought the Savior with an ardent and faithful love, they merited to find Him whom they sought. But they also have shown by their words as well as by their deeds with what effort of mind the shepherds of intelligent flocks, yea, all the faithful must seek Christ. "Let us go over to Bethlehem," they say, "and let us see this word that is come to pass." Therefore, dearest brethren, let us also go over in thought to Bethlehem, the city of David, and in love recall to our minds that there the Word was made flesh, and let us celebrate His Incarnation with honors worthy of Him. Having thrown off carnal desires, let us with all the desire of our mind go over to the heavenly Bethlehem, that is, the house of living bread, not made by hands, but eternal in heaven, and in love let us recall that the Word was made flesh. Thither He has ascended in the flesh; there He sits on the right hand of God the Father. Let us follow Him with the whole force of our strength and by careful mortification of heart and body let us merit to see Him reigning on the throne of His Father, Him whom they saw crying in the manger.

"And they came in haste; and they found Mary and Joseph, and the Infant lying in the manger." The shepherds came in haste and found God born as man, together with the ministers of His nativity. Let us hasten too, my brethren, not with footsteps, but by the advances of good works, to see the same glorified humanity together with the same ministers remunerated with a reward worthy of their services; let us hasten to see Him refulgent with the divine Majesty of His Father and of Himself. Let us hasten, I say, for such happiness is not to be sought with sloth and torpor, but the footsteps of Christ must be eagerly followed. For, offering His hand, He desires to help our course and delights to hear from us: "Draw us, we will run after thee in the odor of thy ointments." Therefore, let us follow swiftly with strides of virtue that we may merit to possess. Let no one be tardy in converting to the Lord; let no one put it off from day to day; let us beseech Him through all things and before all things that He direct our steps according to His word and let not injustice dominate over us.

"And seeing, they understood the word that had been spoken to them concerning this Child." Let us also, most dearly beloved brethren, hasten in the meantime to perceive by a loving faith and to embrace with complete love those things that are said to us concerning our Savior, true God and Man, so that by this we may be able to comprehend Him perfectly in the future vision of knowledge. For this is the only and the true life of the blessed, not only of men, but even of the angels to look continually upon the face of their

Creator, which was so ardently desired by the Psalmist who said: "My soul hath thirsted after the living God; when shall I come and appear before the face of God?" The Psalmist has shown that the vision of Him alone, and on abundance of the things of earth, could satisfy his desire when he said: "I shall be satisfied when thy glory shall appear." But since neither the idle nor the slothful, but those who perspire in works of virtue, are worthy of divine contemplation, he carefully premised these words: "But as for me, I will appear before thy sight in justice.   St. Bede the Venerable

Dearly beloved, he is a true venerator and loving observer of today's feast who thinks nothing false in reference to our Lord's Incarnation, nor anything unworthy of His Divinity. For the evil is of equal danger whether the reality of our nature be denied Him or the equality to the glory of His Father. Therefore, when we attempt to understand the mystery of Christ's Nativity, by which He was born of a Virgin Mother, let the darkness of our human minds be driven far away, and let the fog of worldly wisdom depart from the eye of illumined faith.

For divine is the authority in which we believe: divine is the teaching which we follow. Because, whether we turn our interior attention to the testimony of the law, or to the utterances of the prophets, or to the clarion of the Gospel, that is true which John, filled with the Holy Spirit, intoned: "In the beginning was the Word, and the Word was with God, and the Word was God. The same was in the beginning with God. All things were made by Him, and without Him was made nothing."

And similarly is that true which the same teacher added: "And the Word was made flesh, and dwelt among us: and we saw His glory, as it were the glory of the only begotten of the Father." In both natures, therefore, it is the same Son of God, taking to Himself the things that are ours and not losing His own, renewing man by man, but remaining immutable in Himself.

For His divinity, which is common to Him and the Father, suffered no loss of omnipotence, nor did His form of servant dishonor His form of God, because the supreme and eternal Essence, who lowered Himself for the salvation of the human race, has indeed translated us into His own glory, but He did not cease to be that which He had been. Wherefore, when the only begotten Son of God confesses that He was less than the Father, to whom He says that He is equal, He demonstrates the reality of both forms in Himself: so that the inequality proves the human form, and the equality declares the divine form.   St. Leo, *Pope*

GREAT AND WONDERFUL MYSTERY! The Child is circumcised and is called Jesus. What does this connection signify? It seems that circumcision is more for the sake of one who needs salvation than for the Savior; and it is more proper that the Savior should circumcise than be circumcised. But recognize here the mediator of God and men, who from the very beginning of His birth associated the human with the divine, the lowest with the most sublime. He is born of a woman, but of one in whom the fruit of fecundity so ripens that the flower of virginity fades not. He is wrapped in swaddling clothes, but these very clothes are honored by the praises of the angels. He is hidden in a manger, but proclaimed abroad by a radiant star from heaven. So too the circumcision proves the truth of His assumed humanity, and His Name which is above every name indicates the glory of His majesty. As a true son of Abraham He is circumcised; as the true Son of God He is called Jesus.

Not like other men does my Jesus bear this name, vainly and without reason. In Him it is not the shadow of a great name, but the truth. Indeed the Evangelist testifies that from heaven came the name by which He was called by the Angel before He was conceived in the womb. And mark the depth of these words: "After Jesus was born." He is then called Jesus by men, who was so called by the Angel before He was conceived in the womb. Indeed the same Jesus is Savior both of angels and of men: of angels from the beginning of creation; but of men from the time of His Incarnation.

"His name," the Evangelist says, "was called Jesus, which was called by the angel." In the mouth, then, of two or three witnesses every word stands; and that very Word which in the Prophet was shortened, in the Gospel is more clearly read as the Word made Flesh.

Rightly indeed is the Child who is born to us called Savior when He is circumcised, because, you see, from this very time He began to labor for our salvation, shedding His immaculate blood for us. Truly it is not for Christians to ask now why Christ Our Lord wished to be circumcised. He was circumcised for the same reason for which He was born, and for which He suffered: none of these things on account of Himself, but all for His chosen ones. He was neither begotten in sin nor freed from sin by circumcision, nor did He die for His own sin, but rather in atonement for our crimes. "Which was called," says the Evangelist, "by the angel before he was conceived in the womb." By His own very nature He is the Savior. With this name was He born; it was not given Him by any creature, human or angelic.

St. Bernard

Rejoice in the Lord, beloved! again I say, rejoice! for in but a brief time after the solemnity of Christ's Nativity, the feast of His manifestation has shone upon us; and Him whom on that day the Virgin bore, on this, the world acknowledged. For the Word made flesh so disposed the beginnings of our redemption that while the Infant Jesus was manifest to believers He was hidden from persecutors.

Then verily did the heavens show forth the glory of God and unto all the earth the sound of truth went forth, when to the shepherds there appeared a host of angels telling of the Savior's birth and the Magi were led by a guiding star to worship Him, that from the rising of the sun to its setting the true King's generation should shine forth, since the kingdoms of the East would learn the truth of things through the Magi, and the Roman Empire also would not be left without this knowledge.

The very cruelty of Herod, striving to crush at His birth this King whom he feared, was made a blind means to help carry out this dispensation of mercy. While he was intent on his awful crime and pursued the unknown child by an indiscriminate murder of infants, his infamous act served to spread wider abroad the heaven-told news of the birth of the Lord. Not only the novelty of the heavenly message but also the bloody impiety of the persecutor proclaimed loudly these glad tidings. Then the Savior was taken into Egypt that that nation, given up to ancient errors, might be marked by a hidden grace for its approaching salvation; and that she who had not yet cast out of her mind superstition and error, might receive Truth as a guest.

Let us then, beloved, acknowledge in the Magi, the adorers of Christ, the first-fruits of our calling and faith; and let us, with exultant soul, celebrate the beginnings of a blessed hope. For then we began to enter into an eternal inheritance when the secrets of the Scriptures—speaking to us of Christ —were laid open, and the truth, whom the Jews' blindness receives not, gave forth its light to all nations. Let that most holy day be honored by us, on which the author of our salvation appeared. Him whom the Magi revered in His cradle, let us adore—almighty in heaven. And as they from their treasures offered the Lord mystic semblances for gifts, so let us from our hearts bring gifts which are worthy of God.

Sᴛ. Lᴇᴏ, Pope

Bᴇғᴏʀᴇ ᴛʜᴇ ʟᴏʀᴅ came to be baptized by John in the Jordan, he knew Him, judging by his words where he said: "Comest thou to me to be baptized? Rather I ought to be baptized by thee." But behold, he had known the Lord; he had known the Son of God. How are we to prove that he already knew that He would baptize in the Holy Spirit? Before He came to the river, when many came to John to be baptized, he said to them: "I, indeed, baptize you with water; but He who shall come after me, He is greater than I, the latchet of whose shoe I am not worthy to loose; He shall baptize you with the Holy Ghost and with fire." This he already knew.

What, therefore, does he learn through the dove—lest he afterwards be found a liar (which God forbid that we should think)—except that there was to be some such prerogative in Christ, that, although many ministers would baptize, whether just or unjust, the holiness of the baptism would not be attributed except to Him upon whom the dove descended, of whom it was said: "He it is that baptizeth with the Holy Ghost"? When Peter baptizes, it is Christ who baptizes; when Paul baptizes, it is Christ who baptizes; when Judas baptizes, it is Christ who baptizes.

For if the holiness of the Baptism depended on the merits of the one baptizing, as these differ in merits, so also would the Baptisms differ, and one would be thought to receive a better Baptism if he received it from one having greater holiness. The saints themselves, that is, the good who are related to the dove, the good who are admitted to the lot of the city Jerusalem, the good men in the Church of whom the Apostle says, "The Lord knoweth who are his," these just men differ from one another by diversities of graces and are not all equally just.

There are some men holier than others, some better than others. Why, then, for example, if one is baptized by a just and holy man, and another is baptized by one of inferior merit with God—of lower rank, of lesser continence, of inferior life—is that baptism which they receive one, the same, and equal, unless because it is always Christ who baptizes?

St. Augustine

Readings for After Christmas

WHEN I pay diligent attention to the reading of the Epistles of St. Paul, often twice, or even three or four times during the separate weeks (whenever we celebrate the memory of the Martyrs), I rejoice in gladness, delighting in that spiritual trumpet, and I am stirred up and burn with desire, knowing it to be a friendly call to me, and I seem almost to behold him present and to hear him speaking. Yet, still I am sad and troubled that not all men know this man as he is; yes, some are so ignorant of him that they do not even know the number of his Epistles! Lack of intelligence, however, does not cause this, but the fact that they do not wish to keep the holy man's writings constantly in their hands.

For what we know, if anything, we do not know owing to any superlative talent or keenness of mind, but because, being strongly drawn towards this great man, we never cease from reading his works. For it is true that he who loves someone usually knows better than others what the one loved has done, for he makes greater effort to learn all about the beloved. St. Paul himself shows that this is true when he says to the Philippians: "I have the right to feel so about you all, because I have you in my heart, all of you, alike in my

FLIGHT INTO EGYPT *by Giordano*

The Metropolitan Museum of Art
Gift of Mr. and Mrs. Harold Morton Landon, 1961

chains and in the defense and confirmation of the gospel." Wherefore, if you also will desire to listen attentively to the reading, nothing else will be required of you. For true is the word of Christ who declares: "Seek, and you shall find; knock and it shall be opened to you."

Moreover, since very many among those who gather here with us have undertaken the education of their children, care for their wives, and management of their family, they are not able on that account to give themselves wholly to this work; but do you move yourselves to seize on those things, at least, which others have gathered; be as zealous in heeding those things which shall be spoken, as you are devoted to saving money. For although it may be a little thing to demand nothing from you but only zeal, it will nevertheless be a thing desired if you contribute at least that.

St. John Chrysostom

By the very fact that the Lord, having been invited, went to the marriage feast, He wished to show, even aside from the mystical signification, that He Himself instituted matrimony; for there were to come those of whom the Apostle spoke, prohibiting marriage and saying that matrimony is an evil instituted by the devil. The same Lord, when asked in the Gospel whether it were lawful for a man to put away his wife for any cause, said that it is not lawful, save on account of fornication. In which reply, if you recall, He said this: "What God hath joined together let no man put asunder."

Those, moreover, who are well instructed in the Catholic faith know that God instituted matrimony. Indeed, as the joining together is from God, so divorce is from the devil. One is permitted, however, on account of fornication, to put away his wife; for she first did not wish to be a wife who did not preserve conjugal fidelity to the marriage bond.

Neither are those without nuptials who vow their virginity to God, notwithstanding the fact that they enjoy a greater degree of honor and sanctity in the Church, for they together with the whole Church participate in those nuptials in which the Spouse is Christ.

And hence, when the Lord was invited, He came to the marriage for this reason, that conjugal chastity might be confirmed, and that the sacrament of matrimony might be manifested; for the spouse of that wedding, to whom it was said, "Thou hast kept the good wine until now," was also a figure of the Lord, for Christ has kept the good wine, that is, His Gospel even until now.   St. Augustine

Great multitudes met the Lord when He descended from the mountain, for they had not been able to follow Him as He went up. And first there came to Him a leper. This poor creature's disease had prevented him from hearing the Savior's long discourse on the Mount. It is to be noted that he is the person specially named as being cured. The second one was the Centurion's servant; the third was Peter's mother-in-law, who was sick of a fever at Capharnaum; the fourth were they who, being troubled with evil spirits, were brought to Christ, from whom He, by His word, cast out the evil spirits, at the same time that He healed all that were sick.

"And behold, a leper came and adored Him, saying." Fittingly after preaching and instruction there was presented an occasion for a sign, so that by the persuasion of a miracle the instruction just given might be confirmed in the minds of the hearers. "Lord, if thou wilt, thou canst make me clean." He who beseeches the Lord to have the will, does not doubt that He has the power.

"And Jesus, stretching forth His hand, touched him, saying: 'I will; be thou made clean.'" As soon as the Lord put forth His hand the leprosy departed. Consider how humble and free from arrogance is His answer. The leper had said: "If thou wilt"; the Lord replied, "I will." The leper had affirmed: "Thou canst make me clean"; the Lord rejoined and said: "Be thou made clean." This latter sentence must not be joined, as some Latinists thought, to the former, and read: "I wish to make thee clean"; but must be taken separately, so that He says: "I will"; then He commands: "Be thou made clean."

"And Jesus said to him: 'See thou tell no man.'" And indeed what need was there for him to express in words what he showed clearly in his body? "But go, show thyself to the priest." For various reasons did He send him to the priest. First, for humility's sake, that He might show reverence to the priests. For it was prescribed by law that whosoever was freed from leprosy should offer gifts to the priests. Moreover, that when the priests saw the leper cleansed, they might either believe in the Savior or refuse to believe; if they believed, that they might be saved; if they refused to believe, that they might have no excuse. Finally, that He might give no foundation for the charge that was so often brought against Him, that is, that He did not observe the law.

St. Jerome

We refresh the body with food lest it should become weak and fail us; we chasten it by abstinence lest it should grow heavy and become lord over us; we strengthen it by exercise lest it waste away through lack of use; but very soon we give it rest lest it faint with weariness; we protect it with clothing lest the cold should blight it; and we strip it of the same garments lest the heat should afflict it.

In all these many cares what do we do but serve the corruptible, at least that the multiplicity of cares spent on the body may sustain that which the anxiety of our changeable infirmity presses down? Thus it is well said by St. Paul: "For creation was made subject to vanity—not by its own will but by reason of him who made it subject—in hope, because creation itself also will be delivered from its slavery to corruption into the freedom of the glory of the sons of God."

"Creation was made subject to vanity—not by its own will." For when man of his own free will gave up his state of unchangeable happiness, the just sentence of death was passed upon him and, though not willing, he became subject to the state of change and corruption. But creation itself also will be delivered from its slavery to corruption when it shall rise again incorruptible and be made partaker of the glory of the children of God.

Here, then, the elect are still subject to sorrow, being yet bound by the sentence of corruption; but when we shall have put off this corruptible flesh, we shall be loosed from these bonds, as it were, of sorrow, by which we are bound. For though we already desire to appear before God, we are still hindered by the burden of this dying body. Rightly, then, are we called prisoners, since we are not yet free to go where we will, that is, to God. Well, therefore, did St. Paul, yearning after eternal things, but still weighed down with the burden of this corruptible body, cry out: "I desire to be loosed and to be with Christ." He would not have felt this desire to be loosed unless he saw that he was bound.

St. Gregory, *Pope*

This is a saying made for man, and worthy of all acceptation, that Christ Jesus came into this world to save sinners.

Listen to the words of the Gospel: "The Son of man is come to seek and to save that which was lost." If man had not been lost, the Son of man would not have come. Therefore man had gone astray; God came, having become man, and man was found. Man had gone astray through his own free will; God-made-man came by grace which sets free.

Do you ask how free will avails to evil? Call to mind a sinner. Do you ask how the God-Man is able to help? Consider in Him the grace that liberates. Nowhere is it better and more plainly shown than in the first man how much the free will of man avails to evil when it is taken possession of by pride and used without God's help.

The first man went astray; and where would he be unless the second man had come? And because the former was a man, therefore the latter was also a man; hence this is a saying made for man. Nor is there any place where the benignity of grace and the liberality of the omnipotence of God so appears as in the Man that is Mediator between God and men, the Man, Christ Jesus.

For what do we say, my brethren? I speak to those who have been brought up in the Catholic Church or who have been gathered into the peace of that Church. We know and hold that the Mediator between God and men, the Man Christ Jesus, as regards His manhood is of the same nature as we. For our flesh is not of a different nature from His, nor is our soul. He took upon Himself that same nature which He had ordained to save.   St. Augustine

The kingdom of heaven is the preaching of the Gospel and a knowledge of the Scriptures which lead to life, concerning which it was said to the Jews: "The kingdom of God shall be taken from you, and shall be given to a nation yielding the fruits thereof." Such a kingdom, therefore, is like

CHRIST AND THE WOMAN OF SAMARIA

by Rembrandt

The Metropolitan Museum of Art
Bequest of Lillian S. Timken, 1959

to a grain of mustard seed which a man receiving, sowed in his field.

The man who sows the seed in his field is understood by many to be the Savior because he sows in the souls of the faithful; by others he is understood to be that man himself who sows in his own field, that is, in himself and in his own heart. Who is it that sows but our senses and our soul which, receiving the grain of preaching and nourishing it when sown, makes it by the moisture of faith to sprout forth in the field of the heart?

The preaching of the Gospel is the least of all exercises. Indeed for its very first doctrine the Gospel does not have even the semblance of truth, preaching as it does a man-God, Christ who died, and the proclamation of the stumbling block of the Cross. Compare such a doctrine with the tenets of philosophers, with their books and the brilliancy of their eloquence and the arrangement of their words, and you will see how much less than all these seeds is the seed of him who sows the seed of the Gospel.

Yet the former, when they have sprung up, show themselves without vigor, without spirit, without life; but altogether languid, degenerate, and soft, they develop into herbs and plants which quickly dry up and waste away. But this latter preaching (of the Gospel), which in the beginning seems small, when it is sown in the soul of the faithful or in the whole world, springs up not into a herb, but develops into a tree; so that the birds of the air (which we must understand to be the souls of the faithful or deeds of virtue performed in the service of God) come and dwell in its branches. I consider the branches of this tree of the Gospel, which sprang from the mustard seed, to be the various dogmas on which each of the above-mentioned birds rests.

St. Jerome

THE KINGDOM OF HEAVEN is likened to a householder who hired laborers to tend his vineyard. Who has the likeness of this householder more than our Creator who governs those whom He has created, and possesses His chosen ones in this world as a master does the servants of his house? He it is who has the vineyard, namely, the universal Church, which, from the just Abel to the last of the elect who shall be born at the end of the world, has produced so many saints, as it were, as it has sent forth branches.

This householder, therefore, in order to cultivate his vineyard, hired laborers in the morning and at the third, sixth, ninth, and eleventh hours; for from the beginning of the world even to its end He does not cease to gather preachers to instruct His faithful people. Now the early morning of the world was from Adam to Noe; and the third hour, from Noe to Abraham; the sixth hour, from Abraham to Moses; the ninth, from Moses to the coming of our Lord; the eleventh, from the coming of the Lord till the end of the world. In which last hour the holy Apostles have been sent as preachers, and albeit they came late, they have received a full reward.

For the instruction of His people, therefore—as it were to cultivate His vineyard—the Lord never ceases to send out laborers. For, indeed, when He nurtured the moral uprightness of His people, in the beginning through the patriarchs, later on through the doctors of the law, and finally through the Apostles, He worked as it were through the instrumentality of laborers in the cultivation of His vineyard; on the other hand, each one who in any way or measure, with upright intention, has been a preacher by good example, is a laborer in that vineyard.

Therefore, the workman of the morning, be it of the third, sixth, or ninth hour, is a figure of that ancient and Hebraic people who from the beginning of the world—in their chosen ones—did not desist from laboring in the cultivation of the vineyard in so far as they ceased not to be zealous in worshipping God with the true faith. But at this eleventh hour the Gentiles are called to whom it is also said: "Why stand ye here all the day idle?"   St. Gregory, *Pope*

We read that the Lord was angry. For although He thought, that is, He knew, that man, being placed on the earth and bearing a body, was not able to be without sin (because the earth is, as it were, a certain place of temptation, and the flesh a lure to corruption); still, even though men possessed a mind capable of reasoning and the power of the soul infused into the body, without any deliberation they rushed to their ruin, from which they did not wish to recall themselves.

God does not think as man—as if some new thought should come to Him—nor does He become angry, as if He were changeable; rather these things are said in order that the awfulness of our sins might be demonstrated, which merit even the divine displeasure—as if our fault increases to such an extent that even God, who by nature is not moved by anger or hatred or any passion, would seem to be provoked to wrath.

He threatened, moreover, to destroy mankind. "From man," He says, "even to beast, and from the creeping things even to the fowls of the air I shall destroy them." What offense had the irrational things given? Yet, because they had been made for man, when he for whom they had been made was ruined, it had to follow that they also be destroyed, for there was no one to use them. But in a higher sense this is made manifest, that man is a being capable of reason. For man is defined as an animal—living, mortal, rational. Thus when the highest species of animal has been destroyed, why should the lower species remain? Why should anything be preserved alive when virtue, the basis of salvation, was no more?

However, with regard to the destruction of the rest of things (besides man) and to the manifestation of the divine love, Noe is said to have obtained a hearing before God. At the same time it is shown that the offense of other men does not overshadow the just man, since this latter alone is preserved for the propagation of the race. He is praised not for his nobility of birth, but for the merits of his justice and perfection. For the family of an upright man is a race of strength, because just as men are the offspring of men, so virtues are the offspring of minds. The families of men are ennobled by the splendor of their lineage, while the grace of souls is glorified by the splendor of their virtue.

ST. AMBROSE

Readings for Lent

OUR REDEEMER, foreseeing that the minds of His disciples would be perturbed at His Passion, foretold to them long before both the ignominy of that same Passion and the glory of His Resurrection, so that when they would see Him dying, as He had foretold, they would not doubt that He would also rise again. But because the disciples, being as yet carnal, could not grasp the words of the mystery, He had recourse to a miracle. Before their very eyes the blind man received his sight, so that heavenly deeds might strengthen in the faith those who could not grasp the words of the heavenly mystery.

But the miracles of our Lord and Savior should be so understood, dearly beloved brethren, that on the one hand the deeds themselves are truly believed, and on the other, that they contain some mystic interpretation for our instruction. Indeed His works show forth one thing by their power and speak of another in symbol. For behold, who this blind man was historically we do not know, but yet we do know what he signifies mystically.

Truly blind is the human race which, once expelled from the joys of Paradise in the person of its first parent, now suf-

319

CHRIST AFTER THE FLAGELLATION

by Bartolome Murillo

Museum of Fine Art, Boston
Ernest W. Longfellow Fund

fers the darkness of its own damnation, being ignorant of the brightness of divine light! It is, nevertheless, so illuminated by the presence of its Redeemer that it already sees by anticipation the joys of the internal light and makes strides on the way of a life of good works. It must be noted, however, that the blind man is illumined when Jesus is said to approach Jericho. Now the word Jericho means *the moon*; but the moon in sacred writing is used for carnal fickleness inasmuch as, while it decreases in its monthly phases, it signifies the changeableness of our mortality.

Therefore, whilst our Maker draws nigh to Jericho, the blind man returns to the light; for whilst divinity took on the weakness of our flesh, the human race received the light which it had lost. When God suffers human things, then man is lifted to divine things. And the blind man is rightly described as sitting by the wayside and as a beggar. For Truth Itself says: "I am the Way."   St. Gregory, *Pope*

From these precepts it is clearly shown that all our attention is to be directed to interior joys, lest, whilst seeking a reward in exterior things, we conform ourselves to this world and lose the promise of that happiness (which is more genuine and lasting the more interior it is) in which God has chosen us to be made conformable to the image of His Son. We must, moreover, note in this chapter of the Gospel that pride can have a place not only in the splendor and pomp of earthly things, but even in unkempt mourning garments. And this latter is more full of dangers since it hides under the name of worship of God.

He who is conspicuous for immoderate care of his body, for his dress, or for the brilliance of other things is easily convicted of being a votary of the splendor of the world by these very traits, and misleads no one by deceitful imitation of sanctity. But, because our Lord commanded us to beware of wolves in sheep's clothing, saying, "By their fruits you shall know them," he who, professing Christianity, draws the eyes of men to himself by his unusual filth and soiled apparel (provided he is not constrained by necessity, but does this of his own accord) can be judged from the rest of his actions whether he acts thus from contempt of superfluous care or from a certain secret ambition.

For when, by a few tests, those very advantages which they have obtained or desire to obtain by that subterfuge begin to be taken away, then it is made manifest whether they are wolves in sheep's clothing or sheep in their own. Yet a Christian does not have to delight the gazes of men by undue superfluities because of the fact that very often hypocrites also don a very poor and needy garb in order to deceive the unwary; just as those sheep need not put off their own clothing if it happens at times that wolves hide themselves in them.   St. Augustine

"But i say to you: Love your enemies, do good to them that hate you." Many men in their ignorance, not thinking of the virtues of holy persons, consider the commandments of God which have been prescribed to be impossible, and they say that it is virtuous enough not to hate one's enemies, but that to be commanded to love them is more than human nature can bear. It must, therefore, be understood that Christ did not command the impossible, but rather the perfect things. David performed these things towards Saul and towards Absalom; Stephen the Martyr also prayed for his enemies who stoned him, and Paul wished to be cursed in place of his persecutors. These things, too, Jesus taught and did, saying: "Father, forgive them, for they know not what they do."

"That you may be the children of your Father who is in heaven." If one is made a child of God by keeping the commandments, he is then not a child by nature, but through his free will. "Therefore when thou dost an alms-deed, sound not a trumpet before thee, as the hypocrites do in the synagogues and in the streets that they may be honored by men." He who sounds a trumpet in working charity is a hypocrite. He who saddens his face when fasting, in order to show the emptiness of his stomach by his countenance, is also a hypocrite. He who prays in the synagogue and on the streets in order to be seen by men, is likewise a hypocrite.

From all these examples it is gathered that they are hypocrites who do a thing in order to be honored by men. It seems to me that he also is a hypocrite who says to his brother: "Let me cast out the speck from thy eye"; for it appears that he does this for glory, so that he might seem to be a just man. Wherefore it is said to that man by the Lord: "Hypocrite, take out first the beam from thine own eye." For it is not the act of virtue that has value before God, but the reason for that act. And if you shall stray from the right path but a little, it does not matter whether you go to the right or to the left, since you have lost the true way.

St. Jerome

About to preach to you, dearly beloved, the holiest and greatest of fasts, what beginning could I more fittingly use than the words of the Apostle, through whom Christ Himself has spoken, saying. "Behold, now is the acceptable time, now is the day of salvation." For though there is no season which is not full of divine gifts and though free access to God's mercy is ever provided for us by His grace, yet now the minds of all should be moved with greater zeal to spiritual progress and be animated with fuller confidence—now when the return of that day on which we have all been redeemed invites us to every work of piety, so that, cleansed both in body and in mind, we may celebrate that mystery which surpasses all others—the Lord's Passion.

Such great mysteries justly lay claim to such a lasting devotion and abiding reverence that we should remain such in the sight of God as we ought to be found on the Paschal feast itself. But because such fervor is had but by few, and since the more severe discipline is relaxed because of the frailty of the flesh and our attention is divided among the many actions of this life, even the hearts of religious men must necessarily become soiled by the dust of worldly things. Hence it has been provided in the great wisdom of the divine plan that, in order to restore purity of mind, we should be chastened by the training of these forty days, during which pious works should redeem and chaste fasting melt away the faults of other times.

Therefore, dearly beloved, since we are about to enter upon these mystic days, instituted in a most sacred manner for the purifying of both soul and body, let us take care to obey the Apostolic precepts, cleansing ourselves from all defilement of flesh and spirit, so that, chastened by the struggles that go on between flesh and spirit, the soul, which under God's direction should be the established ruler of the body, may obtain the grace of self-control, that, giving no offense to any man, we may not be exposed to the reproaches of those who revile us.

For we shall justly be blamed by unbelievers, and the tongues of the wicked will arm themselves with our vices to the injury of religion, if the manners of those fasting do not show forth the purity of perfect continence. For the excellence of our fast does not consist merely in abstinence

---

---

from food, nor is meat fruitfully denied to the body unless the mind be recalled from evil. ST. LEO, *Pope*

IF, WITHOUT HAVING OBSERVED the commandments, one is able to attain eternal life by faith alone—which without good works is dead—how will that be true which He will say to those whom He will place on His left: "Go ye into eternal fire which has been prepared for the devil and his angels"? not rebuking them for their unbelief but because they have not done good works. For lest anyone promise himself eternal life by reason of his faith—which without good works is dead—He went on to say that He would separate all nations, even those which, being mingled together, were using the same pastures, that it might be evident that it was those who had believed in Him but had not taken pains to do good works—as though they could attain unto eternal life by means of that same dead faith—that would say to Him: "Lord, when did we see thee suffering such and such afflictions and did not minister to thee?"

Shall they perhaps who have not performed works of mercy go into eternal fire, and they who have taken away the things of others not go? Or, shall those not go who by corrupting the temple of God within themselves have been unmerciful to themselves—as though works of mercy were of any profit without love when the Apostle says: "If I distribute all my goods to the poor, but have not charity, it availeth me nothing"? Or can anyone who does not love himself love his neighbor as himself? For "he that loveth iniquity hateth his own soul."

Nor can that be said here by which some deceive themselves: that the fire has been called eternal but not the burning itself. They think that those to whom they promise

salvation through fire by reason of their dead faith, will pass through fire which is eternal, but, though the fire itself is eternal, their burning—that is, the action of the fire upon them—is not everlasting. Wherefore our Lord, foreseeing this, concluded His sentence with these words: "They will go into everlasting fire, but the just into eternal life." Therefore, the burning as well as the fire will be eternal. And Truth says that they will go into it whose good works, and not faith, He has declared wanting.   ST. AUGUSTINE

THE LORD spoke to the Jews, saying: "I go." To Christ our Lord death was a journeying to Him from whom He had come, yet from whom He had not departed. "I go," He said, "and you shall seek me," not with desire, but in hatred. After He had withdrawn from the eyes of men, there were those who hated Him and those who loved Him: the former persecuting Him, the latter desiring to possess Him. The Lord Himself has said in the psalms by the mouth of the prophet: "Means of escape have failed me, there is none that seeketh me"; and again in the psalm He said: "May they be put to shame and confusion who seek to take my life."

He judges them guilty who sought Him not; He condemns those who did seek Him. Now it is good to seek Christ, but in that manner in which the disciples sought after Him; it is also an evil thing to seek after Christ, in the manner in which the Jews sought after Him. The disciples sought after Him that they might possess Him; the Jews, that they might destroy Him. Finally what did He, continuing His words, say to these latter since they sought after Him in an evil way and with a perverse heart? "You shall seek me, and (lest you think that you seek me rightly), you shall die in your sin." This is to seek after Christ in an evil manner—to

CRUCIFIXION *by Francisco de Zurbarán*
The Art Institute of Chicago

die in one's sin; this is to hate Him through whom alone one can be saved.

For although men whose hope is in God ought not render evil even for evil, these rendered evil for good. Therefore the Lord announced to these beforehand, and, foreknowing all things, He pronounced sentence that they should die in their sin. Then He added: "Whither I go, you cannot come." These same words He addressed to His disciples in another place. Yet to them He did not add: "You shall die in your sin." What then did He say? The same that He said to the Jews: "Whither I go, you cannot come." Christ did not take away hope, but only predicted a delay. For when He spoke thus to His disciples, they were unable at the time to come whither He was going, but they would come later. These Jews, however, to whom He had in prophecy said, "You shall die in your sin," would never be able to come.

St. Augustine

Consider what it is that the mother of the sons of Zebedee is asking, together with and on behalf of her sons. She is truly a mother, the extent of whose desires in her anxiety for the honor of her sons is indeed immoderate, but nevertheless pardonable, especially as she, a mother advanced in years, deeply religious, and deprived of consolation, suffered her sons to be absent from her at the very time when she needed their help and support, and preferred to her own pleasure the reward of followers of Christ for her sons. They, when called by the Lord, at His first word (as we read) leaving their nets and their father, followed Him.

Therefore this mother, so very generous in the duty of motherly solicitude, besought the Savior, saying: "Let these my two sons sit, one on thy right hand, and the other on thy left hand in thy kingdom." Although it be an error, still it is an error of love. For the maternal heart knew no patience. Although she is over-eager in her wish, nevertheless, it is hardly a desire which merits punishment, for it is a yearning not for money, but for grace. Nor is it a shameful petition which pleads not for herself, but for her children. Consider the mother; realize that she is a mother.

Christ considered the mother's love whose comfort in her old age was in the reward of her sons, and, though worn by maternal cares, suffered the absence of her dearest treasures. Do you also consider the woman, that is, the weaker sex which the Lord had not as yet strengthened by His own suffering. Consider, I say, the child of that first woman, Eve, whom the Lord had not yet redeemed by His blood, falling because of the heritage of unbridled desire which has been passed on to all men. Christ had not as yet purified by His own blood that desire for honor, immoderate beyond bounds, which had grown in the affections of all men. Therefore the woman was at fault, but it was a weakness inherited from Eve. St. Ambrose

You see that a divine inheritance is given to those who seek it. Think not that it was a fault of the father that he gave the portion of his inheritance to the youth. In the kingdom of God there is no weakness of age, neither is faith increased by years. He who asked certainly judged himself fit. Would that he had not departed from his father! Then he would not have experienced the drawback of his youth. But after leaving his paternal home and wandering about in a strange country, he "began to be in need." Rightly is he who has left the Church said to have squandered his patrimony.

"He went into a far-off land." What is a more distant journey than to go out of one's self, to be separated not by vast regions, but by morals; to be cut off not by earthly distance, but by the pursuits of the soul; and to be, as it were, divorced from the society of the saints by the burning chasm of earthly lust? He who has separated himself from Christ is indeed an exile from his fatherland; he is a citizen of this world. But we are not strangers nor pilgrims but fellow citizens of the saints and members of the household of God, since we who were once far away have been brought near by the blood of Christ. Let us not envy those wandering in the regions afar off, for we too were once in that territory as Isaias teaches. For there you read: "A light has risen to those who sat in the region of the shadow of death." Therefore this far-off region is the shadow of death.

But we, before the fact of whose soul stands Christ the Lord, live in the shadow of Christ. And therefore the Church says: "I sat down under his shadow in great delight." The man who lives riotously wastes all the beauties of his nature. In like manner you, who have received the image of God, do not destroy it by irrational uncleanness. You are the work of God; say not then to a wooden idol, "Thou art my father," lest perhaps you become like it; for it is written, "Let those who make idols become like them."   St. Ambrose

Why do you correct your brother? Because you are sorry that he has offended you? God forbid! If you do it out of love for yourself, you accomplish nothing; if you do it out of love for him, you are acting perfectly. Finally, notice in these same words for love of whom you are to do this—for yourself or for him. "If he shall hear thee," He says, "thou shalt gain thy brother." Accordingly, act for the sake of him that you may win him. By so doing you are the one who profits; he would have been lost unless you had corrected him. Why is it, then, that men contemn these sins, and say: "What serious things have I done? I have sinned against a man." Do not contemn the fact that you have sinned against a man.

Do you want to know that in offending a man you perish? If the one against whom you have sinned will correct you between you and himself alone, and you hear him, he gains you back. What does this mean—he gains you—except that you would have perished had he not won you back? For if you were not lost, how could he gain you? So let not one think little of it when he has offended against his brother. For the Apostle says somewhere: "Now when you sin thus against your brother and wound his weak conscience, you sin against Christ, because we are all become members of Christ." How can you keep from sinning against Christ when you offend a member of Christ?

Therefore let no one declare: "I have not sinned against God, but against my brother. I have offended a man—it is a small sin, or no sin at all." Perhaps you say, "It is a small sin," because it is quickly passed over. You have offended your brother; make satisfaction and you will be healed. In a moment you have performed a fatal deed, and as quickly you have found a remedy for it. Which of you, my brethren, can expect the Kingdom of Heaven when the Gospel declares: "He who shall say to his brother, 'thou fool,' is guilty of hell-fire"? It is a very terrifying thing, but behold your means of reparation: "If you bring your gift to the altar, and there remember that your brother hath something against thee, leave there thy gift before the altar. . ." God is not angered because you postpone the offering of your gift; God seeks you yourself rather than your gift.

St. Augustine

Mysteries are already beginning. For Jesus is not tired without reason; the strength of God is not wearied without cause; He is not fatigued for nothing by whom the wearied are refreshed; nor is He exhausted to no purpose in whose absence we are wearied and in whose presence we are strengthened. Still, Jesus is tired and spent from His journey, and He sits down, and He sits beside the well, and He sat thus at the well, being wearied, about the sixth hour. All these things point to something; they indicate something; they bring us to attention; they excite us to action. Therefore may He who has deigned so to arouse us, saying, "Knock and it shall be opened to you," open to us and to you.

Jesus is exhausted by His travel for our sake. We have found Jesus strong; now we find Him weak. Strong and weak,—strong, because "in the beginning was the Word, and the Word was with God, and the Word was God. The same was in the beginning with God." Do you wish to see how powerful the Son of God is? "All things were made by Him and without Him was made nothing"; and without labor were they made. Therefore what is more mighty than He by whom were made all things without labor? Do you desire to know Him weak? "The Word was made flesh and dwelt amongst us." The strength of Christ has created you; the weakness of Christ has re-created you, the power of Christ has caused to exist that which was not, the weakness of Christ has kept from perishing that which was. In His power He has formed us; in His weakness He has sought us.

ST. AUGUSTINE

WE KNOW that by fasting Moses ascended the mountain. Nor would he have dared to mount the smoking summit or enter the darkness unless he had been fortified by fasting. By fasting he received the commandments written by the finger of God on the tablets. Likewise, upon the mountain fasting was the promoter of the law that had been given; but below, gluttony led the people to idolatry and contaminated them. "The people sat down," it says, "to eat and drink and they rose up to play." While the servant of God devoted himself to continual fast and prayer, one drunken revelry of the people rendered his labor and perseverance of forty days empty and void.

For the tablets were written by the finger of God, which fasting received, drunkenness shattered, since the most holy Prophet considered a wine-bibbing people unworthy to receive the Law from God. In one moment, on account of their gluttony, that people, though instructed in the worship of God by the greatest miracles, most shamefully fell into the idolatry of the Egyptians. From which, if we consider both at the same time, we may see that fasting leads to God, and delights destroy salvation.

What contaminated Esau and made him the servant of his brother? Was it not one meal, on account of which he sold his birthright? Did not prayer, accompanied with fasting, give Samuel to his mother? What made the brave Samson unconquerable? Was it not fasting, with which he was conceived in the womb of his mother? Fasting conceived, fasting nourished, and fasting made of him a man. The Angel wisely prescribed this for his mother, admonishing that whatever came from the vine she should not touch, neither wine nor any strong drink should she take. Fasting begot prophets, it confirmed and strengthened powerful men.

Fasting makes wise legislators; it is the best guardian of the soul, a sure friend of the body, strength and arms for the brave, training for athletes and contestants. Furthermore, fasting repels temptations, excites to piety, dwells with sobriety and is a promoter of temperance; it brings

THE DESCENT FROM THE CROSS

by Rembrandt

National Gallery of Art, Washington, D.C.
Widener Collection

strength in time of war and teaches calmness in time of peace; it sanctifies the Nazarite; it perfects the priest; for it is not right to touch the sacrifice without fasting, not only now in the mystic and true adoration of God, but not even in that in which the sacrifice was offered in figure according to the Law. Fasting made Elias the spectator of a grand vision, for when he had cleansed his soul by a fast of forty days in the cave, he merited to see God, as far as this is permitted to man. Moses, receiving the Law again, had also a second time practiced fasting. The Ninivites, unless the very beasts fasted with them, would by no means have escaped the threats of ruin. Whose corpses fell in the desert? Were they not theirs who longed for flesh meats?

St. Basil the Great

The miracles which our Lord Jesus Christ wrought are in very deed divine works, and they admonish the human mind to understand God from visible things. For, after all, He is not such a substance as can be seen with the eyes. His miracles by which He rules the whole world and ministers to every creature, have by their frequency become commonplace, so that scarcely anyone thinks it worth while to attend to the wonderful, yes, stupendous works of God in any grain of seed. In accordance with His mercy He has reserved to Himself certain miracles outside the ordinary course and order of nature, which He works at an opportune time, that they to whom the daily miracles have grown common might be astonished by witnessing not greater things, but uncommon ones.

For the governing of the whole world is a greater miracle than the feeding of five thousand men with five loaves of bread. Yet no one marvels at the one; but at the other, men are in admiration, not because it is greater, but because it is rare. For who is it that even now feeds the whole world but He who from a few grains creates the harvest?

He worked, therefore, as God. For by the same power whereby He multiplies the harvests from a few grains, so also did He multiply in His hands the five loaves. The power, indeed, was in the hands of Christ. And those five loaves were as seeds, not indeed entrusted to the earth, but multiplied by Him who made the earth.

This prodigy, then, was brought under the realm of the senses, that thereby the mind might be uplifted; and it was displayed before the eyes, whereby the intellect might be exercised, that we might admire the invisible God through His visible works, and, raised aloft to faith and purified by faith, might yearn even to see that invisible Being whom, though invisible, we learned to know from visible things. And yet it does not suffice to view only these points in the miracles of Christ. Let us ask those very miracles what they tell us of Christ. Oh, yes, they have a tongue if they are only understood. For since Christ Himself is the Word of God, even a deed of the Word is a word for us.   St. Augustine

THE STUPENDOUS and wonderful things that our Lord Jesus Christ has done are both works and words. They are works because they have been done; they are words because they are signs. If therefore this deed signifies something, let us consider what it is. The blind man is the human race. This blindness befell the first man through his sin, from which we trace the origin not only of death, but also of evil. If infidelity is blindness and faith is sight, whom did Christ find faithful when He came? At one time the Apostle, born of the race of the prophets, said: "We were once by nature children of wrath, as also were the rest."

If children of wrath, then also children of judgment, children of punishment, children of hell. If we are so by nature, how is this but that the first man by sinning brought this affliction on human nature? If he brought this penalty on human nature, then every man is born blind according to the spirit.

But then the Lord came. What did He do? He effected a great mystery. He spat on the ground and made clay of the spittle (for the Word was made flesh), and spread clay upon the eyes of the blind man. The man was therefore treated with the clay, but he did not as yet see. The Lord then sent him to the pool which is called Siloe. It was left for the Evangelist to give us the name of this pool which is, according to the interpretation, *Sent*. You all know who it is that is *sent*. Had this One not been sent, none of us would be free from our iniquity. The blind man therefore washed his eyes in that pool which according to the interpretation is called " (the One) Sent," that is, he was baptized in Christ. If Christ therefore gave sight to the man when He, so to speak, baptized him in Himself, then the rubbing of clay on his eyes perhaps signifies making him a catechumen.

You have heard a sublime mystery. Ask a man: "Are you a Christian?" He answers, "No." "Are you a pagan or a Jew?" If he should say, "No," then ask him if he is a catechumen or one of the faithful. If his answer is that he is a catechumen, then he has had clay spread on his eyes; but he has not yet been washed. But whence was it that the clay was spread on? Ask him and he will tell you that it was when he came to believe. Ask him in whom he believes. By the very fact that he is a catechumen he says, "In Christ". Behold now I speak both to the faithful and to catechumens. What is it that I have said about the spittle and the clay? I have said that the Word was made flesh.

The Catechumens hear this, but it is not sufficient for them that their eyes have been covered with the clay (that is, that they believe); let them hasten to the font if they seek the Light.   St. Augustine

Among all the Christian solemnities, beloved, we are not unaware that the Paschal mystery is the principal one, for the worthy and fitting reception of which the arrangement of the whole cycle prepares us; but the present days, which we know to be close on that most sublime mystery of divine mercy, demand our devotion above all. During these days greater fasts were with reason ordained by the holy apostles through the teaching of the Holy Spirit, in order that through the common fellowship of the cross of Christ we also might do something in that which He did for us, as the Apostle says: "If we suffer with him, we shall also be glorified with him." Certain and secure is the hope of promised happiness where there is participation in the suffering of the Lord.

There is no one, beloved, to whom, through circumstance of time, the communication of this glory will be refused, as if the tranquility of peace is void of opportunity for virtue. For the Apostle foretells, saying, "All who wish to live piously in Christ will suffer persecution," and therefore never is there wanting the tribulation of persecution if the practice of piety be not lacking. And the Lord says in His exhortations: "Whoever does not take up his cross and follow me, is not worthy of me."

Nor should we doubt that this saying applies not only to the disciples of Christ, but also to all the faithful and to the entire Church which, in the person of those who were then present, heard for all time the way of her salvation. As therefore it is the duty of the whole body to live piously, so also is it the duty of all time to bear the cross. Rightly is each one persuaded to bear this cross, for it is borne by each one according to his proper disposition and capacity. There is only one name for persecution, but there is not just one type of struggle, and usually there is more danger in a hidden foe than in an open enemy.

Blessed Job, instructed in the fluctuating goods and evils of this world, piously and truly said: "Is not the life of man on earth a temptation?" For not by the mere pains and sufferings of the body is the faithful soul assailed, but when the health of his members is preserved, he is likewise oppressed by serious illness if he is weakened by the pleasure of the flesh.

But when "the flesh lusteth against the spirit and spirit against the flesh," the rational mind is strengthened by the protection of the cross of Christ, and, when enticed by evil desires, it does not consent, for it is transfixed by the piercing steel of continence and by the fear of God.

St. Leo, *Pope*

WHEN I think of the penance of Mary Magdalene, it seems more fitting to weep than to speak. For what stony breast do not the tears of this sinner soften to repentance? She beheld what she had done, and she would not be moderate in what she must do in recompense. She made her way among the guests; she came under no compulsion; she brought her tears to the banquet. Learn with what sorrow she was inflamed who did not blush to exhibit her repentant tears among the diners.

This woman whom Luke names as a sinner, John calls Mary, that same Mary, we believe, whose deliverance from seven devils was recounted by Mark. What else is signified by seven devils but the very zenith of vice? Just as all time is expressed by seen days, so the number seven is understood as all-comprehensive. Therefore, since Mary had *seven* devils, she was full of every kind of wickedness.

But once having glimpsed the stains of her depravity, entirely unashamed before the guests, she hastened to the font of mercy to be cleansed. Because she was inwardly so heartily repentant, she considered external embarrassment to be as nothing. Brethren, which should we admire the more—Mary coming, or the Lord receiving? Receiving, shall I say, or drawing? Rather I should say both drawing and receiving, for He who received her outwardly in His meekness, drew her inwardly through His mercy.

ST. GREGORY, *Pope*

Readings for Easter

ALTHOUGH all solemnities, dearly beloved, which are celebrated in the Church for the honor of God, are holy and venerable, nevertheless, this day of the Lord's Resurrection has a festivity all its own. For indeed, while all the other days hold in themselves gladness for the living, this day holds joy for the dead and for those who have recently lost loved ones in death.

For this festivity is common alike to the lower regions as well as to those that are above, for the Lord, rising again from the dead, brought festivity there where He conquered death, and there too whither He has returned as the Victor over death. Well, therefore, does the Psalmist speak especially of this day saying: "This is the day the Lord has made; let us be glad and rejoice therein."

For, announcing the Lord's Resurrection, he indicated that it was a day of salubrious exultation, not to the heavens alone, but also to the lower regions. When the Lord descended into the blackness of hell, even there, at the time when the Savior illumined it, it was without doubt a most bright day. Whence the Evangelist beautifully says: "And the light shone in the darkness, and the darkness did not

CHRIST AND THE PILGRIMS OF EMMAUS

by Velazquez

The Metropolitan Museum of Art
Bequest of Benjamin Altman, 1913

comprehend it." Although the Lord descended into the darkness, He did not, however, feel its gloom.

He retained in that horror of night the inviolable splendor of His majesty; He shone in the splendor of His eternal nature, and so the Light was not overwhelmed by the night, but the night by the Light. Let us be glad, therefore, most dearly beloved, and let us rejoice in the Lord, for today is given to us by the Lord the Light of salvation, according to that which the same Psalmist says in one of the following verses: "The Lord is God, and he hath shone upon us."

St. John Chrysostom

Mary magdalene, who had been a sinner in the city, by loving the Truth washed away with her tears the stains of her crime, and the word of the Truth was fulfilled by whom it was said: "Many sins are forgiven her, because she has loved much." She who had remained cold in her sin, afterwards became fervent by her ardent love. For after she had come to the tomb and did not find our Lord's body there, she believed that it had been taken away and announced the fact to the disciples, who, coming, saw for themselves and believed it to be as the woman had told them. And it is written of them: "The disciples therefore departed again to their home." And then it is added: "But Mary stood at the sepulchre without, weeping." Thus does St. John describe her patient vigil.

Wherefore it must be considered how great a force of love enkindled the soul of the woman who did not depart from the tomb even though the disciples left. She was seeking One whom she had not found; in her search she wept, and, inflamed with the fire of her love, she burned in her yearning for Him whom she believed had been taken away. Thus did it happen that she alone then saw Him—she who had remained behind to look for Him; for truly, the virtue of a good work is perseverance, and it is declared by the voice of Truth: "He who shall persevere to the end, he shall be saved."

"Now as she was weeping, she stooped down and looked into the sepulchre." Certainly she had already seen that the tomb was empty; she had already announced that the Lord had been taken away—why is it that she bends down again, that she desires to look again? It does not satisfy one who loves to have looked but once, for the strength of love multiplies the reasons for the search. Therefore she sought before and did not find; she persevered in her search, and so it came about that she did find. This delay was made that her desires, by not being fulfilled at once, might increase, and, increasing, might meet with Him to whom they aspired.

ST. GREGORY, *Pope*

STRAIGHTAWAY upon reading this Gospel a question agitates the mind: How was it that the body of our risen Lord was a real one since it was able to pass through closed doors into the presence of His disciples? But we ought to know that the operation of God is not wonderful if it is comprehended by reason; neither has faith any merit in regard to that for which human reason offers demonstration. Nevertheless, those very works of our Redeemer, which can in themselves by no means be fully understood, must be considered in connection with another operation of His, so that to wonderful things even more wonderful facts might give credibility.

For it was that same body of the Lord that came in to the disciples through closed doors which had become known to human eyes by His birth from the closed womb of the Virgin. And what wonder is it if that body which, coming (into the world) to die, proceeded from the Virgin's womb without breaking the seal thereof, after the Resurrection and now destined to live forever, should have passed through closed doors? But because the faith of the onlookers wavered with regard to that body which could be seen, He immediately showed them His hands and side; the flesh which He had brought in through closed doors He submitted to be handled.

Wherefore He manifests two admirable and, according to our human reasoning, exceedingly opposite marks in as far as He showed His body after its Resurrection incorruptible, yet palpable. For what is palpable necessarily is also corruptible; and what is incorruptible cannot be palpable. But in a wonderful, nay, inestimable manner did our Redeemer after His Resurrection exhibit His body both incorruptible and palpable so that He might invite us to a reward by showing it as incorruptible, and that by showing it as palpable He might strengthen our faith. It was for this reason, then, that He manifested Himself both incorruptible and palpable: to show that His body after the Resurrection was truly of the same nature but of another glory.

He said to them: "Peace be to you. As the Father hath sent me, so I also send you," that is, "As God the Father hath sent me who am God, so I, as man, send you who are men." The Father sent the Son and decreed that He should be made flesh for the Redemption of the human race. It is evident that He wished Him to come into the world to suffer; but nevertheless He loved the Son whom He sent to suffer. So also our Lord did not send the chosen apostles into the world to the joys of the world, but, as He Himself was sent, to sufferings. Therefore, just as the Son is beloved of the Father and nevertheless is sent to suffer, so also the disciples are beloved of the Lord, and, notwithstanding this, are sent into the world to suffer. Rightly, therefore, is

[*Continued on page 360*]

The Apostles

"And going up a mountain, he called to him men of his own choosing, and they came to him. And he appointed twelve that they might be with him and that he might send them forth to preach. To them he gave power to cure sicknesses and to cast out devils. They were Simon, to whom he gave the name Peter; and James the son of Zebedee, and John the brother of James (these he surnamed Boanerges, that is, Sons of Thunder); and Andrew, and Philip, and Bartholomew, and Matthew, and Thomas, and James the son of Alpheus, and Thaddeus, and Simon the Cananean, and Judas Iscariot, he who betrayed him." (Mark 3:13-19)

IT IS significant that the Gospels record carefully and explicitly, one by one, the names of all twelve of the Apostles. In the plan of God they are an absolutely indispensable link in the chain of events that make up the history of our salvation. The Lord God came down to our world, became one of our human family, walked among us, spoke to us in a way we could easily understand. But we would never have heard his voice were it not for the Apostles. They were "with him from the beginning". They alone, therefore, knew what he was really like; they alone heard all that he had to say to us. And so it was that the Lord sent them forth in a very special way. (The word "apostle" means "one who is sent".) They did indeed go forth.

The Acts of the Apostles records some of the history of their many journeyings. Strengthened by the power of the Holy Spirit, enlightened by the clear light of the same Spirit, they went everywhere they could to tell as many people as possible the good news of our redemption. They were looked up to and listened to because they had been with the Lord. After their mission was accomplished, their lives were snuffed out one after the other by civil authorities for daring to suggest that our hope for the future lay not with governments or emperors but with Christ.

PETER
Peter Paul Rubens
Museo del Prado, Madrid, Spain

JAMES
Peter Paul Rubens
Museo del Prado, Madrid, Spain

JOHN
Peter Paul Rubens
Museo del Prado, Madrid, Spain

ANDREW
Peter Paul Rubens
Museo del Prado, Madrid, Spain

PHILIP
Peter Paul Rubens
Museo del Prado, Madrid, Spain

BARTHOLOMEW
Peter Paul Rubens
Museo del Prado, Madrid, Spain

MATTHEW
Peter Paul Rubens
Museo del Prado, Madrid, Spain

THOMAS
Peter Paul Rubens
Museo del Prado, Madrid, Spain

JUDE
Peter Paul Rubens
Museo del Prado, Madrid, Spain

SIMON
Peter Paul Rubens
Museo del Prado, Madrid, Spain

MATTHIAS

Peter Paul Rubens

Museo del Prado, Madrid, Spain

PAUL
Peter Paul Rubens
Museo del Prado, Madrid, Spain

it said: "As the Father hath sent me, so I also send you."
That is, "When I send you among the scandals of persecutors, I love you with that same charity with which the
Father loves me, whom He decreed should come to undergo
sufferings.   ST. GREGORY, *Pope*

DURING THESE HOLY DAYS dedicated to the Resurrection
of the Lord, in as far as we are able with His help, let us
treat of the resurrection of the flesh. For this is our faith;
this gift was promised us in the flesh of our Lord Jesus
Christ, and in Himself He has given us the example. For
He willed not only to foretell what He promised us for the
end of time, but also to demonstrate it to us. Those, indeed,
who were then present, when they saw Him, and were
frightened and thought they saw a spirit, grasped the solid
substance of His body.

For He spoke to them not only with words for their ears,
but likewise by a form for their eyes; indeed, it was of
little avail to offer Himself to their sight had He not also
offered Himself to be examined and touched. For He says:
"Why are you perturbed, and why do doubts arise in your
hearts?" For they thought they were looking at a spirit.
"Why are you afraid," says He, "and why do doubts arise
in your hearts? See my hands and my feet; touch them and
see, because a spirit does not have bones and flesh, as you
see me to have."

Men disputed against this evidence. But what else would
men do, who think of things which are of men, than to dispute about God against God? For He is God; they are men.
But God knows the thoughts of men that they are vain. In
carnal man the one rule which determines what shall be
understood is what can be seen. What they are accustomed
to see they believe; what they are not accustomed to see

they do not believe. But God works miracles beyond ordinary custom because He is God.

Greater, indeed, are the miracles that daily so many men are brought into life who were not, than that a few who had been living have arisen from the dead, and yet these miracles are not given much consideration, but have become ordinary because of their frequency. Christ has arisen; that is certain. He was body, and He was flesh; He hung on the cross, gave up the ghost, and His flesh was laid in the sepulchre. He who had lived in it showed that flesh to be living. Why do we wonder? Why do we not believe? It is God who has done these things.   St. Augustine

THE FACT THAT the disciples were slow to believe in the Resurrection of the Lord was not, as I shall point out, so much a weakness of theirs as it was our future strength. For as the Resurrection was made manifest to those who doubted by many proofs, what else can we do when, while reading, we come to know these proofs but be strengthened by their hesitancy? For Mary Magdalene, who believed so readily, proves less to me than Thomas, who doubted for a long time. He, because he doubted, touched the place of the wounds, and took away from our heart the wound of doubt. To penetrate into the truth of the Lord's Resurrection we must take into consideration what Luke refers to, saying: "Eating together with them, he commanded them that they should not depart from Jerusalem"; and after a few words: "While they looked on, he was raised up and a cloud received him out of their sight." Note the words; mark the mysteries: "eating, he was raised up." He ate, and He ascended, evidently in order that as a result of the eating the reality of His flesh might become manifest.

But Mark relates that before the Lord ascended into heaven He upbraided the disciples for their infidelity and hardness of heart. What else must we consider here but that the Lord upbraided His disciples at that time when He left them corporally for this reason, that the words which He said while departing might remain the more deeply engraved on the hearts of His hearers.   St. Gregory, *Pope*

"He who believes and is baptized, shall be saved; but he who believes not shall be condemned." Someone perhaps may say to himself: "I have already believed; I will be saved." He speaks truly if he holds to the faith in his actions. For that faith is true which does not contradict in deeds what it professes by words. Hence it is that St. Paul says of certain false believers: "They profess that they know God, but in their works they deny him." Therefore John says: "He who says that he knows God, and does not keep his commandments, is a liar."

Since this is the case, we ought to acknowledge in our lives the truth of our faith. For then are we truly faithful if we fulfill by our deeds what we promise by our words. Indeed, on the day of Baptism we promised to renounce all the works and all the pomps of the old enemy. Then let each of you draw the eyes of your mind to a self-examination; and if each keeps after Baptism what he promised before it, being now certain that he is faithful, let him rejoice.

Yet, behold, if what he promised he has in no wise kept, if he has fallen away into doing evil deeds and desiring the pomps of this world, let us see if he knows how to bewail what he has done wrongly. For before the merciful Judge he who returns to the truth is not considered as a liar even after he lies; because Almighty God, while gladly receiving our repentance, in His judgment conceals that which we have done amiss.   St. Gregory, *Pope*

Readings for Pentecost

THE HEARTS of all Catholics realize, dearly beloved, that today's solemnity must be ranked among the principal feasts, and there is no doubt that the greatest reverence is due to this day which the Holy Spirit has consecrated with the outstanding miracle of the gift of Himself.

For this day which has dawned upon us is the tenth from that on which the Lord ascended above every height of the heavens to sit at the right hand of the Father, and the fiftieth from His Resurrection, on which began the dispensation of grace. This day holds within itself great mysteries of both ancient sacraments and new, whereby it is made most plain that grace has been foretold by the Law and the Law fulfilled by grace.

For as formerly, after the Hebrew people had been freed from the Egyptians, the Law was given on Mount Sinai on the fiftieth day after the sacrifice of the lamb, so now, after the Passion wherein the true Lamb of God was slain, on the fiftieth day from His Resurrection, the Holy Spirit has come down upon the apostles and upon the faithful. And thus with ease the observant Christian may recognize that the beginnings of the old Testament have ministered to the

CHRIST AT THE SEA OF GALILEE *by Jacopo Tintoretto*

foundations of the Gospel, and that the second pact was established by the same Spirit as had been the first.

From this day, then, the trumpet of the preaching of the Gospel has sounded; from this day showers of spiritual gifts, rivers of blessings have watered every desert and all the dry land. For, to renew the face of the earth (with a spiritual progeny), the Spirit of God moved over the waters; and, to dispel the ancient darkness (of sin), flashes of the new light glittered when, in the splendor of sparkling tongues, alike the lightsome word of the Lord and the fiery speech was received, in which there was—for bringing about understanding and for destroying sin—the ability to enlighten and the power to burn.   St. Leo, *Pope*

It seems desirable, most dearly beloved, to pass briefly over the words of the Gospel lesson, that afterwards we may be able to rest for a longer time in contemplation of so grand a solemnity. For today, with a sudden sound, the Holy Spirit came down upon the disciples and transformed their love for carnal things into love for Him; while fiery tongues appeared without, within, their hearts were made to burn; while in the vision of fire they received God, they were sweetly aflame with love. For the Holy Spirit Himself is love; whence John says: "God is love."

Whoever, therefore, desires God with a pure mind truly already possesses Him whom he loves. For no one, indeed, could love God without possessing Him whom he loves. But behold, if any of you were asked whether he loves God, with a full faith and an unwavering affection he would answer: "I do love." Yet in the very beginning of the reading you heard what the Truth says: "If anyone loveth me, he will keep my words." The proof, therefore, of love is the demonstration of it in action. Wherefore in his Epistle the same John says: "He who saith, 'I love God,' and keepeth not his commandments, is a liar."

Truly, then, do we love God and keep His commandments, if we refrain from forbidden pleasures. For one who still gives himself up to illicit desires surely does not love God, for he contradicts Him in his own will. "And my Father will love him, and we will come to him and take up our abode with him." Ponder, dearest brethren, how great a dignity this is: to possess in the guest chamber of your heart the presence of God.

Certainly, if some wealthy or influential friend were to come to one's house, the whole dwelling would in all haste be cleansed lest perhaps there be something to offend the eyes of that guest upon his entrance. Let him, therefore, who prepares the house of his mind for God wash away the squalor of evil deeds. But see what the Truth says: "We shall come and take up our abode within him." For into the hearts of some He comes without *taking up His abode* there, because through compunction they indeed experience a reverence for God, but in the time of temptation they forget the very thing for which they had been sorry; and so they return to committing sins as though they had not felt the least compunction for them.

ST. GREGORY, *Pope*

THE ASCENSION
Andreas Herman Hunnaeus
Aagerup Church, Aagerup, Denmark

Readings for After Pentecost

THE BOUNDLESS FAVORS of the divine goodness shown to the Christian people confer an inestimable dignity upon it. For there is not, nor has there been at any time, so wonderful a nation having its gods so near to it as our God is to us. For indeed, the only-begotten Son of God, willing that we should be partakers of His Divinity, has assumed our nature, so that, having been made man, He might make men gods. And still more, that which He has assumed from us He has offered in its entirety for our salvation. For He offered on the altar of the cross His own body as an oblation for our reconciliation; He shed His own blood both as a ransom and as a purifying laver, so that we, being bought back from wretched slavery, might be cleansed from all sin. And in order that the remembrance of such a great gift should remain constantly with us, He left His own body for food and His own blood for drink to be partaken of by the faithful under the species of bread and wine.

O precious and admirable banquet! Life-giving and filled with every sweetness! For what can be more treasured than this banquet? This banquet in which, not the flesh of bullocks and goats—as was formerly in the Law—but Christ, true God, is served to us to be partaken of! What is more marvelous than this Sacrament? For in it bread and wine are converted substantially into the body and blood of Christ; and He, perfect God and man, is contained under the species of a little bread and wine.

He is, consequently, eaten by the faithful, but He is by no means broken into parts; what is more, when the Sacrament is divided, He remains entirely in each particle. Moreover, in the Sacrament the accidents remain without their subject that faith may play its part when the visible is taken invisibly, hidden under a different exterior form (that is, when the body and blood of Christ, which of themselves are visible, are received in the Eucharist under the appearances of bread and wine), and the senses, which judge of accidents known to them, may be rendered free from deception.

Likewise, there is no sacrament more salutary than this by which sins are purged away, virtues increased, and the mind enriched with an abundance of all spiritual charismata. It is offered in the Church for the living and the dead, that what has been instituted for the salvation of all may be of profit to all. Finally, no one is able to describe the sweetness of this Sacrament by which spiritual sweetness is tasted at its very source, and there is recalled the memory of that supreme charity which Christ displayed during His Passion. Wherefore, in order that the immensity of this charity might be more deeply fixed in the hearts of the faithful, Christ, when about to pass from this world to the Father, having celebrated the Pasch with His disciples, instituted this Sacrament at the Last Supper as an everlasting remembrance of His Passion, the fulfillment of the ancient types, and the greatest of the miracles worked by Him; and He left it as a special comfort for those who are saddened by His absence. St. Thomas Aquinas

IN ORDER THAT the Church might be formed from the side of Christ, sleeping on the cross, and that the Scripture might be fulfilled which says, "They shall look upon him whom they have pierced," it was permitted by divine providence that one of the soldiers should open His sacred side by piercing it with a lance, so that, by the blood flowing forth with water, the price of our redemption would be shed, which, once poured out from the fountain, that is, from the secret recesses of His Heart, would give to the Sacraments of the Church the power to confer the life of grace, and would be to those already living in Christ a draught of the living fountain, springing forth unto life eternal. Arise, then, O soul, well-pleasing to Christ; cease not to watch; place your youth at His wounded side that you may draw waters from the fountains of the Savior.

For once we have come to the Heart of the most sweet Lord Jesus (and it is good for us to be here), we are not easily torn away from it. Behold how good and how pleasant it is to dwell in this Heart. Your heart, O dearest Jesus, is a goodly treasure, a precious pearl, which we have found in the torn field of Your body. Who will snatch away this pearl? Yea, I will rather give up all other pearls; I will change all my thoughts and affections, and I will buy for myself that one pearl, casting my every thought into the Heart of my good Jesus which will nourish me without fail.

Hence, O sweetest Jesus, having found this Heart, both Yours and mine, I will pray to Thee, my God: "Admit my prayers into the sanctuary of Thy hearing; yea, more, draw me entirely into Thy Heart. For this purpose was Thy side wounded, that we, being removed from exterior disturbances, could dwell therein. Over and above this it was also wounded to show us by means of a visible wound the invisible wound of love." How could the ardor of this love be better manifested than by His permitting not only His body, but His very Heart also to be wounded with a lance? The bodily wound makes known the spiritual wound.

Who will not love that Heart so wounded? Who would not return love to such a lover? Who would not embrace such purity? In so far as we can, therefore, let us while still in the flesh love in our turn this Lover; let us embrace our wounded One whose hands and feet, whose side and Heart wicked husbandmen have dug; and let us pray that He may deign to wound with the dart of His love and to bind up with the bond of that same love our heart, still so hard and impenitent.

ST. BONAVENTURE

YOU HAVE HEARD, my brethren, in the Gospel lesson that sinners and publicans approached our Redeemer; they were received, moreover, not only to converse but also to dine with Him. When the Pharisees saw this, they were indignant. Gather from this fact that true justice has compassion, but false justice feeleth scorn.

Although even good men rightly make it a point to be angry at sinners, still it is one thing when done as a mark of pride, quite another when done out of zeal for discipline. Good men become angry indeed, but they are not scornful; they have little hope, but they do not despair; they inflict punishments, but lovingly; for even if exteriorly in their punishment they overdo corrections, still interiorly they preserve sweetness through charity.

They place before themselves in their own mind those whom they are wont to correct; even those whom they judge they consider better than themselves. By so doing they keep a guard over their subjects by correction, and a guard over themselves by humility. On the other hand, those who are wont to make a show of false justice despise everyone else;

being without mercy, they are most uncondescending towards the weak; and the more they believe themselves not to be sinners, so much the worse sinners do they become.

Of the number of these were certainly the Pharisees, who, upbraiding the Lord because He received sinners, closed up by their own barren heart the very font of mercy. But because they were so sick that they knew not their own malady, and in order to appraise them of their condition, the heavenly Physician cared for them with soothing remedies; He offered them His own benign example; and in their heart He assuaged the swelling of their wound.

St. Gregory, *Pope*

John adds: "One of the soldiers opened his side with a lance, and immediately there came out blood and water." O love that melts all things! How is it for our redemption you have abandoned our Lover? For in order that the deluge of love might flood all things, great abysses have burst over us, namely, the innermost depths of the Heart of Jesus, which the cruel lance, penetrating to the limit, did not spare. Blood and water flowed out: the blood unto redemption, but also water came forth for cleansing. From these the Church was formed out of the side of Christ, so that she might learn that she was one eternally with Christ and loved by Him, and that she might recognize how displeased He was with that guilt for which the divine blood so flowed forth from the Man-God, alive and dead. For we are of no small account if the divine blood was poured out for us.

Literally the water did not flow out indistinguishable from the blood. For it could not have been ascertained by the unwise if it flowed forth mixed with the blood. And perhaps all the blood ran out from that divine body as a sign of the love completely expended, after which the water followed.

And indeed in this a deep mystery has occurred: that first the redeeming price should come out of that body, then the water, in which is signified the multitude of the redeemed peoples. For many waters are many peoples; yet those who belong to the Christian Faith are one faithful people, so that there are not waters, but water which emanated from the side of Christ as the Apostle says in the tenth chapter of the first letter to the Corinthians: "We being many are all one bread and one body, who partake of one bread and one chalice." And again in the letter to the Ephesians in the fourth chapter, he says, "One God, one faith, one baptism."

It should be carefully noted, however, that the side of Christ is said to have been opened, not wounded; because a wound properly speaking is only associated with a living body. For John the Evangelist says, "One of the soldiers opened his side with a lance," so that we could learn by the opened side the love of His Heart even unto death, and that we could enter into that ineffable love through that side whence it came to us. Let us therefore draw near to His Heart, that deep heart, that secret heart, that heart knowing all things, that heart thinking all things, that heart loving, yea, rather burning with love. And let us understand that opened gate at least in the greatness of its love; and, made like that heart, let us penetrate that secret hidden from all eternity, but now revealed in death, so to speak, by that opened side. For the opening of the side declares the opening of the eternal temple wherein is consummated the eternal happiness of all men.   St. Bernadine of Siena

Ponder carefully how unspeakable was that love by which the most high God, with great torment to His Heart and with the whole world's scorn, underwent for you, vile worm, the cruelest of deaths on the cross. Note that Christ the

Savior showed the greatest generosity to all His own. At one time, standing in the midst of the people, He cried out: "If any man thirst, let him come to me and drink." He showed himself ready to come to the help of all in all their needs. Consider that He freely gave up His Heart's precious blood when His sacred side was opened and He poured out whatever blood remained in His body.

Therefore, that I be not wholly ungrateful, I often place before my eyes these perennial fountains of gifts and every good, since there is concerning them that sweetest of promises: "You shall draw water with joy out of the Savior's fountains, and you shall say in that day, 'Praise ye the Lord.'" To those thrice-blessed clefts in the rock that is not to be rent will I fly; in them will I put my nest secure, having no other wish than that in my trials and troubles I take heart in recalling the Lord's wounds.

And do you in every temptation take care to flee to Christ's lovable Heart; put before your mind His goodness and love, and compare with it your own worthlessness, malice, infidelity, arrogance. How great is the love of that Christ who gathers all to Himself: "Come to me all you that labor and are burdened, and I will refresh you." He presents Himself all ready and desirous, for love of us, to bear the burdens of each and every one. Wherefore with great confidence throw your sins into the abyss of His love, and straightway you will find yourself relieved of your burden.

St. Peter Canisius

Let us not think that we shall have an excuse if at times we find associates in our sins, for this will rather increase the guilt. While it is true, indeed, that the serpent was punished more than the woman, so also was the woman punished more than her husband. Jezabel also suffered greater punishment than Achab, who seized the vineyard. She, in fact, contrived this whole affair and was the occasion of the king's falls. Therefore you also, if you are the cause of the ruin of others, will pay more severely than they who have been seduced by you. For to sin personally does not imply as much evil as to lead others to sin.

Consequently, whenever we see men sin, not only are we not to encourage them, but we should even draw them out of that trap of their evil doing, lest we should receive punishment for another's downfall. Let us likewise be constantly mindful of that terrible judgment-seat, of the river of fire, of the unbreakable chains, of the profound darkness, of the gnashing of teeth, and of the poisonous worm. "But," you will say, "God is lenient." Are these things then all talk, and is not the rich man, the scorner of Lazarus, punished, nor the foolish virgins rejected by their spouse? Will they, then, who have not feared Christ, not go into the fire prepared for the devil? Will he who wears soiled raiment not perish, bound hand and foot? Will he who exacted the hundred denarii from his fellow-servant not be delivered to the torturers? Will that which is said of adulterers—especially that their worm will not die and their fire will not be extinguished—not be true?

Is God but threatening these things? You answer, "Yes." And how, I pray, do you dare to speak such a thing in public and to proffer this opinion on your own initiative? I, to be sure, shall be able to prove the contrary, both from those things which God has spoken, and from those things which He has done. But if you do not believe on account of future things, then at least believe on account of those things which have already happened. For those things which have happened and have come into very act surely are not only threats and words.

Who, then, deluged the whole world by causing the flood, and effected that awful storm and the complete destruction of our race? Who cast those lightning-bolts and fiery darts upon the land of the Sodomites? Who drowned all the army of Egypt in the sea? Who burned the synagogue of Abiron? Who slew those seventy thousand men in one moment of time because of David's sin? Has not God brought about all these things and more?   St. John Chrysostom

Do not be slow in turning to the Lord, and do not put it off from day to day, for you do not know what the coming day will bring. There is, in fact, danger and fear in postponement, while salvation is certain and assured if there be no delay. Hence, cultivate virtue; because thus, even if you die as a youth, you will take your leave with confidence, and if you arrive at an old age, you will depart from this life with great ease and no worry; you will possess a double happiness in that you have refrained from wickedness in life, and have cultivated virtue. Do not say, "There will be a time when it will be suitable to convert," for these words greatly exasperate God.

For why, when He Himself has promised time eternal to you, do you not want to labor in this present life that is short and of a moment's duration? You act so lazily and indolently as if you were looking for a life shorter than this. Do not these daily revelries, do not these banquets, these impure persons, the theatres, the riches pay witness to your unspeakable desire for evil-doing? Consider well that, as often as you have sinned against purity, so often have you condemned yourself, for sin is such that, as soon as it has been perpetrated, the Judge passes sentence on it.

Have you been drunk? Have you glutted your stomach? Have you stolen? Stop at once on the down-grade, and turn yourself in the opposite direction. Give thanks to God that He has not snatched you away in the midst of your sins; do not seek to gain a little more time in order to do evil. Many people, while they were living evil and vicious lives, have perished and have passed to their evident damnation. Be fearful lest the same thing happen to you!

"But to many," you will say, "God has given time for them to confess their fault in extreme old age." What then? Will it be given to you? "Perhaps He will grant it," you say. Why do you say, "Perhaps"? Does it happen often? Mark that you are concerned with your soul; then also consider the other possibility, and say: "But what if He does not grant it?"— "But what if He does," do you say? All right! Then He grants it, but the first consideration is surer and more advantageous than this other. St. John Chrysostom

Sacred scripture is placed as a kind of mirror before the eyes of the mind so that our internal appearance may be beheld therein. For there we recognize the ugly things, there the beautiful things in ourselves; there we realize how far we have advanced, or how far we are from progress. It tells of the deeds of holy men, and encourages the hearts of the weak to imitate them; by making mention of their victorious works, it strengthens our weakness against the onslaughts of vices, and through its accounts it is effected that our minds become less afraid in their conflicts the more we view the triumphs of so many brave men set before us.

Sometimes, too, Holy Scripture not only declares these men's virtues to us, but also makes note of their falls, in order that in the victory of the strong we may see what we are to seize upon to imitate, and likewise, in their falls, what we are to fear. For example, Job is pictured as being made great in temptation, while David in his trial is prostrated;

accordingly the virtue of great men nourishes our hope, and the mishaps of great men serve us as a guard of humility, so that while the former (their virtues) bolster us up in our joy, the latter (their falls) weigh upon us in our fear. Thus the soul of him who listens to Scripture, being grounded by the one in the confidence of hope and by the other in the lowliness of fear, neither grows proud in overconfidence because it is laden with fear, nor, when burdened with anxiety, does it despair, because it is strengthened in the assurance of its hope through the example of virtue.

"There was a man in the land of Hus, whose name was Job." Where the holy man dwelt is told that the merit of his virtue might be revealed. For indeed, who does not know that Hus is in the land of the Gentiles? Now the Gentile people live in subjection to vices because of the fact that they had no knowledge of their Creator.

Hence it was told where Job dwelt that this might add to his praise, that he was good among evil men. For it is nothing especially praiseworthy to be good among the good, but to be good among evil men is worthy of praise. Just as it is a greater fault not to live as a good man among the good, so it is of the greatest credit to have lived as a good man even among the evil.   St. Gregory, *Pope*

I know well enough, dearly beloved, that many among you are so careful in those things which pertain to the observance of the Christian Faith that they do not have to be encouraged by our exhortations. This fact tradition has for a long time upheld and custom has established; neither is our zeal unaware of it, nor does our love overlook it. Yet, because it is the duty of the priestly office to have a common concern for all the children of the Church, we arouse one and all to that which is of profit both to the ignorant and to the learned, whom we love equally, so that, by chastisement of soul and body, we may celebrate with a lively faith the fast which the return of this seventh month points out to us who wish to follow Christ.

Now, then, this observance of continence is assigned to the four seasons in order that in the passing course of the whole year we might realize that we are constantly in need of purification and must be always taking care, since we are cast about in the changing ways of this life, that the sin which is contracted through the weakness of our flesh and the corruption of our desires may be blotted out by fasts and alms-giving.

Let us go hungry for a while, dearly beloved, and take from our usual fare some small thing that may be of service to the poor who are in need of help. Let the conscience of the benevolent be delighted with the fruits of their own generosity, and in spreading joy you will receive that by which you yourself will be gladdened. The love of neighbor is the love of God, which, in the unity of this double charity, constitutes the fullness of the Law and of the Prophets, so that no one is to doubt that he has offered to God that which he has bestowed on his neighbor, since the Lord, our Savior, declared when He was speaking of feeding and aiding the poor: "That which you did to one of these, you did unto me." [*Matthew 25:40*]

So let us fast on Wednesday and Friday; then on Saturday let us celebrate the Vigil at the tomb of the blessed Apostle Peter, by whose merits and prayers we believe we shall be helped to please our merciful God through our fast and devotion.　　　　　　　　　　　　　　St. Leo, *Pope*

Should some come up to you and say, "Do not fast often lest you become weak," do not believe them nor give ear to them. For by them the enemy suggests these things. Be mindful of that which is written—how, when the three young men and Daniel and other youths were taken captive by Nabuchodonosor, king of Babylon, and it was ordered that they should eat of the king's own table and drink of his wine, Daniel and the three young men were unwilling to be defiled with the king's table, but spoke to the eunuch who had received them in his care: "Give us some vegetables, and we shall eat." To whom the eunuch answered: "I fear the king, who hath appointed you meat and drink, lest your faces appear leaner than the other youths who are fed from the royal table, and he punish me."

They said to him: "Try thy servants for ten days, and give us vegetables." So he gave them vegetables to eat and water to drink; and he brought them before the king, and their faces appeared fairer than the other youths who were fed from the royal table. Do you see what fasting does? It heals sickness; it dries the humors of the body, puts demons to flight, drives out lewd thoughts, makes the mind cleaner, makes the heart pure, sanctifies the body, and finally presents man before God's throne.

Think not that these things are said rashly; you have witness of this very matter given by the Savior in the Gospels. For when the disciples asked how unclean spirits might be cast out, the Lord replied: "This kind is not cast out but by prayer and fasting." Whoever, therefore, is troubled by an unclean spirit, if he recognizes it and uses this remedy— fasting—I declare the oppressed evil spirit will straightway depart, fearful of the strength of fasting. For the demons mightily delight in surfeit, drunkenness, and bodily luxuries.

There is great strength in fasting, and great and notable things are done by it. By what other way would men accomplish such marvelous things, would miracles be performed by them, would God grant through them health to the sick, except, to be sure, through spiritual exercises of humility of mind and a good life? For fasting is the food of angels, and whoever employs it is to be reckoned of angelic rank.

St. Athanasius

Our lord here warns us that we must weigh the worth of flattering words and a seeming meekness by the fruits which they that manifest such things bring forth in their deeds, and that, to see what a man is, we should look not at his words, but at his deeds. For in many there is concealed the fierceness of a wolf under sheep's clothing. But as thorns do not produce grapes, nor thistles, figs, and as evil trees do not bring forth good fruit, so neither in these men, the Lord teaches, is there found the fruit of good works, and therefore all are to be judged by their fruits.

For lip-service alone will not procure for us the Kingdom of Heaven, nor will he who will say, "Lord, Lord," be an heir thereof. What recompense is there in saying to the Lord, "Lord"? Will He not be the Lord unless He be called so by us? And what is the holiness of this service, this calling of a name, when obedience rather to God's Will, not the invocation of a name, will discover for us the way to the heavenly kingdom?

"Many will say to me in that day: 'Lord, Lord, have we not prophesied in thy name?'" Here the Lord condemns the deceit of false prophets and the shams of hypocrites, who take to themselves glory by reason of the power of their words, their prophesying in teaching, their casting out of devils, and such like mighty works. Because of these things they promise themselves the Kingdom of Heaven, as though what they speak or do were anything of their own and not rather the power of God which, when invoked, brings all things to a successful end; for it is reading that brings knowledge and the name of Christ that agitates the devils.

That blessed eternity must be merited by us; we must give something of our own by willing what is good, by shunning every evil, by obeying the heavenly precepts with our whole heart, that by such acts we may be friends of God. Let us therefore do what God wills rather than boast of what He can do. And we must repudiate and thrust away those who have turned from the knowledge of Him to works of iniquity.

ST. HILARY

THE PHARISEE might at least have said: "I am not like *many* men." Who are the "rest of men" save all but himself? "I," he says, "am just; the rest are sinners. I am not like the rest of men, unjust, robbers, adulterers." And notice for yourself how from the publican nearby there arose the occasion for greater arrogance. "Such as," he says, "that publican." "I," he adds, "stand alone; he is of the rest of men. I am not such a one as he because of my good works, by reason of which I am not a sinner."

"I fast twice a week; I give tithes of all I possess." Seek in his words what he asked of God; you will find nothing. He came up to pray; he does not wish to beg for aught of God but rather to praise himself. It is not enough for him to ask nothing of God, and instead, to praise himself; yea, more, he even insults him who is praying.

The publican stood afar off, yet he was near to God. The consciousness of his own sinful heart held him back; piety drew him forward. The publican indeed stood afar off, but the Lord heard him from very near. For the Lord is high and regardeth the lowly, but the exalted, as was this Pharisee, he knoweth from afar. The exalted He knoweth indeed from a distance, but He does not overlook them.

Hear further of the humility of the publican. That he stood at a distance is not all; he did not even raise his eyes to heaven. That he might be looked upon, he did not look up; he dared not raise his eyes. His conscience oppressed him, but hope raised him up. Hear further: He struck his breast. Of himself he sought punishment; therefore was the Lord indulgent to him who was so penitent. He struck his breast, saying: "Lord, be merciful to me, a sinner." Behold what sort of man it was who asked! What wonder that God forgives sins when they are so acknowledged by the sinner.

ST. AUGUSTINE

FIRST there is cured the man with dropsy, in whom the excess swelling of the flesh rendered the duties of the soul burdensome and extinguished the ardor of the spirit. After that, humility is taught, when at the wedding banquet, desire for a better place is curbed. Mercifully, nevertheless, in order that kindly persuasion might exclude bitterness of coercion, that reason might bring about the effect of persuasion, and correction amend the will.

To this humility, as to its next-door neighbor, kindness is joined. And by the Lord's own saying it may thus be recognized if it be shown to the poor and the weak; for to be hospitable to those able to return your hospitality is to be moved by avarice. And finally, just as a salary is prescribed to a soldier only as a recompense, as it were, for the riches that must be contemned, so also he who, intent on lower desires has procured for himself earthly possessions, cannot attain to the Kingdom of Heaven, for the Lord said: "Sell all that thou hast and follow me."

Nor yet he who bought the oxen; for Eliseus killed what oxen he had and divided them amongst the people. And he who has taken a wife will think on the things of the world, and not of God. Not because marriage is disapproved, but because virginal chastity is called the greater honor; for the unmarried woman and the widow think on those things that are the Lord's—how they may be holy in body and soul.

And therefore it is that the Apostle tells us that we must flee avarice, lest, weighed down in pagan fashion with iniquity, malice, lewdness, and avarice, we be unable to come to Christ's kingdom. For "no unclean person, or covetous one (which is idolatry) has any inheritance in the kingdom of Christ and God."   ST. AMBROSE

TODAY'S GOSPEL shows that Christ by human actions effected divine mysteries, and with visible things carried out invisible activities. "He entered into a boat," it tells us, "and passed over the water, and came into his own city." Is this not He who, having driven back the waves, laid bare the depths of the sea that the people of Israel might pass dryshod between the stilled waters as through the hollows of the mountains?

Is this not He who inclined the crests of the sea to the feet of Peter so that the watery way might present to his feet a solid footing? Then how does it happen that He here refuses for Himself this service of the sea in order to make the crossing of such a small lake by the hire of a ship? "He went up," it says, "into a boat, and crossed over the sea."

But why do you wonder, brethren? Christ came to take on Himself our infirmities and to confer on us His strength; to seek that which is human, to give what is divine; to receive injuries, to bestow honors; to take away all troubles, to restore what is healthful. For a physician who will not bear infirmities will not know how to heal, and he who will not make himself infirm with the infirm man cannot give him health.

Christ therefore, had He held fast to His own glorious prerogatives, would have had nothing in common with men; and had He not taken on Himself the weaknesses of flesh His taking on of flesh alone would have been of no avail. "He went up into a boat," it says, "and crossed over the water and came into his own city." The Creator of all things, the Lord of the world, after He had for our sakes clothed Himself with our flesh, began to have an earthly fatherland, to be a citizen of the Jewish commonwealth; He, the Parent of all parents, began to have parents, so that love might invite us, charity draw us on, affection conquer us, and affability win us whom despotism had driven away, fear had scattered, and the civil power had made exiles.

ST. PETER CHRYSOLOGUS

IT IS AN ORDINARY THING with the Syrians, and especially the Palestinians, to join parables to every discourse, so that what cannot be grasped by the hearers through simple injunction, may be understood by means of a similitude and example. Therefore under the comparison of the king and lord and the servant who, owing a debt of ten thousand talents, had obtained indulgence from his master upon asking, the Lord commanded Peter that he also should forgive his fellow-servants when they erred in lesser things. .

For if that king and lord so easily forgave his servant who owed him ten thousand talents, how much more ought servants forgive their fellow-servants lesser debts? In order that this be made clearer, let us speak by way of example. If anyone of us should commit adultery, murder, or sacrilege, these greater crimes—signified by the ten thousand talents—are forgiven to those who ask if they themselves forgive others who commit lesser crimes.

But if, on the other hand, we are irreconcilable because

of an insult, and because of a bitter word we have perpetual strifes, would it not seem to us that we are rightly cast into prison, and thus through our own example bring it about that forgiveness of our greater transgressions be not granted to us?

"So also my heavenly Father will do to you, if you do not each forgive your brother from your hearts." This is an ominous declaration, if the decision of God is bent and formed according to our own mind—if we do not forgive our brethren little things, the great things shall not be forgiven us by God. And because everyone can say, "I have nothing against him; he (the brother) knows it; he has God as his judge; I do not care what he wants to do; I have forgiven him," God strengthens His word and rejects all simulation of a feigned peace, saying: "If you do not each forgive your brother *from your hearts*."   St. Jerome

Frequently the Pharisees are embittered against Him, but can gain no occasion from past events with which to prosecute Him. In fact, vice could not intrude itself upon His deeds and words; yet because of their disposition to evil-doing, they exerted themselves to the most careful search in order to find a charge. Now He had been calling all men from the crimes of the world and from the superstitions of man-made religions to the hope of the Heavenly Kingdom.

Thereupon they tried to catch Him through the dilemma of their proposed question as to whether one might violate secular authority, or whether he was obliged to pay tribute to Caesar. He, aware of the interior secret of their thoughts (for God does not have to search for any of the things which are hidden within man), commanded that a denarius be brought to Him, and He asked them whose inscription and image was on it.

The Pharisees replied that it was that of Caesar. He told them the things which were Caesar's should be rendered to Caesar, but that the things which were God's should be rendered to God. O answer filled with miraculous power! O perfect solution of this heavenly reply! He so moderated all things between a contempt of the world and the disrespect that would have been offered to Caesar that He freed the minds devoted to God from all worry and human obligations when He decided that only the things which were Caesar's must be rendered to him. For if nothing of Caesar's lies in our possession, we will not be held by the obligation of rendering to him what is his.

Hence if we depend on his power, if we make use of his authority, and as hirelings subject ourselves to a dependence on another's estate, it is beyond the complaint of injustice that we pay to Caesar that which is his. On the other hand, we are obliged to render to God the things that are His: our body, our soul, our will. For we have these things in their perfection and growth from God. Consequently it is just that they give themselves back completely to Him to whom they consider themselves due both in their origin and in their perfection.   ST. HILARY

Readings About Mary

HAIL MARY, FULL OF GRACE, holier than the saints, more exalted than the heavens, more glorious than the Cherubim, more honorable than the Seraphim, and venerable above every creature. Hail, O dove, bringing to us the olive twig, preserving us from a spiritual deluge, and announcing to us the haven of salvation; thou whose silvered wings and whose pinions in green shimmering gold are radiant with the brightness of the most holy and illuminating Spirit. Hail, most delightful and rational paradise of God, planted this day in the East by His most benevolent and omnipotent right hand, sending forth for Him the sweet fragrance of the lily, and producing the ever-fresh rose for the cure of those who have drunk the destructive and fatal bitterness of death in the West; thou paradise in which the life-giving tree blossoms forth unto the knowledge of truth, from which those who have tasted obtain immortality.

Hail, O divinely built, immaculate, and most pure palace of God, the most high King, adorned round about with the magnificence of this same divine King, hospitably receiving all with mystical delights, in which, shining with manifold beauty, is the nuptial chamber, not made with hands, of the

spiritual Spouse; in which the Word, desirous of recalling the erring human race, took to Himself flesh that He might reconcile to the Father those who by their own free will had become estranged from Him. Hail, most fertile and secluded mountain of God on which the rational Lamb, who bore our infirmities and sins, was fed; O mountain from which the Rock, uncut by any hand, rolled down, broke the altars of the idols and became the cornerstone, wonderful in our eyes. Hail, holy throne of God, divine shrine, house of glory, ornament of exceeding beauty, elect treasure, propitiatory of the whole world, the heaven which speaketh forth the glory of God. Hail, vessel of pure gold, containing the delight of our souls, namely, Christ, who is our manna.

O Virgin most pure, most worthy of all praise and homage, consecrated temple of God, excelling in estate all creatures, land unbroken, meadow unplowed, most flourishing vine, fountain gushing forth waters, Virgin with Child, Mother who knew not man, hidden treasury of innocence, perfection of sanctity, by thy most acceptable and, because of thy maternal authority, thy most powerful prayers to our Lord and God, Creator of all things, thy Son, begotten by thee without a father, deign to guide the helm of the Church and to bring it to a tranquil port.

Gloriously clothe our priests with justice and with the joy of an approved, pure, and sincere faith. Direct in tranquility and prosperity the scepters of orthodox princes, who, in preference to purple and the splendor of gold and in preference to pearls and precious stones, have chosen thee to be the diadem, the royal cloak, and the most steadfast adornment of their kingdom. Overthrow those unfaithful nations which blaspheme thee and the God born of thee; give strength to the submissive people that they may perse-

THE ASSUMPTION OF THE VIRGIN *by El Greco*
The Art Institute of Chicago

vere in the sweet yoke of obedience according to the precept
of God. With the triumphs of victory crown this thy city
which considers thee its watch tower and foundation; protect the habitation of God by surrounding it with strength;
preserve always the beauty of the temple. Free those who
sing thy praise from all danger and distress of soul, grant
redemption to the captives, show thyself the solace of pilgrims destitute of home or any protection. Stretch forth thy
helping hand to the whole world that with joy and gladness
we may in the most splendid manner conclude thy solemnities, together with that feast which we have recently celebrated in Christ Jesus, the King of all and our true God, to
whom is glory and strength, together with the Father, the
holy Principle of life, and the coeternal, consubstantial, and
co-reigning Spirit now and always, unto all ages. Amen.

St. Germanus

What shall I say, or what shall I declare concerning the
excellent and holy Virgin? For with the exception of God
alone, she stands far above all; she is more grand by nature
than the Cherubim and Seraphim themselves and all the
angelic army; no heavenly or earthly tongue is in the least
able to praise her, nay, not even the tongue of angels. O
blessed Virgin, pure dove and heavenly spouse. Mary,
heaven, temple, and throne of the Divinity, who possesses
Christ—the Sun shining in heaven and on earth! Bright
cloud, who drew Christ as most brilliant lightning from
heaven that He might illumine the world.   St. Epiphanius

Readings About The Saints

THE HOLY MAN, St. Benedict, having returned to Subiaco, long continued to shine by his virtue and miracles, and assembled a great number of solitaries who consecrated themselves to the service of God, so that, with the aid of our Lord Jesus Christ, he built twelve monasteries, placing in each twelve Religious with an Abbot to govern them. He retained with himself only a few of his disciples who, he thought, still needed his presence to be better formed to perfection.

It was at this time that many persons in Rome, conspicuous for their nobility and virtue, began to visit him and offer their children that he might mould them to piety, and teach them to live for God alone. Aequitius and Tertullus, who had the honor of being Roman Patricians, came to see the saint and confided to his care their two children; the former offered his son Maurus, and the latter, his son Placidus. Maurus was distinguished for spotless innocence of life, and merited, though young, to be chosen by his master to assist him in his functions. As to Placidus, being only a boy, he was subject to the weaknesses inseparable from tender age.

On another occasion, a certain Goth, a man of much simplicity, presented himself to Saint Benedict to become a monk, and the man of God most gladly received him among his disciples. One day the saint ordered a hook to be given him to cut some bush and thorns occupying the place intended for a garden. The place given him to clear was situated on the border of a lake, and as he worked with might and main, the iron slipped off the handle and flew into the lake which was so deep that there could be no hope of recovering the lost blade. The Goth, seeing his iron lost, went, trembling with fear, to the monk, Maurus, and told him the loss the monastery sustained and underwent penance. Maurus made the matter known at once to Benedict, the servant of God, who, as soon as he had heard it, went to the shore. He took the handle from the Goth and immersed it a little in the water. Immediately the blade returned from the bottom of the lake and adjusted itself to the handle. The hook having been thus restored, Benedict returned it to the Goth, saying: "Take thy hook, go to work, and trouble thyself no further."

The venerable Benedict being one day in his cell, the boy Placidus, one of his religious, went out to fetch water from the lake, but, when dipping his pitcher into the water, not taking sufficient heed, his body followed the vessel and he fell into the lake. The waves immediately bore him out from the land as far as the usual flight of an arrow. The saint, who was in his cell, knew of the sad accident at that very instant, and at once calling Maurus, his disciple, said to him: "Brother Maurus, run with all speed; the boy who went to fetch water fell into the lake and has been already carried off a long distance."

A thing wonderful and unheard of since that instance of the Apostle Peter! Maurus having asked and received the blessing, ran to the lake to execute the order of his Abbot. Thinking he was treading upon dry land, he advanced to the very place whither the waves had carried off the child, and laying hold of him by the hair, brought him back with great haste to the shore. Having reached the land, he began to reflect on what he did, and casting a look behind, saw that he had been running over the waves. He was astonished thereat and very much afraid, seeing that he had performed what he would not have dared to undertake if he had been aware of what he was doing. Having returned to the monastery, he narrated the whole occurrence to the Abbot. The venerable Benedict did not attribute this miracle to his own merit, but to the obedience of the disciple. Maurus, on the other hand, said he was only fulfilling a command, and could have no share in a miracle which he unconsciously performed. During this pious dispute arising from the humility of the holy Abbot and his disciple, the boy rescued from peril presented himself as arbitrator, and put an end to the contest thus: "When I was being drawn out of the waves, I saw the Abbot's robe above my head, and it seemed to me that it was he who delivered me from the water." This is narrated by Pope St. Gregory. An ancient tradition says that the monk Maurus was sent into Gaul by the same holy Father. There, according to the same tradition, he founded a monastery at Glannofol; after having governed it for a long time, he died in the Lord in a good old age, renowned for his sanctity and miracles.   St. Gregory, Pope

"THINK YE that I came to send peace on the earth? Not so, I tell you, but separation." But what of that saying, "Behold the Lamb of God"? What of this other, "As a sheep that is led to slaughter and as a lamb that is dumb in the presence of its shearer, so he did not open his mouth"? And of this one, "Say to the daughter of Sion: 'Behold, thy King cometh to thee in meekness'"? Why is it that this Lamb strikes so harshly in His preaching? Why does He grow so violent in word who in His passion holds His peace with such patience and who in death submits in all humility?

And indeed, brethren, Christ entered into the world in all things meek and gentle: for He is sweetly born into our race; in the cradle He allows Himself to be fondled lovingly, being Himself even more affectionate. He shows Himself as a little boy and even relaxes on a human lap; being caressed on the neck of His Mother, He returns the caress with a whole-hearted embrace of love. He always acts like a poor man; He always goes about as a solitary, because the poor man is always approachable; the solitary is accessible to all.

And how is it that He by His words spreads about such a great fire which inflames so greatly and so much, and spreads abroad so widely? Water begets fire—thus one must think—a union of things so contrary! Water begets flame, and the flame increases the water. What is this? How reconcile such discord? Herein is made known the action of the divine Husbandman; for absolutely everything springs forth by His heat, and by His moisture is nourished.

Whence God, the origin of all, by the mingling together of fire and water begets us and nourishes us, for whom He longs, wishes, seeks, and desires with such ardent affection. "Think you," He says, "that I came to send peace on earth?" No! Why? Because heavenly union is in this earthly separation. No one can be attached to the earth and joined to heaven. Precious, therefore, and dear is this earthly separation which so separates us from earthly things that it makes us participate in those that are divine.

ST. PETER CHRYSOLOGUS

MAY THE HOLY SPIRIT teach us at this time what we should say, for we are about to speak the praises of Saint Meinrad, the everglorious martyr, whose birthday, as you know, we keep today. And these, that is, the birthdays, the Church celebrates in such wise that she calls the precious death of the martyrs birthdays. What is this, brethren? When he was born we know not; but because today he suffered, today we keep his birthday. Yet that former day, even though we knew it, we would not keep. For on that day he contracted original sin; but on this he overcame every sin.

For us the suffering of the most blessed martyr Meinrad has made this day a feast; the fame of his victory has brought us, his devoted clients, to this place. But the celebration of the martyrs' solemnities should be an imitation of their virtues. It is easy to celebrate a martyr's honor; it is a great thing to imitate the faith and patience of a martyr. Let us so do the latter that we may desire the former; let us so celebrate the latter that we may the more prize the former. Why do we praise the faith of a martyr? Because even to death he battled for the truth and therefore he conquered. The alluring world he spurned; to the raging world he yielded not; therefore, a victor, he approaches God. Errors and terrors abound in this world. Our blessed martyr overcame the errors with wisdom, the terrors with suffering.

Spurn the world therefore, Christians, spurn, spurn the world. The martyrs spurned it, the Apostles spurned it. Blessed Meinrad, whose memory we keep today, spurned it. Do you wish to be rich? honored? healthy? All these he spurned in whose memory you have come together. Why, I beg, do you love so much what he whom you so honor spurned? Surely, if he had not spurned these things, you would not so honor him. Why do I find you a lover of those things whose scorner you venerate? Without doubt if he had loved them you would not venerate him. Do not love them; for he has not entered and closed the door against you. Do you spurn them too and enter after him.   ST. AUGUSTINE

MEN WHO ARE ILL patiently allow themselves to be cut by the surgeons, to be cauterized, and to be annoyed by different compounds of bitters, so that they may be restored finally to temporal health; how much better has this blessed man perseveringly suffered all the bitterness of temporal torments that he might be crowned with mercy and compassion, and that his desire might be satiated with riches? In the wine-press, therefore, he wished to be trodden upon so that as a ripened grape he might change into wine and give the wine of pomegranates to his Beloved to drink—which inebriated religious minds know is to tread manfully and to pant with unflinching eyes for things eternal.

Therefore he, who in the beginning of his life has despised worldly riches, who has likewise tamed the lusts of the body, who in the carrying on of his warfare has suffered many injuries, by keeping nothing back for himself in the consummation of the sacrifice, has offered himself as a holocaust, drinking of that precious chalice which he had seen first placed before him by his Host while sitting at the great table of sacred reading. His death, however much it may appear despicable in the sight of reprobates, is nevertheless precious in the eyes of Him who "is wonderful in his saints."

For He, in the first place, has called His soldier; He has Himself justified him; He has made him great; He has granted him to fight; He has granted him to conquer. Far different is this warfare from warfare in the world, in which they are reckoned as victors who achieve what they wrongly desire, who are made glad when they have committed evil and exult in their most infamous acts.

In a Christian's martyrdom, then, the penalty is manifest, the victory hidden, according to which the Psalmist cries out in the person of the martyrs, "Grant us help from trouble, for vain is the help of man. Through God we shall do mightily," as if they would declare, "Our victory, our glory is within; it is not without. On the outside we are despised; within, beloved."   ST. AUGUSTINE

SCHOLASTICA was the sister of the venerable father Benedict. She had been consecrated to almighty God from her very infancy, and was accustomed to visit her brother once a year. The man of God came down to meet her at a house belonging to the monastery, not far from the gate. It was the day for the usual visit, and her venerable brother came down to her with some of his brethren. The whole day was spent in the praises of God and holy conversation; and at nightfall they took their repast together. Whilst they were at table and it grew late, as they conferred with each other on sacred things, the holy woman thus spoke to her brother: I beseech thee, stay the night with me, and let us talk till morning on the joys of heaven." He replied: "What is this thou sayest, O sister? On no account may I remain out of the monastery." The evening was so fair that not a cloud could be seen in the sky.

Therefore, when the holy woman heard her brother's refusal, she clasped her hands together, and, resting them on the table, she hid her face in them and prayed to the almighty God. As soon as she raised her head from the table, there came down so great a storm of thunder and lightning and torrents of rain that neither the venerable Benedict nor the brethren who were with him could set foot outside the place where they were sitting. Indeed the holy woman, bowing her head in her hands, had shed a torrent of tears on the table; and as she wept, the clear sky produced rain. The rain fell in torrents immediately after the prayer, and such was the accord between the prayer and the storm that, when she raised her head from the table, the thunder came, since it was in one and the same instant that she raised her head and that the rain fell.

Then the man of God, seeing it was impossible to reach the monastery in lightning and thunder and torrential rain, was sad, and said complainingly, "Almighty God forgive thee, sister; what hast thou done?" But she replied: "I asked thee a favor, and thou wouldst not hear me; I asked it of my God, and He heard me. Go now if thou canst; send me away and go back to the monastery." But it was not in his power to leave the shelter; so that he who would not have stayed willingly had to stay unwillingly. And so it came about that they passed the whole night without sleep, entertaining each other with discussions about the mysteries of the spiritual life.

On the morrow the holy woman returned to her own cell and the man of God to the monastery. When lo! three days after, as he was in his cell, raising his eyes, he saw the soul of his sister going up to heaven in the shape of a dove. Full of joy at her being thus glorified, he thanked almighty God in hymns of praise, and told the brethren of her death. He straightway bade them go and bring the body to the monastery, and he had it buried in the tomb he had prepared for himself. Thus it was that as they had ever been one soul in God, their bodies were united in the same grave.

St. Gregory, *Pope*

"Come to me all you that labor." Now why do we all labor, if not because we are mortal men, frail, weak, carrying about vessels of clay that are continually causing difficulties for one another? But if the vessels of the flesh do cause distress, let the avenue of charity be broadened. Why then does He say, "Come to me all you that labor," unless that you might not labor? In this case His promise is clear, for since He has called for laborers, perhaps they will ask about the reward to which they are called. "And I," He says, "will refresh you.

"Take up my yoke upon you and learn of me," not how to make a world, not how to create all things, visible and invisible, not how to work wonders in the world and to raise the dead, but—"for I am meek and humble of heart." Dost thou wish to be great? Begin from the very least. Art thou planning on constructing a great and lofty edifice? Then first of all give thy thought to the foundation of humility.

Now when one wishes and determines to construct a building, the higher the building is to be, the deeper does one dig the foundation. As the building is under construction, it rises in the heights, but he who digs the foundation is forced down into the depths. And therefore the edifice is lowly before it is majestic; the pinnacle is reached only after humiliation.

What is this pinnacle of the edifice which we are striving to erect? To what height is the summit to reach? Without delay I answer, "Even to the sight of God." You see how exalted it is, how great a thing to behold God. He who desires, understands both what I say and what he hears. There is promised to us the sight of God, of the true God, of the most high God. This in very truth is something good—to see Him who sees. Those who worship false gods easily see these gods, but they see gods who have eyes and see not. But to us is promised the vision of the God who lives and sees.

ST. AUGUSTINE

DEAREST BRETHREN, you have heard that at a single command Peter and Andrew, leaving their nets, followed the Redeemer. Up to that time they had not seen Him perform any miracles; they had heard nothing from Him concerning a reward of eternal joy, and still, at a single bidding of our Lord, they forgot about that which they seemed to possess. What great miracles of His have we seen, with how many scourges are we afflicted, by what great anxieties of threatening things are we disheartened, and nevertheless we contemn Him who calls us to follow!

He who counsels us in our manner of life already sits enthroned in heaven; already has He bowed the necks of the Gentiles to the yoke of the Faith; already He has laid low the glory of the world; already, with the world's disasters increasing more and more, does He announce the approaching day of His severe judgment, and yet our proud mind still does not wish to abandon of its own accord that which it is daily losing unwillingly.

What, then, dearly beloved brethren, what shall we say in His judgment, we who are not turned from the love of this present world by His counsels, nor corrected by his chastisements? But perhaps someone will say in his silent ruminations: What or how much did either of these fishermen, who possessed almost nothing, forfeit at the call of the Lord?

In this matter, dearest brethren, we must consider the disposition rather than the personal wealth. He forsakes much who keeps nothing for himself; he forsakes much who gives up every little thing, his all. But we, on the other hand, hold with love the things we have, and even out of desire seek those things which we do not have. Therefore, Peter and Andrew forsook much when both forfeited even their desire to possess.   ST. GREGORY, *Pope*

Index

ACKNOWLEDGMENTS

Confraternity of Christian Doctrine, Washington, D.C.
for the quotations from the Bible.

Grail Publications, St. Meinrad's Abbey, St. Meinrad, IN for the
selections from the breviary homilies, taken from *Liturgical Readings*.

Loyola University Press, Chicago, IL, for permission to use
the following prayers from *Challenge* and *For Jesuits*.

   Challenge:
      Prayer to the Holy Spirit, page 52
      Prayer to St. Joseph, page 80
      Prayer to St. Anthony of Padua, pages 90-91
      Prayer for my Father, page 103
      Prayer for my Mother, page 103-04
      Prayer for Success in Study, pages 106-07
      Prayer for God's Protection, page 181
      The Spirit of an Apostle, page 204
      Prayer to St. Thérèse, page 207
      In Gratitude—A Prayer for Nuns, page 209
      Prayer for the Right Partner in Marriage, page 220
      Prayer for Religious Vocations for Girls, page 221
      Prayer for Unmarried Persons, page 223
      Prayer for a Happy Death, page 229

   For Jesuits:
      For My Father, pages 382-83
      For My Mother, page 383
      Grievances, pages 417-18
      Discernment, page 426
      A Teacher's Prayer.

Editor's note: For ease of use, the numbering of the Psalms and the titles of the
books of the Bible follow the New American Bible convention.